Britain at the Polls, 2001

Britain at the Polls, 2001

edited by
Anthony King

with
John Bartle
Ivor Crewe
David Denver
Philip Norton
Patrick Seyd
Colin Seymour-Ure

CHATHAM HOUSE PUBLISHERS
SEVEN BRIDGES PRESS, LLC

NEW YORK · LONDON

Seven Bridges Press
135 Fifth Avenue
New York, NY 10010-7101

Publisher: Ted Bolen
Managing Editor: Katharine Miller
Composition: ediType
Cover Design: Stefan Killen Design
Cover Art: PhotoDisc, Inc.
Printing and Binding: Victor Graphics, Inc.

Library of Congress Cataloging-in-Publication Data

Britain at the polls, 2001 / Anthony King ... [et al.].
p. cm.
Includes bibliographical references and index.
ISBN 1-889119-74-1
1. Great Britain – Politics and government – 1997- . 2. Political
parties – Great Britain. I. King, Anthony Stephen.
JN231 .B696 2002
324.941'086 – dc21

2001004995

Manufactured in the United States of America

10   9   8   7   6   5   4   3   2   1

Contents

Figures and Tables

Preface

THE BRITISH GENERAL ELECTION of 1997 was one of the most exciting elections in recent history. It led to a landslide victory for the Labour Party after eighteen consecutive years of Conservative government. By contrast, the 2001 general election was one of the dullest in recent history. Apart from the fact that John Prescott, the 62-year-old deputy prime minister, threw a punch at a demonstrator, nothing happened. There were no events, no crises, no excitements, above all, no movements in the opinion polls that suggested, even for a moment, that the Conservative Party stood a chance of winning. In the end, as John Bartle points out in Chapter 7, Labour's victory was not on quite the grand scale that everyone had predicted; but it was a convincing victory all the same, and throughout the campaign everyone knew that, whatever the final margin, Labour was certain to come out ahead.

The fact that the election was dull, however, does not mean that it was uninteresting. On the contrary, it had three features that make it of unusual interest. The first is the simple fact that it had the effect of returning to power a Labour government for a second full term. That had never happened before, and in early August 2003 Tony Blair, if he decides to remain at Number 10, will become the longest-serving ever Labour prime minister. This book asks, among other things, how Blair and his colleagues managed to make the Labour Party re-electable in a way that none of their predecessors had succeeded in doing. It also asks how, simultaneously, the Conservatives contrived to put in their second worst electoral performance since Britain became a democracy (indeed since long before Britain became a democracy). It is at least possible that Labour is in the course of becoming Britain's hegemonic political party in the way that the Conservatives were for much of the last century. If that happens, it will be an astonishing outcome: many people in the 1970s and 1980s were prepared to write off the Labour Party as washed up, as having long since passed its political pull-by date. How wrong they were.

The second interesting feature of the election is more subtle. Labour in 2001 won handsomely over the Conservatives and secured a majority in Parliament almost as large as its majority following the 1997 election. But, except possibly during its first few months, the Blair government was never especially popular or well respected. Much of its support was always grudging, and it was clear that many voters were backing Labour *faute de mieux*. There was a widespread sense that, if Labour won in 2001, as it seemed bound to do, it would be finishing second in an unpopularity contest. The fuel crisis of September 2000, discussed in Chapters 1 and 7, showed just how fragile support for the Blair government was. Discontent with Labour specifically, but also with "them" in general, seemed constantly to be bubbling just below the surface of British political life. On election night itself, the most remarkable result anywhere in the country was the victory of Richard Taylor, a retired consultant physician with no previous political experience, standing as an independent in the Worcestershire constituency of Wyre Forest. His cause was local and specific: the defence of a local hospital threatened with being downgraded. But he almost certainly owed his victory — he ousted a Labour government minister — to widespread public feelings of alienation from the whole of the political class.

The third interesting feature of the election, almost certainly arising partly out of the second, was the low turnout: the lowest since 1918 and the lowest in normal peacetime circumstances since the nineteenth century. In fact, turnout in Britain in 2001, given that the British turnout figure is given as a percentage of the registered electorate rather than of the total adult population, was probably not a great deal higher than in the United States in 2000. Despite Labour's landslide victory, only one registered elector in four actually voted for his or her local Labour candidate. There was much talk in the Blair government during its first term of "reconnecting" British politicians with the British people and of "revitalizing" British democracy. Whatever efforts were made along these lines clearly failed. The reasons for the low turnout in 2001 are, as yet, not entirely clear; but the low turnout, which is discussed in Chapter 7, marks out the 2001 election from every other general election since the war.

This volume in the "Britain at the Polls" series, like its predecessors since 1974, does not set out to be a definitive work of reference. That particular task is left to David Butler and Dennis Kavanagh, whose *The British General Election of 2001* is scheduled to be published in November 2001. Nor does it provide a detailed survey-based account of voting behaviour (and non-voting behaviour) during the election. That task is left to the participants in the British election study, led by David Sanders and Paul Whiteley of the University of Essex and Harold D. Clarke of the University of North Texas. The aims of *Britain at the Polls, 2001* are rather to provide students and general readers, in North America as well as Great Britain, with an analytic description of the whole of the 1997–2001 period, with accounts of the major developments within each of the major political parties, with a "first-cut" explanation of the election outcome and with some reflections on the election's long-term significance. An additional chapter is devoted to the sequence of important constitutional changes introduced by the Blair government.

The preface to the 1997 volume in the series, *New Labour Triumphs,* concluded by noting that, following New Labour's landslide victory, two tantalizing questions remained. How would Tony Blair and New Labour actually govern? And what lessons would the Conservatives draw from their defeat and especially from the magnitude of their defeat? Answers to both these questions are provided in what follows. In the event, New Labour remained true to itself and governed with extreme caution. The Conservatives by and large behaved as though they had learned nothing.

Anthony King
July 15, 2001

CHAPTER 1

Tony Blair's First Term

Anthony King

UNTIL SHORTLY BEFORE the end of its first term, the most striking thing about Tony Blair's Labour government was that there was nothing striking about it. It was the first "normal" Labour administration in British political history. All previous Labour governments—those headed by Ramsay MacDonald, Clement Attlee, Harold Wilson and James Callaghan — had been associated with dramatic economic crises, with the devaluation of the currency and, under Wilson and Callaghan, with widespread industrial unrest. Fear of the consequences of installing Labour in power had been a major factor in keeping Labour out of power for eighteen years between 1979 and 1997. But, following this extended period of political exile, Labour under Blair won in May 1997 — and nothing happened. The currency did not collapse. The workers did not take to the streets. The markets did not panic. Life carried on as normal. Labour, it turned out, could govern after all.

The contrast between the years 1997–2001 and the time of previous Labour administrations cannot be overemphasized. Ramsay MacDonald's minority Labour administration collapsed amidst mutual recrimination under the weight of the Great Depression in 1931; the United Kingdom abandoned its attempt to remain on the gold standard shortly afterwards. Clement Attlee's postwar Labour government did survive for a full term but presided over fuel shortages during the harsh winter of 1946–47 and then in 1949 devalued the pound by a massive 30 per cent, from $4.03 to $2.80. Harold Wilson's administration between 1964 and 1970 also survived for a full term, but it, too, devalued the pound—in 1967, by nearly 15 per cent, from $2.80 to $2.40 — and under Wilson Britain suffered wave upon wave of industrial unrest. The Labour governments of Harold Wilson and James Callaghan between 1974 and 1979 presided over low growth, record inflation, rising unemployment and more or less continual industrial disruption, culminating in the "Winter of Discontent" in 1978–79. Moreover, although the Callaghan government did not formally devalue sterling, the value of the British currency against the U.S. dollar fell in the autumn of 1976 to an all-time low of

$1.59, and the government was placed in the humiliating position of having to borrow from the International Monetary Fund. By 1979 Labour was inextricably associated in millions of voters' minds with chaos, uncertainty, disruption and, in many cases, considerable personal inconvenience. The principal beneficiaries, for nearly two decades, were the Conservatives, initially under Margaret Thatcher, later under John Major.

It was Tony Blair's overriding objective from the moment he became Labour leader in 1994 to reassure voters that, under him, things would be different — and, in the event, they were. Britain under Labour quietly prospered. Nothing like it had happened before.[1]

LABOUR AND THE ECONOMY

The genius presiding over Labour's economic success between 1997 and 2001 was Gordon Brown, Tony Blair's chancellor of the exchequer, his principal political rival and his most probable successor as prime minister.[2] A drab and stony-faced Scot whose demeanour in public usually resembled that of an out-of-sorts bank manager, Brown had served as shadow chancellor for five years while Labour was in opposition. As soon as the party returned to power, he took personal charge of every aspect of the government's economic policy. It was he who determined both the volume of taxation and the detailed ways in which taxes would be levied. It was he who determined not only the total volume of government expenditure but its allocation among departments. In addition, he made himself the overseer of the government's reforms of the social security system. The Treasury was not only his personal fiefdom: it was the base from which he launched raids deep into the territory of his cabinet colleagues. Despite his lack of personal charm, or perhaps because of it, Brown by 2001 was easily the most highly regarded chancellor of the exchequer of the entire postwar period.[3]

From the moment he took office, he had a great deal going for him. The United States economy remained buoyant throughout the 1990s and during the early years of the new century, and the economies of Britain's European neighbours, though less buoyant, never looked like going into deep recession. By the time Labour came to power in 1997, it was also clear that the economic downturns in east Asia and parts of Latin America were not going to cause a global downturn on the scale that had once been feared. Closer to home, Brown inherited from the outgoing Conservative administration an economy marked by low inflation, falling unemployment and rapidly falling deficits in the public finances. The Blair government, in other words, inherited a stronger economy than any previous Labour government. Kenneth Clarke, the Conservatives' chancellor from 1993 to 1997, claimed a good deal of the credit for his successor's subsequent economic success. He had solid grounds for doing so.

But Gordon Brown could have dissipated this enviable economic inheritance. He could have set off on a lavish spending spree and either raised taxes sharply or else not raised them enough, thereby greatly increasing the scale of government borrowing. In other words, he could have done what most previous Labour chancellors of the exchequer had done. But he did not. On the contrary, he was cautious, if anything ultra-cautious. His watchword, endlessly repeated, was "prudence", and he made it his central task to attempt to damp down the wild swings from boom to bust — and back again — that had characterized the British economy for decades, most notably under the Conservatives in the late 1980s and early 1990s. He did not imagine that he could completely abolish the trade cycle, but steady, sustained growth was to be the aim. In the words of Brown's 1999 budget report:

> Over the past three decades, the UK economy has exhibited high volatility in output and inflation. Instability has made it hard for individuals and firms to plan and invest and has damaged the long-term growth of the economy. The Government has reformed the framework for macroeconomic policy to promote economic stability.... Stability is essential for high levels of growth and employment.[4]

Brown arrived at the Treasury in 1997 armed with two pledges that were intended simultaneously to reassure wavering voters, to reassure the financial markets and, not least, to make it impossible, once Labour was back in power, for any Labour ministers and MPs who were less prudent than himself to press successfully for higher direct taxes and higher government spending. The first pledge was that under no circumstances would a new Labour government raise the top level of income tax above its existing rate of 40 per cent. The middle classes and the well-off were not to be hammered; business men and business women could sleep soundly in their beds at night. The second pledge was that, at least for its first two years, a new Labour government would adhere strictly to the tight limits on public expenditure laid down by the out-going Conservative administration. Taken together, the two pledges were meant to lock in Labour financially and, even more important, to be seen to be doing so. They proved a great success under both headings.

Brown also arrived at the Treasury in 1997 with an important non-pledge: a decision that he had already taken but not announced publicly. Ever since the Second World War and the nationalization of the Bank of England, it had been the responsibility of successive chancellors of the exchequer to set interest rates. In other words, the British chancellor was a one-man equivalent of the U.S. Federal Reserve Board. This arrangement had both advantages and disadvantages from the chancellor's point of view. On the one hand, it gave whoever held the office effective control over the most important single instrument of U.K. monetary policy. On the other hand, fine-tuning interest rates was a major distraction and took up an inordinate amount of successive chancellors' time. In addition, the fact that it was an elected politician who set interest rates meant that the individual in question would inevitably be tempted to set the rates to suit the government's immediate political convenience and that, even if he were not so tempted, the markets would believe that he was. The view was widely held that the Conservative chancellor, Kenneth Clarke, would have pushed up interest rates in 1996–97 but for the imminence of a general election which the Conservatives seemed in danger of losing. Brown was determined on change. He did not believe, as a matter of principle, that chancellors should set interest rates; he also believed that the financial markets would be innately suspicious of the motives — and the good sense — of any Labour chancellor. Accordingly, he announced on May 6, 1997, only four days after taking office, that henceforth U.K. interest rates would be set not by him or his successors but by a wholly independent Monetary Policy Committee of the Bank of England. The markets were astonished — and delighted. Brown had, within days, made his mark.

His caution and steadiness over the next four years paid dividends, both economic and political. The figures in Table 1.1 speak for themselves. The United Kingdom maintained a steady if not spectacular rate of economic growth. The annual inflation rate fell and remained in the region of 2–3 per cent. Public sector borrowing also fell as a proportion of gross domestic product (GDP), with the government able to repay substantial chunks of the national debt. Above all, especially from the point of view of a Labour administration, unemployment, which had already fallen under the Conservatives, continued to fall under Labour. By the spring of 2001, unemployment had, according to one measure, fallen below one million, and underlying unemployment in Britain was substantially lower than in Germany, France, Italy and Spain. A widely publicized OECD report described as "enviable" the performance of the U.K. economy under Gordon Brown's tutelage.[5]

Brown was thus a conservative chancellor, but he was not only that. While retaining a tight grip on public spending, especially in the early years, he gradually reordered the system of taxation and state benefits so that the poor made substantial gains while the better-off gained less, if anything. He introduced a generous Working Families Tax Credit and also a Minimum Income Guarantee to ensure that poorer old-age pensioners did not fall below the poverty line. The government also introduced Britain's first-ever statutory minimum wage. Partly as a consequence of the government's actions, partly as a result of falling unemployment, the authoritative Institute of Fiscal Studies reckoned that by 2000 the poorest tenth of Britons had become 8.8 per cent better off since 1997 while the richest tenth had actually become 0.5 per cent worse off.[6] Brown did not announce that he was redistributing income, but he was.

Having stuck rigidly to the Conservatives' spending limits during his first two years, Brown also began, from 1999 onwards, to loosen the reins on public expenditure. Prudence had initially been his only watchword; his phrase now was

Table 1.1 Economic Indicators, 1997–2001

		Growth of GDP (%)	Inflation (%)	Unemployment (%)	Public sector debt as % of GDP
1997	Q2	0.9	2.6	7.3	48.0
	Q3	1.0	2.8	7.0	
	Q4	0.5	2.8	6.7	
1998	Q1	0.7	2.6	6.5	45.4
	Q2	0.7	2.9	6.4	
	Q3	0.5	2.5	6.4	
	Q4	0.2	2.5	6.3	
1999	Q1	0.4	2.5	6.3	43.2
	Q2	0.7	2.3	6.1	
	Q3	1.3	2.2	6.0	
	Q4	0.8	2.2	6.0	
2000	Q1	0.4	2.1	5.9	40.5
	Q2	0.9	2.1	5.6	
	Q3	0.8	2.1	5.5	
	Q4	0.4	2.1	5.4	
2001	Q1	0.3	1.9	5.1	

Sources: Growth of GDP: Office for National Statistics, *Gross Domestic Product by Gross Value Added 1948–2001* (online dataset: <http://www.statistics.gov.uk>), 2001; Inflation: Office for National Statistics, *Retail Price Index: Index Numbers of retail Prices 1948–2001* (online dataset: <http://www.statistics.gov.uk>), 2001; Unemployment: Office for National Statistics, *Labour Force Survey: Summary, 1987–2001* (online dataset: <http://www.statistics.gov.uk>), 2001; Public sector debt as a % of GDP: Bank of England, *Statistical Abstract,* Table 15.1 (<http://www.bankofengland.co.uk>), October 2000.

Note: Growth is shown as the percentage increase in Gross Domestic Product compared with the previous quarter. Inflation is shown as the figure for the annual Retail Price Index, underlying rate (excluding mortgage interest payments). Unemployment is shown as the International Labour Organization rate, including all adults to retirement age.

"prudence with a purpose". Spending on education and the National Health Service rose scarcely at all in real terms in the new government's first three years, and spending on transport and housing actually fell; but Brown announced massive spending increases in his 2000 annual budget and again in 2001. For example, education spending was planned to rise from £46.0 billion in 2000–01 to £58.1 billion in 2003–04 and health spending from £44.7 billion to £57.1 billion.[7] The chancellor hoped — and believed — that the increased spending could be paid for largely out of increased tax revenues, but he was also quietly introducing a number of new taxes and raising the rates of others. He kept his promise not to raise the top rate of income tax, and he actually lowered the standard rate; but the duties on fossil fuels, for example, rose far faster than the rate of inflation and total taxation as a proportion of GDP showed a modest but measurable increase. The Conservatives in opposition accused the chancellor of introducing "stealth taxes", Britain's fiscal equivalent of the American stealth bomber.

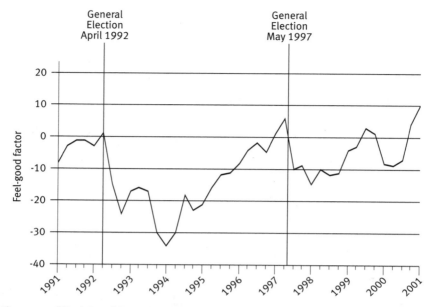

Figure 1.1 "Feel-Good Factor", 1991–2001

Sources: Anthony King and Robert J. Wybrow, eds., *British Political Opinion 1937–2000: The Gallup Polls* (London: Politico's, 2001), 309–12; *Gallup Political and Economic Index,* Report No. 487, March 2001, 8.

Note: The "feel-good factor" is defined as the proportion of Gallup's respondents saying that they believe their household's financial situation will get "a lot" or "a little" better during the coming twelve months minus the proportion saying that they believe it will get "a little" or "a lot" worse.

Increased taxes, whether stealthy or not, appeared, however, to have little or no effect on the public's high regard, not merely for Gordon Brown as chancellor but for the Blair government's overall economic record. The Labour Party before the election had been determined to reassure voters that it was capable of managing the economy effectively, and Blair and Brown after the election were equally determined to make the same point. They succeeded. Two separate measures attest to their success. One, set out in Figure 1.1, plots quarter by quarter the so-called feel-good factor — the proportion of people believing their household's financial situation will improve over the coming twelve months minus the proportion believing it will deteriorate — over the whole of the decade from the spring of 1991, with the Conservatives still in power, to the spring of 2001, roughly four years after Labour's return to power. As can be seen, there was no dramatic improvement in the feel-good factor on Labour's return to power in May 1997;

on the contrary, it deteriorated somewhat, especially in 1998. But, as can also be seen, the feel-good factor at its worst under the new Labour government never fell as low as under the Conservatives in the mid 1990s, and it became increasingly buoyant as the 2001 election approached.

The other measure of the Labour government's success contrasts the public's confidence in Labour's ability to manage the economy with the Conservative Party's ability to do the same. The British Gallup Poll in all its political surveys asks the question: "With Britain in economic difficulties, which party do you think could handle the problem best — the Conservative Party or the Labour Party?" Between 1964 and 1992, there was only one month in which Labour led the Conservatives on this issue, but Labour pulled ahead towards the end of 1992 and stayed there throughout the remainder of the 1992 parliament; and, with a very brief blip in September 2000, Labour, now in power, also remained there throughout the 1997 parliament. The figures are set out, again quarter by quarter, in Table 1.2 (p. 8). The table is further testimony to Gordon Brown's success in managing the economy in his first four years as chancellor — so much so that on the eve of the 2001 election Gallup revised the opening of its standard economic-competence question to read: "If Britain were in economic difficulties..." The economic skies did begin to lower in the early months of 2001, as darker clouds began to blow in across the Atlantic, but Britain still seemed better placed to weather any future economic storms than many of its European neighbours.

NEW LABOUR IN POWER

Its successful management of the economy was probably the single most important way in which the new Labour government under Blair distinguished itself from its predecessors. But it was not the only way. Blair had declared in the early hours of May 2, 1997, "We have been elected as New Labour and we will govern as New Labour." And he kept his word, even if it was not always entirely clear what his word meant for practical purposes.

In the first place, the Blair government differed from all of its Labour predecessors in what might be called its "class orientation". To an extent that Americans and others sometimes found hard to believe, the British Labour Party had always been precisely that, a Labour party, with its electoral appeal aimed at the manual working classes and its policies aimed mainly at furthering working-class interests. Labour had always tended to be a somewhat exclusive party, one that built walls around itself and communicated with the outside world only when necessary. Inside the walls, all was warm and snug (if often disputatious). Outside the walls, the world was cold and threatening; the inhabitants of that outside world were to be treated with suspicion, if not downright hostility. Old Labour was a party that kept its distance: from the rich, from business, from every non-Labour political party.

Table 1.2 Economic Competence, 1991–2001

		Labour best party to handle economy	Conservatives best party to handle economy	Labour advantage
1991	Q1	32	51	-19
	Q2	30	46	-16
	Q3	29	46	-17
	Q4	30	45	-15
1992	Q1	31	42	-11
Conservative government re-elected				
	Q2	31	48	-17
	Q3	36	41	-5
	Q4	39	28	11
1993	Q1	40	30	10
	Q2	41	26	15
	Q3	40	25	15
	Q4	41	26	15
1994	Q1	43	25	18
	Q2	44	23	21
	Q3	48	22	26
	Q4	49	20	29
1995	Q1	49	20	29
	Q2	49	21	28
	Q3	46	24	22
	Q4	48	24	24
1996	Q1	46	23	23
	Q2	46	24	22
	Q3	43	26	17
	Q4	44	26	18
1997	Q1	47	37	10
Labour government under Tony Blair elected				
	Q2	56	31	25
	Q3	58	30	28
	Q4	58	28	30
1998	Q1	52	33	19
	Q2	53	32	21
	Q3	52	33	19
	Q4	54	31	23
1999	Q1	52	31	21
	Q2	54	31	23
	Q3	53	32	21
	Q4	53	31	22
2000	Q1	51	31	20
	Q2	45	35	10
	Q3	46	38	8
	Q4	46	37	9
2001	Q1	51	31	20

Sources: King and Wybrow, eds., *British Political Opinion,* 116–19; *Gallup Political and Economic Index,* Report No. 487, March 2001, 9.

Note: Labour's advantage on economic competence is calculated by subtracting the proportion of respondents saying that, with Britain in economic difficulties, the Conservatives would handle the problem best from the proportion saying that Labour would. A considerable proportion often reply "neither" or "don't know".

New Labour, in power as well as on the road to power, was different, consciously so. Inclusivity was in; exclusivity was out. New Labour sought electorally to appeal to the whole nation, not merely to the working classes but to those sections of the middle and even the upper classes that were either liberal in their general political outlook or else were, for whatever reason, disaffected from the Conservatives. "We are a broad-based movement for progress and justice," Tony Blair wrote in the 1997 Labour manifesto. "New Labour is the political arm of none other than the British people as a whole."[8] In power, the new Labour government took every opportunity to demonstrate its continuing concern with the views and aspirations of the upwardly mobile and progressive middle classes. Business tycoons and pop stars attended parties at 10 Downing Street; focus groups in middle-class marginal constituencies reminded ministers constantly of what "middle England" was thinking. Occasionally there were lapses — as when Gordon Brown, in strikingly Old Labour language, rounded on an Oxford college for failing to admit a student from a northern comprehensive school — but they were few.

More specifically, the Blair government was the first-ever Labour government to be openly, even ostentatiously pro-business. Pro-Labour business men and business women appeared, as representatives of business, in Labour party political broadcasts. Business people and their representatives were welcome at Number 10. Blair was even eager to recruit business people into the ranks of the government itself, partly as a gesture to the business world but partly also because he believed they tended to be better managers and more creative than most politicians. Lord Simon of Highbury, former group chief executive and chairman of BP (British Petroleum), became minister for trade and competitiveness in Europe. Lord Sainsbury of Turville, former head of one of Britain's largest supermarket chains, became minister of science in the Department of Trade and Industry (as well as one of the largest donors to Labour party funds). The government and business organizations like the Confederation of British Industry continued to have their differences, of course (over the minimum wage, for example); but ministers were instructed to be, and were, continuously sensitive to business interests. Tony Blair's belief in business as an activity, and his admiration for business men and business women, matched that of Margaret Thatcher.

Moreover, the Blair approach was a substantial success in its own terms. Winning the 1997 general election, Labour secured the support of more than one third of the professional, executive and managerial classes, equal to the Conservatives and far more than at any previous election. Four years later, support for Labour among these high earners remained at an almost equally high level. Even more remarkable in some ways was the fact that large numbers of business people no longer regarded the Labour Party and Labour ministers as the enemy. Some of them were positively sympathetic; more regarded Labour in power as simply a fact of life, a fact that they were not bothered by and could easily live with.

New Labour's new, warmer relationship with business was made possible, not only by Gordon Brown's prudent economic management but also by the fact that, whatever else it was, Tony Blair's government was not, in any meaningful sense of the word, a socialist government. Traditional British socialism had been founded on two pillars, one ideological, one organizational. The ideological pillar, embodied originally in Clause 4 of the Labour Party's constitution, committed the party to "the common ownership of the means of production, distribution and exchange". In practice, that meant state ownership of large sectors of industry. Previous Labour governments, as recently as the 1960s and 1970s, had nationalized the bulk of the steel industry, aircraft production and shipbuilding; Labour administrations had also extended state ownership into newer fields like computers and North Sea oil. However, Blair and his colleagues set off in a completely different direction. Not only did Blair, as leader of the Labour Party in opposition, strip the original version of Clause 4 from the party's constitution, but in government he set out actually to reduce the state's direct involvement in industry, not to extend it. An earlier Labour pledge to renationalize the railways, privatized under John Major, was dropped, and the Blair government insisted that improvements on the London Underground be financed, not by direct government subsidies to the existing Underground management, but by means of a complex public–private partnership. The New Labour government even engineered the partial sell-off to the private sector of the national air-traffic control system. The private sector could scarcely grumble. Thatcher herself would have been proud. Secretly, she probably was.

The other pillar of traditional British socialism had been the close organizational links between the Labour Party and Britain's trade unions. A Conservative politician once described the Labour Party as "a wholly owned subsidiary of the trade union movement", and he was not far wrong. The unions financed the Labour Party; they also controlled the vast majority of votes at the party's annual policy-making conference. Labour's close association with, and identification with, the unions had been one of the reasons for the party's dismal electoral performance at the 1979 election and throughout the 1980s. The unions were unpopular. Their unpopularity inevitably rubbed off on the party.

Blair by no means severed the links between the party and the unions (though there was occasional talk of a complete separation), but he succeeded in putting the party–union relationship on a completely new footing. Before coming to power, he and his supporters persuaded the annual conference to limit the extent of the unions' financial contributions to the party's coffers and, correspondingly, to reduce their voting strength at the conference. The National Executive Committee, scourge of previous Labour administrations, was reorganized and largely deprived of its policy-making functions. The unions could no longer use their effective control of the executive to embarrass Labour governments and promote policies, invariably left-wing policies, against the party leadership's wishes. Perhaps more important, Blair in opposition sought to establish a certain psychological distance between him and the unions. He appeared only intermittently at union conferences and took every opportunity to assert that the unions could expect "fairness, not favours" from a future Labour government. The opinion polls showed clearly that, by 1997, a majority of voters were persuaded that a government led by Tony Blair would not be in hock to the unions.

Blair, in fact, was not anti-union. He believed that it was wrong in principle and dangerous politically for the unions — or any other single interest group — to have control of a major political party. He also believed that much of the unions' behaviour in the 1960s and 1970s had been deeply anti-social (as well as damaging to Labour). But he was personally friendly with many individual trade-union leaders, and he had much sympathy with the unions in their role as champions of the underdog. He was disposed to champion what he saw as the unions' legitimate rights. When he said "fairness, not favours", he meant "fairness" as well as "not favours". Blair may not have been — he was not — as close to the union movement as most of his predecessors as Labour leader, and the unions certainly did not see him as one of their own; but they nevertheless saw him as a friend, not a lover perhaps, but a friend.

In the event, the new Labour government's treatment of the unions was as even-handed as Tony Blair had suggested it would be. He and his colleagues were not so pro-union as to antagonize the business community, but they were sufficiently pro-union as not to antagonize the unions themselves. On the one hand, the new government kept in place all of the Thatcher government's major trade-union legislation. Secondary picketing remained illegal. Unions had to ballot their members before undertaking any form of industrial action. Any union that broke the law would still face heavy fines and the sequestration of its property. But, on the other hand, the Blair government introduced the national minimum wage, long advocated by the unions. It also acceded, unlike the previous Conservative government, to the pro-union "social chapter" of the 1992 Maastricht Treaty. It went on to accord the unions, for the first time in their history, a statutory right to employer recognition. If more than 50 per cent of employees already belonged to a union, recognition was automatic; if more than 40 per cent voted for union representation in a ballot, the union was in. The unions were not delighted by the Blair government's performance so far as they were concerned; but they, like business, were reasonably well satisfied.

The Blair government was thus Britain's first-ever non-socialist Labour government; and it differed from its predecessors in other conspicuous ways. One was its emphasis on work — work as a means to greater material prosperity, but also as a good in itself. An American journalist famously said, following a visit to the Soviet Union in the 1920s, "I have seen the future, and it works."[9] Gordon Brown is alleged to have remarked, "I have seen the future, and it's work." To be sure, previous Labour governments had advocated full employment and when in power had actively sought to promote it, but at the same time they were inclined to take the view that being out of work was a personal misfortune rather than a matter of personal choice and that the state should therefore treat those who were unemployed generously and in a non-intrusive, non-invasive manner. The underlying premise was that, if work were available for all, all who were available for work would try to find it. Labour had historically rejected the Conservative notion that some, at least, of the unemployed were layabouts and scroungers. It had also rejected the notion that over-generous benefits — and benefits that were too easily obtained — could cause the recipients to become dependent, emotionally as well as materially, on the state rather than on themselves. Old Labour, in that sense, was soft.

New Labour was harder. Influenced to a great extent by American ideas — and to an even greater extent by American language — Blair and Brown took up an American-sounding cause: that of welfare reform. And central to the government's variegated welfare-reform programme was work: the availability of it, the demand for it, the incentives that could be offered to encourage people to go into it. New Labour still believed that full employment was a desirable goal; and as time went by Gordon Brown, in particular, became more and more forthright in stating that Labour's long-term aim remained the restoration of full employment. But in the meantime both he as chancellor of the exchequer and Blair as prime minister believed that much existing unemployment was essentially voluntary, that the poor who were unemployed would remain poor so long as they remained unemployed and that work afforded individuals status, a sense of self-worth and opportunities for personal advancement. This approach to the unemployed came naturally to the sons of a Conservative lawyer (Blair) and a Presbyterian minister (Brown). But, in addition, Blair and Brown believed that work, education and training were inextricably linked: that Britain could remain a world-class industrial power only if it possessed a highly educated, well-trained labour force and that anyone without work should be encouraged, even required, to undergo proper training, not merely for his or her own sake but for the country's.

The new government's policies matched its rhetoric. The centrepiece of its welfare-to-work programme was the so-called New Deal, initially aimed at the young unemployed, later extended to single mothers, the disabled and (in the form of New Deal Plus) people over the age of 50. Entrants into the New Deal initially underwent a period of intense personal counselling. If by the end of this period they had not moved on to education or a job, they were offered four options: a period of formal education, a job (with the employer subsidized at the rate of £60 a week), work with a voluntary body or work on an environmental project. Crucially, the New Deal embodied an element of compulsion, at least for the young: it made no allowance for a fifth option, the option of remaining indefinitely on unemployment benefit.[10] As Blair, Brown and others put it, they were offering unemployed youth "a hand up, not a handout". As the Working Families Tax Credit developed, it was also intended to provide an incentive for wage-earners in families to remain in work rather than become dependent on government benefits.

As with work, so with crime. Fairly or unfairly, Old Labour had always been seen as a party soft on crime, more concerned with reforming the criminal than with punishing him, more concerned with keeping people out of prison than with locking them up. New Labour was determined to break with that tradition, partly because Blair, Brown and other senior colleagues were stern by disposition, partly because many of them, including Jack Straw, the new home secretary, represented deprived inner-city areas where crime was rife, and partly because Blair and Brown believed, correctly, that Labour's alleged softness on crime damaged the party at the polls. While still in opposition, someone, either Tony Blair or Gordon Brown (credit was disputed), coined the phrase "tough on crime, tough on the causes of crime". Once in power, New Labour set out to act on at least the first part of that phrase.

It began by completely outlawing the private possession of handguns, a move that met with scarcely any opposition among the public and passed the House of Commons by 384 votes to 181. That move might have been labelled left-wing, though it actually had widespread support among Conservatives; but, in both tone and substance, most of the rest of the new government's agenda was anything but left-wing. Under Jack Straw, the Home Office — Britain's equivalent of the U.S. Justice Department — became a veritable legislation factory. The titles of the most important pieces of legislation capture the flavour of the factory's output: the Crime and Disorder Act 1998, the Criminal Justice (Terrorism and Conspiracy) Act 1998, the Youth Justice and Criminal Evidence Act 1999, the Criminal Justice and Court Services Act 2000, the Regulation of Investigatory Powers Act 2000 and the Terrorism Act 2000.[11] The new government extended electronic tagging of offenders, effectively lowered the age of criminal responsibility to 10, began the process of restricting the right of defendants to opt for jury trial, implemented the previous government's proposals for imposing mandatory sentences on repeat offenders, gave the police and local authorities powers to clamp down on noisy neighbours and impose curfews on unruly children and, not least, signalled to the judiciary that it would welcome more, and longer, custodial sentences. Unsurprisingly, the average prison population in England and Wales rose from 55,281 during 1996, the last full year of Conservative government, to 65,008 during 2000, the last year before the election — an increase of nearly 18 per cent in only four years.[12] At the time of the election, ministers were considering abolishing, at least in the most serious cases, the long-standing ban on double jeopardy, which prevented accused persons from being tried twice for the same offence. They were also considering making some defendants' previous convictions known to juries in criminal cases before they reached their verdicts. It was a formidable — or at least a formidable-looking — record.

The Labour government's new approach to the substance of policy was accompanied, in addition, by a new approach to political process: to the ways in which politics and government were conducted. Previous Labour administrations, however radical they had been in what they did, had tended to be rigorously orthodox in how they did it. Labour prime ministers, with the partial exception of Harold Wilson during his first term, remained essentially *primus inter pares* (first among equals). The conventions of collective cabinet government were maintained. Civil servants continued to be ministers', including the prime minister's, principal policy advisers. Indeed it was often commented that Labour governments managed to combine a radical willingness to innovate in terms of policy with a marked degree of institutional timidity. Perhaps they felt that, precisely in order to be able to fly high, they needed a secure base on the ground.

Be that as it may, New Labour under Tony Blair was determined, yet again, to be different — a fact signalled shortly before the 1997 election by one of Blair's aides, who remarked: "You may see a change from a feudal system of barons to a more Napoleonic system."[13] One baron, Gordon Brown, remained, and he was a mighty baron, wielding virtually vice-regal powers within his exclusive and extensive domain; the so-called Blair government in reality was a Blair–Brown duumvirate. However, in the rest of British government outside Gordon Brown's domain, Tony Blair was determined to "strengthen the centre" — that is, to strengthen 10 Downing Street. He was not by temperament a control-freak (though he was often accused of being such), but he mistrusted the abilities of many of the people in the Labour ranks whom he knew he would have to appoint to ministerial office after the election and he shared the widely held view that the British system suffered from excessive departmentalism and fragmentation, with the governmental machine failing to address in a holistic way such problems as child poverty and social exclusion. Like Margaret Thatcher, he had doubts about the capacity of the permanent civil service to innovate and think creatively. He was also, like almost every incoming American president, accustomed to working with *his* people: the small team of individuals, known to him personally and trusted by him, who had helped him to win office in the first place and on whom he could rely. In the British system, the transition from opposition to government is usually, in personal and personnel terms, quite abrupt. Tony Blair, American-fashion, simply brought his people in with him.

The principal private secretary to all previous postwar prime ministers had been a career civil servant, and the principal private secretary who served one prime minister might well go on to serve the next, even of a different party. Blair effected a major change. He maintained a civil servant in post who formally held the title of principal private secretary, but Blair's chief aide in opposition — Jonathan Powell, a former civil servant (who, as it happened, was the younger brother of Sir Charles Powell, one of Margaret Thatcher's principal advisers) — followed the new prime minister into Number 10 as his chief of staff. In that position, Powell absorbed — some would say usurped — many of the principal private secretary's former functions and, in an unprecedented step, was given formal authority to issue instructions to career civil servants. Similarly, the prime minister's press secretary had usually, though not invariably, been a professional civil servant, but Blair brought into Number 10 with him the man who had served under him in the same capacity in opposition, a Labour-inclined ex-journalist named Alastair Campbell. Together with Anji Hunter, Blair's highly political special assistant, Powell and Campbell constituted a formidable troika of power in Number 10, The whole of the Number 10 apparatus was politicized — and personalized — in much the same way. Many career civil servants remained and continued to perform important functions, but the Number 10 Policy Unit, as well as the Number 10 Press Office, became largely the preserve of loyal Blairites, and at a later stage a Strategic Communications Unit and a Research and Information Office, staffed along similar lines, were also established. Advocates of the new arrangements insisted that the creation of, in effect, a powerful prime minister's department was essential and, indeed, long overdue. Traditionalists, such as Britain's leading student of Whitehall politics, Peter Hennessy, deplored Blair's "command and control" governmental style, which, in his view, accorded ill with Britain's traditional constitutional practices (and which, he clearly thought, might cause Blair in the fullness of time to come to a sticky end).[14]

Not only the degree of centralization in Number 10 was new. So was the way in which back-bench Labour members of Parliament comported themselves. The role of back-bench, non-ministerial members of the governing party in the House of Commons has been limited during most of recent British history. Nevertheless, Labour prime ministers in the past have always been buffeted, and occasionally thwarted or defeated, by back-bench dissidents. Back-bench Labour MPs have historically been an unruly lot, and Wilson and Callaghan, in particular, bore the scars of large-scale rebellions, some on major economic, foreign-policy and industrial-relations issues. Blair and his colleagues during their first term had an altogether easier time. The Parliamentary Labour Party was not a body they needed to spend much time worrying about; every political commentator remarked on the PLP's unprecedented quiescence. Occasional rebellions did occur — more than 40 Labour backbenchers rebelled on four occasions, in 1997 over a proposed reduction in lone parent benefits, in 1999 over a proposal to place restrictions on entitlements to disability benefits, in 2000 on a back-bench motion to restore the link between increases in pensions and increases in average earnings and, also in 2000, over the government's plans to part-privatize the national air-traffic control system — but, especially given the controversial nature of much of the Blair government's agenda, such rebellions were remarkably few and attracted remarkably little support.[15]

Why this quiescence? The short answer is that most back-bench Labour MPs seemed to accept that almost the only serious obstacle to Labour's returning to power for a full second term would be noisy and large-scale unrest on the back benches. Both Blair and his parliamentary supporters were well aware that disunity in the Labour Party had cost the party dear in the 1970s and 1980s, and they were also aware that disunity on a comparable scale had helped to destroy the Major government. Their shared fear of disunity gave him, Blair, a weapon with which to keep them, the backbenchers, in order. Paradoxically, it may also have helped that the Labour Party's parliamentary majority, 179, was so enormous. On the one hand, the size of the majority did mean that backbenchers could rebel confident in the knowledge that the chances of the government actually being defeated were remote; but, on the other hand, the enormous size of the majority also meant that an unusually large proportion of Labour MPs now represented marginal constituencies. If the government, because of their activities, got into trouble, they got into trouble. The thought was sobering — and restraining.

And there was another factor, so obvious to British observers that its importance was often overlooked, even by them. The simple fact is that the left wing of the Labour Party had virtually collapsed. From its inception in 1901 until the 1990s, the British Labour Party had always been riven into two factions: the radical left, which sought utterly to transform British society, and the more moderate right, which sought merely to reform it. The battles between left and right had been protracted and bitter, and during much of the 1970s and 1980s the left of the party had been in the ascendant. Now the left had all but disappeared, destroyed by the collapse of communism, by its own disastrous electoral record and by the sheer implausibility, in the circumstances of the 1990s, of much traditional socialist doctrine. One consequence was that the Parliamentary Labour Party was no longer the deeply fractured entity it had once been. Not everyone was New Labour, but almost no one was an Old Socialist. In the 1970s and 1980s, Tony Benn, in particular, had been the standard-bearer of the left, a man of enormous power in the party, who struck terror into the hearts of his right-wing opponents. By the mid 1990s, Benn, still a member of the House of Commons, was almost universally regarded as an amiable old gentleman, eccentric, ineffectual, someone to be listened to with all of the respect due to the elderly, but not someone to be taken seriously. A former big beast of the jungle had been reduced to mascot status. Even right-wing Tories professed to like him.

Tony Blair's approach to politics was, as we have seen, an inclusive approach. Blair reached out to prosperous middle-class sections of the electorate; he befriended business; and he went out of his way, while keeping his distance from them, not to offend the trade unions. Ideologically, too, Blair, like Bill Clinton in the United States, was a self-consciously big-tent politician — a man, as he often said, of the "centre and centre-left", never solely of the left (almost however "left" was defined). During the early phases of his premiership, in 1997–98, he even went so far as to appoint a number of Conservative politicians to important positions. Margaret Thatcher was famously consulted on one occasion. No previous Labour prime minister had been remotely so ecumenical (though Attlee always retained a soft spot for his wartime comrade in arms, Winston Churchill).

Blair's disposition to be inclusive had one remarkable political consequence, one whose significance, if any, is still not clear and may not become clear for a number of years. Although Blair was, by both temperament and conviction, a big-tent politician, his conception of his own tent was not so big as to cover the whole, or even the bulk, of the Conservative Party. He felt akin to some individual members of the party — for example, Chris Patten, a traditional "One Nation" Conservative whom he appointed to the European Commission — but for the most part Blair was a traditional British progressive: radical by instinct, disposed to be egalitarian, disposed to side with the underdog, disliking traditional power and privilege, liberal on issues of gender, religion and race. He was not a man to worship the traditional Labour gods, but he was, as he repeatedly made clear, not a Tory.

On the contrary, Blair regarded it as the single greatest misfortune of twentieth-century British politics that at the beginning of the century the new Labour Party and the old Liberal Party had come asunder and that, close allies before the First World War, they had become implacable enemies thereafter. By universal consent, the twentieth century had been "the Conservative century", in the sense that the Conservative Party had been in power for much the largest part of it; and Blair believed that that would not have happened if the Liberal–Labour coalition — the great progressive coalition, as he saw it — had remained intact. Blair's vision for the future was that the twenty-first century, unlike the twentieth, should be "the progressive century", with the Conservative Party more or less permanently excluded from power. Thus, whereas most members of the Labour Party either ignored the new Liberal Democrat Party — formed in the late 1980s from a merger between the old Liberal Party and the new Social Democratic Party, a breakaway from Labour — or else held it in disdain, Blair felt comfortable with Liberal Democrat politicians and, in particular, with the Liberal Democrats' leader until 1999, Paddy Ashdown.

More than that, Blair believed that the chances of the twenty-first century's being a progressive century would be greatly increased if the Labour Party and the Liberal Democrats could find some way of working together, possibly involving a merger between them, undoing, so to speak, the damage done to progressive politics some eighty years before. David Denver in Chapter 6 of this book discusses in detail the development of relations between the two parties during the

1997 parliament and in the period leading up to the 2001 election. Suffice it to say here that Labour–Liberal Democrat cooperation formed part of what Blair and his allies called "the project" and that, as a symbol of his long-term aims, a joint Labour–Liberal Democrat committee on the constitution, formally designated a cabinet committee, met in Downing Street during most of Tony Blair's first term. It achieved little. Its significance, if it had any, lay in the fact that it existed at all.

New Labour at Sea

The reader could be forgiven if, at this point, he or she concluded that the good ship New Labour had had an easy passage between 1997 and 2001. After all, the economy was buoyant, the new-style Labour Party had managed to bring on board the trade unions, business and large sections of the middle classes, there were no serious signs of mutiny among the Labour Party's crew either above decks in Parliament or below decks in the country, and relations between Captain Blair and his most important passengers, the Liberal Democrats, remained reasonably good, even if they were not quite as cordial under Charles Kennedy from 1999 onwards as they had been under his predecessor, Paddy Ashdown.

But, if that is the impression conveyed so far, it is totally false. During his first term Tony Blair did not run into rough weather on anything like the scale encountered by John Major between 1992 and 1997, but his first four years were remarkably turbulent and choppy nonetheless. Crisis followed crisis, there were few periods of sustained calm, and Blair and those around him often seemed nervous, unsure of themselves, even frantic. Moreover, the public, although it never turned en masse against the prime minister and his government, showed its displeasure in a wide variety of ways. Whatever the final outcome of the 2001 election, the Blair government was not a popular government.

The British Gallup Poll asks every month three relevant questions. The first concerns the incumbent government as a whole and asks: "Do you approve or disapprove of the government's record to date?" The second concerns the incumbent prime minister and asks, in the present instance: "Are you satisfied or dissatisfied with Tony Blair as prime minister?" And the third question, asked since the beginning of 1998, is concerned with the incumbent government's probity and asks: "Do you think that the government has, on balance, been honest and trustworthy or not?"

Figure 1.2 sets out the responses, quarter by quarter, to all three questions for the period from New Labour's election at the beginning of May 1997 until the time of the general election in June 2001. Only the proportions approving of the government's record, satisfied with Blair as prime minister and believing that the government has, on balance, proved honest and trustworthy are shown. As can readily be seen, all three lines on the graph slope sharply downwards. Blair remained more popular than his government has a whole. Even so, his rating fell from above 65 per cent during the whole of his first eighteen months in office to

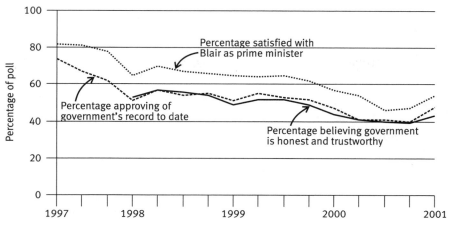

Figure 1.2 Ratings of Government and Blair, 1997–2001

Sources: King and Wybrow, eds., *British Political Opinion,* 177–8, 197–8, 181–2; *Gallup Political and Economic Index,* Report No. 487, March 2001, 11–3.

below 50 per cent during much of the final year of his first term. The approval rating of the government itself, never quite as high, fell from more than 50 per cent during its first few heady months to less than 40 per cent during some months in 2000. The proportion thinking the government was proving honest and trustworthy began well above 50 per cent, then fell to the point where it was usually hovering about 40 per cent and sometimes fell below. The figures suggest that, at least in voters' eyes, something, somewhere was amiss. What was it?

The answer falls under a number of headings, each of which deserves separate exploration.

The Plight of the Public Services

Labour won its massive 1997 election victory in large part because voters believed that the Labour Party, unlike the Conservative Party, would invest in, and improve the quality of, Britain's great public services: the National Heath Service (NHS), the state education system and, to a lesser extent, public transport. Pre-election polls in 1997 showed beyond any doubt that fear for the future of the public services under the Conservatives was one of the main reasons why hundreds of thousands of voters switched to Labour. To some extent, altruism and disinterested concern for others were involved, but more important was the fact that the overwhelming majority of the British population — to the extent of roughly 90 per cent in the cases of the NHS and state education — are personally dependant on state-provided services. New Labour in opposition had gone out of its way to avoid making extravagant promises in connection with the NHS, the education system and so forth, but, even so, the Labour Party had long been closely associated in voters' minds with the public services — the postwar Attlee government had largely created the modern welfare state — and expectations, or at least hopes, were high. They were largely disappointed.

The National Heath Service is an especially exposed service. Not only do most people in Britain depend on it, they make a great deal of use of it; and, because they make a great deal of use of it, the majority of them have some personal experience, either directly or through conversations with friends and relatives, of how well or badly it is performing. The NHS is no ideological abstraction; it is alive, real, close to home. In addition, the British press, especially the tabloid press, relishes NHS-related horror stories: of old ladies' operations being postponed so often that they become inoperable, of accident victims left lying for hours, even days, on hospital trolleys as a result of chronic shortages of beds. Even if the new Labour government had acted quickly to repair the service's deficiencies, it would have taken years to make good the existing backlog of modern hospitals, cancer specialists and trained nurses.

But it did not act quickly. Because of Gordon Brown's insistence on sticking during his first two years to the previous government's spending limits, the rate of increase in NHS spending actually fell between 1997 and 1999. Under John Major, NHS spending had increased in real terms at an average annual rate of 3.3 per cent, already below the postwar average of 3.4 per cent. Under Gordon Brown, the rate of increase fell still further to 2.0 per cent.[16] In practical terms, years of financial stringency under the Conservatives were followed by years of financial stringency under Labour, with the result that parts of the NHS, far from showing significant improvement, actually deteriorated. And the public noticed. So did the newspapers. Not only that, but Lord Winston, the most famous doctor in the country, a television personality who also happened to be a Labour supporter, dismissed New Labour's health policy as "deceitful" and maintained publicly that Britain had the worst health service in Europe, worse even than Poland's.[17]

Once the two years were up, the government would have sharply increased NHS spending in any case, but the evidence of public discontent, not to mention Lord Winston's démarche, brought forward the government's announcements of spending increases and led the prime minister on television to declare that New Labour's objective was nothing less than to match, sooner rather than later, European levels of health spending. Brown in his 2000 budget announced that over each of the next four years the amount of money going into the NHS would increase at an average rate, in real terms, of 6.1 per cent — nearly double the postwar rate.[18] By 2004 the United Kingdom would be spending almost as much on health care as a proportion of gross domestic product (GDP) as its continental neighbours. After extensive consultation, the government in 2000 also launched an ambitious National Plan for the NHS, including detailed targets relating to such matters as maximum waiting times for routine operations, the numbers of new health-care professionals and the cleanliness of hospital wards. But all that was for the future. Two students of social policy, both sympathetic to New Labour, concluded that overall the government in 2001 was left "with a weak record on achievements so far, only able to promise that the best is yet to come over the second term."[19]

The new government undoubtedly fared better, though not a great deal better, in the field of education. Blair in opposition had insisted repeatedly that New Labour had three and only three priorities: "education, education, education". Blair and his education secretary, a former city council leader named David Blunkett (one of the first totally blind people ever to head a major government department anywhere), believed that education provided young people with opportunity: with their best chance, perhaps their only chance, of escaping from social deprivation and poverty. Certainly education had provided Blunkett himself — the son of a shift worker in the gas industry — with the means of self-advancement.[20] Blair and Blunkett also believed, as did Brown, in the crucial importance to the economy of creating a literate, numerate, technically skilled and, above all, adaptable workforce. A few years of schooling at an early age were no longer going to be enough. "Lifelong learning" quickly became the new government's educational catchphrase.

Labour in power did score some successes. Most of those both in and out of the world of education welcomed the introduction in primary schools of literacy and numeracy hours (the implication, correct, being that primary schools had previously failed to teach a large proportion of their pupils the three Rs). Class sizes in primary schools, though not secondary schools, were somewhat reduced, and the proportion of pupils obtaining good results at the end of their secondary education increased slowly but steadily. Although a decline in the standard of the relevant examinations was frequently alleged, there was little hard evidence to prove it. In addition, the proportion of young people attending university steadily increased under the Labour government as it had under the Conservatives. By 2000 roughly a third of 18–21 year olds were entering higher education, nearly double the figure of a generation before.

That said, Labour ministers themselves were dissatisfied with the performance of the educational system as a whole, and there was a great deal of hard evidence that all was far from well. Because of the Brown freeze, little extra money was spent on education during Labour's first two years, and low pay in the teaching profession — teachers' earnings as a proportion of average non-manual earnings had already fallen precipitously under the Conservatives — meant that the profession was failing to attract sufficiently high-calibre recruits and that serious teacher shortages were developing in a number of academic subjects, including science and mathematics. Teacher–pupil ratios in secondary schools deteriorated, and in extreme cases (though, admittedly, they were extreme) teacher shortages forced schools to operate a four-day instead of a five-day week. Too many school buildings, by universal consent, were dilapidated and under-equipped. Moreover, partly because money was not initially forthcoming from the Treasury, education ministers and Blair himself often substituted the language of exhortation for the language of resources. Blair and Blunkett spoke of the need to raise standards in schools, of poor-quality teachers, of failing schools, of the need to "name and shame" schools that were underperforming, of the need, possibly, to involve the private sector on a substantial scale in state education. Their rhetoric — sustained over the whole four years of Blair's first term — sent mixed messages. On the one hand, it testified to ministers' determination to improve educational standards. On the other hand, it forcefully drew attention to the fact that so far they had not had a great deal of success. As in the case of the NHS, Brown in his 2000 budget announced that massive increases in education spending would take place over the next four years; but, also as in the case of the NHS, a typical and grudging verdict was "could do better".

If the state education service was in a bad way, the newly privatized railways were in even worse condition. The previous Conservative government, in privatizing Britain's rail network, had achieved what even many Conservatives later admitted was the worst of all worlds. Ownership and management were both fragmented, with control of the infrastructure — the right of way, signalling and the larger big-city stations — in the hands of a single large corporation, Railtrack, while actual train operations were in the hands of a large number of individual train operating companies. Services on some lines improved but on others deteriorated; investment was not on a sufficient scale to maintain the existing network, let alone to expand and improve it; and day-to-day maintenance standards deteriorated to the point where they were slipshod, even dangerous. In the wake of two previous disasters, at Southall and Ladbroke Grove, both in west London, the climax came in October 2000 when a Great North Eastern express travelling at 115 mph came off the rails at Hatfield in Hertfordshire. Not many people died, only four, fewer than at either Southall (seven) or Ladbroke Grove (thirty-one), but it soon emerged that the cause of the crash was a cracked rail, one that had previously been reported, and that similar cracking, both reported and unreported, was to be found throughout the whole rail network, from the south of England to the north of Scotland. As a result of the inspections and repairs necessitated by the Hatfield disaster, trains all over the country were subject to cancellations and delays — sometimes severe delays — for the following six months. Railtrack lost what little remained of its reputation, the operating companies lost money, and thousands of passengers, especially commuters into big cities, were seriously inconvenienced.[21] Meanwhile, the London Underground, the world's first underground railway and once a source of considerable national pride, decayed visibly as the government could not, or would not, find the means of financing the massive new investment that would be needed to bring it up to the standards of, say, Berlin, Paris or Washington, D.C.

The London Underground was still publicly owned, and the government of the day could therefore still be blamed for its crumbling condition. The railways were no longer publicly owned, and the government could therefore not be blamed, in any straightforward way, for what was going wrong. The significance of the Hatfield crash and its aftermath lay in the fact that it symbolized people's sense that the public services in general, whoever owned them, were simply not up to standard. People not only hoped for more, they expected more, and they were not getting it.

With respect to crime and law and order, their expectations were probably somewhat lower; many people are sceptical about any government's capacity to do much about prevailing levels of crime, whatever they are. But even here the government's record during its first four years was patchy and seen to be so. The number of people locked up increased, but the number of policemen actually fell. More to the point, although the best evidence suggested that overall levels of crime, including violent crime, were tending to fall, opinion polls showed that many voters believed the opposite. Fear of crime, and the belief that crime rates were rising, were fuelled by the tabloid press, notably by the *Daily Mail* and the *News of the World,* which printed lurid accounts of a few peculiarly unpleasant crimes and contrived at the same time to give the impression that such crimes were both typical and common. In fact, a sharp rise in reported street robberies was apparently due to an increase in teenagers stealing one another's mobile phones. The government itself contributed to the widespread sense that the country was in the midst of a crime wave by failing straightforwardly to deny that it was (for fear of appearing soft on crime) and also by responding to press criticism and public concerns with ever more draconian — or at least draconian-sounding — measures. Jack Straw's reputation for toughness depended in part on his giving the impression that there was a great deal to be tough about.

Tony Blair and his colleagues were vividly aware that, in the end, their government would be judged, not on the basis of what it said but on the basis of what it did. "Delivery" therefore became one of New Labour's constant themes. To achieve delivery, the new resources to be pumped into the public services were to be matched by reform and modernization of the services. But the public remained largely unimpressed. The British Gallup Poll asked people from time to time during the parliament whether they thought the Blair government was actually delivering or not. Table 1.3 (p. 24) reports the results of one such survey conducted in August 2000. As can be seen, the government was awarded high marks for reducing unemployment, much lower but still reasonably good marks for improving the quality of education in schools, but marks ranging from poor

Table 1.3 Blair Government and "Delivery"

There is a lot of talk at the moment about whether the present government is or is not "delivering". From what you know, do you think it is or is not delivering on each of the following?	Yes, is delivering	No, is not delivering
Getting people back to work	62	34
Improving the quality of education in schools	50	44
Putting an end to the old stop-go, boom and bust economic cycle	47	37
Improving the National Health Service	40	58
Being tough on crime and tough on the causes of crime	31	66
Improving the quality of public transport	25	70

Source: Gallup Political and Economic Index, Report No. 480, August 2000, 8.

to dreadful in connection with the NHS, public transport (even before the Hatfield crash) and crime. The government's failure to deliver became one of the themes of the Conservative Party's election campaign.

Sleaze

There were also doubts about New Labour's morality, not about its moral code but about ministers' and MPs' actual behaviour. One factor leading to the Conservative rout at the 1997 general election — how large a factor no one can say — was "sleaze": the plethora of unsavoury rumours that swirled around John Major's government, many of them subsequently shown to be well founded, some not. It was said that Conservative MPs were being paid to ask parliamentary questions, that Conservative ministers were abusing their power for personal or partisan advantage and that some Conservative politicians' sex lives did not bear too close examination (though that, of course, is what they got). Tony Blair and his colleagues in opposition and again in the early months of government made much of the fact that Labour in power would maintain much higher standards. "We will clean up politics," the 1997 Labour manifesto announced primly — twice.[22] In other words, New Labour was also to be Clean Labour.

Real life proved rather messier.

- As one manifestation of his new business-friendly approach, Blair appointed Sir David Simon, the chairman of BP, as minister of state for trade and competitiveness in Europe. The rules required that Simon, now Lord Simon of Highbury, should sell or place in a blind trust any of his shareholdings that could give rise to a real or perceived conflict of interest. Most of Simon's shareholdings were in BP, and the trustees of the blind trust would therefore be obliged to sell those shares so that they could create on Simon's behalf a more balanced (and therefore more conflict-of-interest free) portfolio. However, the City of London's rules against insider trading forbade a person like the recently ex-chairman of BP from selling BP shares so long as he might be in a position to benefit from insider knowledge. Simon took official advice, chose not to sell his shares immediately but decided instead that, until he did sell them, no matter relating to BP should be allowed to cross his desk. Simon and his officials behaved honourably throughout, but the Conservatives in the House of Commons enjoyed themselves hugely at the government's — and especially the prime minister's — expense.

- Far more serious was the Bernie Ecclestone affair. Ecclestone, a multi-millionaire and effective overlord of worldwide Formula One motor racing, had been persuaded by a friend to donate £1 million to the Labour Party. The fact that he had donated money to the party, but not the precise amount, would in any case have become public knowledge in due course, but for the time being the matter remained a secret between Ecclestone and party officials. Meanwhile, however, the new Labour government was pressing for a Europe-wide ban on both tobacco advertising and tobacco sponsorship. If such a ban were imposed, one of several sports that would be hard hit — because of the existence of lucrative sponsorship deals — would be Formula One. Ecclestone and two colleagues accordingly requested, and were granted, a private audience with Tony Blair at Number 10. Almost immediately thereafter, the government announced a change of policy to allow Formula One to be exempted from the ban. Immediately after that, it became known that Ecclestone and his colleagues had seen Blair and also that Ecclestone had made a large donation to the Labour Party. Journalists quickly prised out of Ecclestone just how large the donation had been. The algorithm was perfect: man gives money to party; government proposes policy; man goes to see prime minister; policy is changed. In fact, the policy would probably have been changed anyway, but the damage had been done — and would have been even greater if the Labour Party had not agreed to refund Ecclestone his £1 million. Within less than a year of taking office, the new prime minister and his government were thus made to look devious, secretive, stupid (Ecclestone referred to "those clowns" in Downing Street) and possibly even corrupt.[23] Blair was forced to apologize on television. It is doubtful whether New Labour's reputation for probity ever fully recovered.

- Another of Blair's business-friendly appointments was that of Geoffrey Robinson, a wealthy business man and former chief executive of Jaguar Cars, to the number-three ministerial post in the Treasury. While still in opposition, Blair and his family had holidayed in Robinson's substantial villa in Tuscany. Towards the end of 1997, it emerged that Robinson's financial holdings included a beneficial interest in a £12 million off-shore trust based in Guernsey. He had not declared this interest in the House of Commons Register of Members' Interests, and it was also embarrassing that Robinson, a senior minister in a department concerned with trying to eliminate tax avoidance, was himself involved in a large-scale tax-avoidance scheme. As though that were not enough, Robinson was soon afterwards accused of failing to declare in the House of Commons register a payment of £200,000 he had allegedly received several years before as chairman of a company owned by the soon-to-be disgraced and now dead tycoon Robert Maxwell. Robinson denied ever having received the money. Not everyone believed him, but he remained, for the time being, in post.[24]

- There followed the affair of the Lord Chancellor's wallpaper, trivial in itself but suggesting that, now that they were in office, some New Labour ministers were ready to shrug off the cloak of humility that they had worn in opposition. The Lord Chancellor, Lord Irvine of Lairg and one of the prime minister's inner circle, went ahead with the refurbishment of his official residence in the Palace of Westminster at a cost estimated at £330,000, including the sum of £59,000 to be spent on hand-made wallpaper copied from the original designs of the palace's Victorian architect, Augustus Pugin. Irvine chose at the same time to liken himself to his Tudor predecessor as Lord Chancellor, Cardinal Wolsey. The government's more solemn critics refused to see the joke.

- New Labour's claims that it occupied the high moral ground were further undermined in the summer of 1998 by what was briefly known as the "cash for access" affair. A man called Derek Draper, a New Labour hanger-on turned lobbyist, boasted at a reception in Whitehall's Banqueting Hall that he personally knew all the people who counted at Number 10. More than that, he introduced Roger Liddle, an old friend of his who was now a member of the Number 10 Policy Unit, to an American business man whom he had just encountered at the reception. Liddle in turn handed the American his business card with both his home and Number 10 phone numbers, inviting him to give him a call. Unfortunately for Draper and Liddle, the American "business man" was in fact an American freelance journalist, employed by the Sunday *Observer*. When details of the encounter appeared in the paper a few days later, Draper was forced to resign from his lobbying firm. The prime minister did not insist on Liddle's resignation but did tighten up the rules on the relations between government advisers and lobbyists. "We must", he declared, in a phrase that was to come back to haunt him, "be purer than pure."[25]

- One problem with being purer than pure — or at least with being seen to be so — was that Geoffrey Robinson was still a Treasury minister. Unbeknownst to the prime minister, Robinson had, before the 1997 election, lent Peter Mandelson £373,000 towards the purchase of a luxury house in a fashionable part of west London. Mandelson was one of Tony Blair's closest friends and allies, one of the principal architects of New Labour and, by the autumn of 1998, a member of the cabinet as secretary of state for trade and industry. In his departmental capacity, he now found himself responsible for overseeing the official investigations that by this time were taking place into the financial dealings of his creditor-colleague, Geoffrey Robinson. Perfectly properly, Mandelson resiled from any direct involvement with these investigations on the ground that Robinson was his ministerial colleague; but he neglected to inform either the prime minister or his department's permanent secretary that Robinson was not merely his colleague but his creditor — on a lavish scale. Mandelson's enemies did, however, take the trouble to inform selected journalists, and, when the story finally broke, Mandelson and Robinson were both forced to resign. The episode hugely damaged the government's reputation. Mandelson's sin was, on the face of it, venial rather than mortal, and Blair, once informed of the circumstances of the loan, acted swiftly; but Mandelson, a senior minister and close friend of Blair, had been shown to be less than candid, and an association that had already been established in many voters' minds between New Labour and a somewhat louche life-style was further reinforced. The details might be obscure, but the fact that the whole affair appeared somewhat seedy was undeniable.[26]

- The funding of the Labour Party continued to raise issues that were awkward for both the government and the party. Labour's difficulty, like that of the Conservatives, was that its traditional sources of funds were drying up. Fewer individuals belonged to the party than in previous generations. More important, the trade-union movement's donations to the party were on a smaller scale than in the past (partly, though not wholly, because the party wanted to be seen to be less dependent on the unions). The Labour Party instead found itself having to rely for a substantial portion of its income on very large donations from a few wealthy individuals. Bernie Ecclestone was one such individual (though he, uniquely, got his money back). Others, whose names emerged towards the end of the parliament, were Lord Sainsbury of the supermarket chain, who was also a government minister, Christopher Ondaatje, a Sri Lankan-born business man and philanthropist, and Lord Hamlyn, a multi-millionaire publisher. Among them they gave the party in the order of £9 million. Such a high degree of dependence on a few rich individuals would in any case have been slightly embarrassing for Labour (as a similar dependence was for the Conservatives), but in one case the Labour Party set out to evade soon-to-be-implemented legal requirements both by refusing to disclose the donor's name until the party's accounts were published and also by refusing ever to disclose the amount donated because the party's internal rules, pending the implementation of the new requirements, stated only that large donors' names should be revealed, not the precise amount they had donated. Fortunately for Labour and the government's reputation, the donor in question, Lord Hamlyn, agreed within a few days that both his identity and the amount he had donated, £2 million, should be made public. But the attempt at secrecy had already been condemned by prominent Labour MPs as well as by the Conservatives, and a former member of the Committee on Standards in Public Life, which had recommended to the government the imminent disclosure requirements, said Labour's behaviour struck him as "grubby".[27]

- Only a few weeks later Lord Irvine — he of the Pugin wallpaper — found himself in the midst of another fund-raising controversy. As Lord Chancellor, Lord Irvine was not only a senior member of the government: he was responsible for appointing judges and elevating barristers to the position of Queen's Counsel (thus elevating their status and potentially their incomes). For obvious reasons, previous Lord Chancellors had been careful — some, admittedly, more so than others — to distinguish between their political and their judicial roles. However, many in the legal profession were amazed, even horrified, when it was revealed in February 2001 that Lord Irvine, writing on Labour Party notepaper, had invited known Labour sympathizers in the profession to a fund-raising dinner at which the prime minister's wife, Cherie Blair, would be the guest of honour. "We will be making an appeal on the evening for the Labour Party's general election fund," Lord Irvine wrote. "The minimum amount you will be invited to pledge is £200 per person, but we know many of you will take the opportunity to make a significant contribution."[28] Labour party officials denied that Lord Irvine was bringing pressure to bear on would-be judges and QCs, and there was almost certainly no intention to bring such pressure, but, again, the algorithm was obvious: man with power invites you to attend dinner and give money; you attend dinner and give money; your chances of obtaining patronage from the man with power are thereby likely to be increased (and certainly not diminished). Almost no one outside the Labour Party was prepared to defend Lord Irvine's actions. "By jeopardising his independence", a former chairman of the Bar Council said, "he has done something which no other Lord Chancellor would have dreamed of doing."[29] In the House of Lords a few days later, Lord Irvine's behaviour was universally condemned. He himself appeared only slightly contrite.

- In early 2001, only a few months before the general election, Peter Mandelson was in trouble again. Following his resignation over his home-loan affair in 1998, Mandelson had spent a year and a half on the back benches before returning to the cabinet as Northern Ireland secretary in the autumn of 1999. It was a measure of Blair's confidence in Mandelson, and indeed his reliance on him, that he was prepared to give him a second chance. Mandelson proved a considerable success as Northern Ireland secretary, as he had shown every sign of proving a success at the Department of Trade and Industry. But the "Mandelson I" of 1998 was now followed by "Mandelson II". It was alleged that several years earlier Mandelson, when already a minister, had lobbied the Home Office to grant a British passport to a wealthy Indian business man, Srichand Hinduja. Hinduja and his brother, Gopichand, had helped rescue a project close to Mandelson's heart, and it was perfectly natural that Mandelson should have wished to return the favour; but, in the first place, it was against the rules for ministers to lobby one another over passport applications, and, in the second, the Hinduja brothers happened to have been accused by the authorities in their homeland, India, of serious corruption in connection with large-scale arms deals. In fact, Mandelson, well aware of the rules, denied flatly ever having lobbied the Home Office. However, there was considerable confusion about whether or not he had personally been in contact with the Home Office, and Number 10 came to believe that, although he had probably not done anything seriously wrong (and quite possibly nothing wrong at all), he had not been entirely candid in his dealings with Number 10. Equally important, it was by now evident that Mandelson was a man whose presence in the government, for whatever reason, seemed inevitably to arouse controversy. Bluntly, Mandelson was bad news. After a strained and at times emotional meeting at Number 10, Blair sacked Mandelson for the second — and almost certainly the final — time.

- Even then, the last had not been heard of the Hinduja brothers. It emerged that the brothers had long had, and continued to have, close business links with Keith Vaz, a lawyer and Labour MP who in 1999 became minister of state at the Foreign Office in charge of Britain's relations with Europe. During 2000 and 2001 an extended series of newspaper reports alleged that Vaz had accepted money from a business man whom he had subsequently recommended for an honour, that he had taken money from another business man who wanted help with planning applications for a mosque, that officials in his constituency party had no knowledge of substantial contributions made to Vaz's campaign funds, that he had failed to disclose financial links with the Hinduja brothers on whose behalf he had lobbied for a passport before becoming a minister and that he had failed to disclose many of these connections and transactions in the parliamentary Register of Members' Interests. The Parliamentary Commissioner for Standards, Elizabeth Filkin, investigated all the complaints made against him and found against him in one instance; but she complained that, in other instances, Vaz and his lawyers persistently obstructed her enquiries and prevented her from reaching firm conclusions. Yet another enquiry, specifically concerned with Vaz's links with the Hinduja brothers, was under way when the election was called. Vaz was allowed to remain a minister, at least for the time being.

These were not the only episodes that gave the impression that New Labour was failing to live up to the high standards it had set itself. A number of Labour MPs were temporarily suspended from the House of Commons either for failing to declare relevant financial interests or for leaking draft select committee reports, including to ministers. It was claimed that John Reid, Blair's secretary of state for Scotland, had encouraged members of his staff, whose salaries were paid for out of public funds, to campaign for the Scottish Labour Party. Allegations concerning Geoffrey Robinson's business dealings were seldom out of the news for long. There were also, inevitably, reports of incidents involving MPs' and ministers' private lives. A Scottish member of Parliament committed suicide, leaving a note accusing a fellow Labour member of having spread malicious rumours about his health and sexual orientation. Robin Cook, the foreign secretary, threw over his wife of nearly thirty years in a VIP departure lounge at Heathrow Airport. Ron Davies, the Welsh secretary, resigned after an incident on Clapham Common that he afterwards delicately described as "a moment of madness". Although there is no evidence that voters were unduly concerned about these purely private episodes, or that they had any significant effect on the Blair administration's overall standing, the more political episodes — and those that linked politics to money — undoubtedly caused large numbers of people increasingly to question New Labour's honesty and integrity. New Labour was not, after all, turning out to be purer than pure. Clean Labour was turning out to resemble more closely a well-known character in children's fiction: Slightly Soiled.[30]

Spin

If New Labour in power thus quickly became a school for scandal, it also became a school for cynicism. By June 2001 the word "spin" had become indissolubly linked with the Blair government and its political style. New Labour never suffered from a credibility gap on the scale suffered by President Lyndon Johnson in the United States during the Vietnam War, but the fact that the two could be mentioned in the same breath was nevertheless revealing.

The Blair government between 1997 and 2001 was, by a wide margin, more continuously preoccupied with issues of presentation than any of its predecessors.[31] Blair and those around him were desperate to win a second term in office. They were acutely aware of the damage that Old Labour had inflicted on itself as a result of its internal divisions and its lack of interest in relating to the great British public. They were also acutely aware of how badly the outgoing Major administration had suffered from its disunity and its poor relations with the press. Not least, the Blair people believed that their American friend and ally, Bill Clinton, owed both his election in 1992 and his re-election in 1996 not merely to his middle-of-the-road appeal in terms of policies but to his unwavering concentration on connecting with both the media and the public. Bill Clinton's politics was the politics of opinion polls, focus groups, war rooms, rapid rebuttal units, photo opportunities, camera angles, subdued lighting, coordinated colour schemes, fast fades and the twenty-four hour news cycle. Tony Blair's was too. Clinton proved himself to be a consummate actor-manager. Blair had the same ambition.

The centrality of Blair's concern with the media and public relations was apparent in the entire structure and personnel of his Downing Street operation. Not only did Alastair Campbell, Blair's principal press spokesman and adviser in opposition, become, as we have seen, the prime minister's official press secretary in government: he was, and remained, one of Blair's closest friends, advisers and confidants. Often described as the real deputy prime minister, he even attracted a full-length biography, only the second British press secretary ever to do so.[32] He initiated the reorganization of the official Government Information and Communication Service, discussed by Colin Seymour-Ure in Chapter 5, and the creation in Number 10 of the Blairite Strategic Communications Unit. Another of the prime minister's innermost circle until his fall in January 2001 — and, some would say, even thereafter — was Peter Mandelson. A former television producer, his principal preoccupations, like those of Campbell, were with the media and public presentation. In the 1980s he had been the Labour Party's director of communications and, in a less formal way, he still cast himself — and was still cast by Blair — in that role. Blair saw Campbell in person almost every day; Mandelson he spoke to on the phone nearly as often. Philip Gould, a publicist and one of Britain's few full-time political consultants, was the third member of Blair's specialized but highly influential public-relations troika. Gould supervised the prime minister's polling, ran his focus groups and, like Campbell and Mandelson, was constantly turned to for political advice (for example, at the time of Mandelson's first resignation).[33] It is striking that Campbell, Mandelson and Gould feature prominently in the index of every book — and there are a lot of books — about Blair and his administration.[34]

Blair and his public-relations advisers had a number of straightforward objectives. They wanted the new government — in the jargon of the time — to be constantly "on message", to be at all times "singing from the same hymn sheet". There were to be none of the public displays of disunity that had characterized Old Labour and John Major's shambolic Tory administration. In addition, they wanted to control the content of the single message: to compose the tunes and write the words on the hymn sheet. Finally, they wanted to control the timing of government pronouncements, so that they achieved maximum publicity and were not eclipsed by other news developments.

This approach, and the administrative apparatus underpinning it, achieved in its own terms a considerable degree of success. Government initiatives were frequently — and successfully — trailed in one or more of the Sunday papers, then trailed again on BBC Radio 4's *Today* programme, then announced in the House of Commons (or elsewhere), then reported on that evening's television news bulletins; the media-conscious public at least knew that the government had acted (or at least spoken). Flat contradictions between ministers were for the most part avoided. So were major collisions between government announcements and predictable public events. Even the government's severest critics acknowledged that Tony Blair and Alastair Campbell's handling of the death of Princess Diana in a road accident in August 1997 had been superb. The prime minister's brief, dignified tribute to the dead princess — whom he dubbed "the people's princess" — was seen by tens of millions on television and reprinted in newspapers around the world.

There were, however, problems. One was that Blair and Campbell were, in the end, trying to control the uncontrollable. By 1997, as Colin Seymour-Ure shows in Chapter 5, the number of media outlets — especially in the electronic media — had grown almost exponentially since Labour had last been in power. Each was in the business of making its own mark; each was in the business of trying to catch politicians out. An off-the-cuff interview on an obscure local radio station could suddenly become national news. Moreover, ministers themselves could not be controlled. More precisely, not all ministers could be controlled all of the time. Clare Short, the international development minister, and Mo Mowlam, the Northern Ireland secretary and later a Cabinet Office minister, both became famous — and popular — for constantly speaking out of turn. John Prescott, a pugnacious man and the only patently working-class member of Tony Blair's cabinet, also became famous — and popular — for the same reason. In the early months of the new administration, Prescott, who was not over-fond of Peter Mandelson, visited a building site in east London, picked up a jar containing a small crab and announced to the television cameras — and therefore to the world — that he proposed to name the crab "Peter". He proceeded to address the small creature in unflattering terms. Moreover, even if most ministers could mostly be kept on message, many of their political aides — their so-called special advisers — could not. There were a lot of them, far more than under any previous administration, and many of them loved talking to journalists — unattributably, of course. What they said was frequently damaging. If Blair and Campbell often gave the appearance of being control freaks, it was partly because there was so much they wanted to control and because so much of what they wanted to control was actually beyond their control. Campbell, in particular, wore a look of almost permanent anxiety.

The problem of uncontrollability was compounded by the fact that, while most cabinet ministers were wholly loyal to Blair, whether by instinct or calculation, a number of them had their own agendas, their own personal hymn sheets. Gordon Brown, in particular, was determined to speak his mind on economic policy in general and the single European currency in particular. The government's line on the single currency, which would have been somewhat unclear in any case, was additionally blurred by the fact that, whereas Blair usually sounded positive and up-beat, Brown more commonly sounded less positive and more down-beat. This difference in emphasis was not the result of subtle coordination between the two men; it was the result of genuine disagreements and the on-going struggle for turf that characterized the relationship between them. On occasion, it led to considerable public embarrassment. In the case of the euro, what *was* the message that ministers were supposed to be on?[35]

Another problem with government presentation was that people kept making mistakes. Those in and around Number 10 were supposed to be geniuses at public relations. Perhaps they were — but they sometimes behaved like dunces. Gordon Brown's press secretary, Charlie Whelan, was forced to resign when two Liberal Democrat press officers overheard him in a pub briefing journalists on a sensitive issue on his mobile phone. Brown himself brought down the wrath of pensioners on the government's head early in 2000 by refusing to raise the state pension by more than 75p a week. Later in the same year, Tony Blair was slow-handclapped and heckled at a large Women's Institute gathering because his speech, delivered to a largely non-political audience, was thought to be too political in tone; embarrassed and visibly unsure of himself, Blair floundered badly. The prime minister and his people also seriously misjudged the opening of the Labour Party's election campaign a year later. Instead of making a formal announcement on the steps of Number 10, Blair launched the campaign in front of an audience of school-children in a church school in south London. Posed before a stained-glass window and speaking from a lectern that resembled a pulpit, Blair looked more like a bishop conferring a blessing than a politician avid in the pursuit of power. The occasion was variously described in the next day's newspapers as "nauseating and emotionally exploitative" (*The Times*), "deeply cynical" (*Guardian*), "disturbing" (*Daily Telegraph*) and "ridiculous" (*Independent*).[36]

But the main problem with spin and presentation from the government's point of view was that it was so quickly seen through, first by journalists and broadcasters, then by the general public. The selling of the government's story soon became the story. Pronouncements by Her Majesty's Government were no longer solemn and authoritative: they came to be treated with the same generalized scepticism as television and radio commercials. The British Medical Association repeatedly accused the government of spinning the statistics on the numbers of new doctors entering the profession. The Royal College of Nurses made the same accusation with regard to nurses. A widely publicized *Panorama* programme on BBC Television demonstrated that ministers more than once announced new spending on the NHS, then announced it again and then announced it yet again, on each occasion giving the impression that it was new money that was going to be spent. Even some ministers began to complain about the "culture of spin" and Downing Street's involvement in it. In the summer of 2001, a series of leaked memoranda from Philip Gould and the prime minister himself revealed how obsessed with its public image the government was and how this obsession was itself damaging its image. By the time of the 2001 election a mordant journalist was heard to say: "If the government announced that the sun was going to rise in the east tomorrow, I would get out of bed in the morning and instinctively face west."

Opinion polls provided evidence of how mistrustful the general public, and not just journalists, had become. The Gallup Poll in the autumn of 1999 asked the following question:

> Some people are saying at the moment that government ministers quite frequently mislead the public by claiming that additional money will be spent on the NHS or some other public service when the money is not actually new and also by claiming that they are taking new initiatives when all they are doing is pursuing existing policy. Do you agree or disagree that ministers quite frequently try to mislead the public in this way?

Even though the same survey showed Labour to be well ahead of the Conservatives, no fewer than 82 per cent of Gallup's respondents agreed that ministers quite frequently sought to mislead the public in this way.[37] In another survey, conducted immediately after the 2001 election, a massive 92 per cent of Gallup's sample said they hoped that the Blair government in its second term "would place more emphasis on practical achievements and less on presentation."[38]

Events and Personalities

The widespread sense that there was something amiss with the Blair administration, despite its undoubted successes, was fuelled by a number of other circumstances and developments. Some may have been symptomatic of a deeper malaise. Others represented sheer bad luck, of the kind that can befall any government. It was a Conservative prime minister, Harold Macmillan, who, when asked to name the major single challenge facing all prime ministers, replied simply, "Events, dear boy, events." Some events Tony Blair and his colleagues responded to well — notably the Kosovo conflict in 1999, when one insider described Blair's performance in office as "hugely impressive", even "awesome" — but others they responded to less well.[39]

The Blair government in its early months showed signs, quite eccentric signs, of wanting to "rebrand" Britain, as though a country could be rebranded like a tooth-paste or detergent. The notion appeared to be that Britain's image was old-fashioned and fuddy-duddy and that the country should be presented to the world, and to itself, as hip, cool and up to the minute. Out with Big Ben, warm beer and stately homes. In with Brit Art, football (half the cabinet claimed to be football fans) and London Fashion Week. Tony Blair went out of his way to enter-tain — and to be seen to be entertaining — pop stars, musicians, actors, actresses, fashion designers, sports personalities and leading scientists at lavish — or lavish-seeming — parties at Number 10. The establishment was out. The "luvvies" were in. But, of course, it was impossible to rebrand Britain — the country had been around for too long — and in any case it turned out that both the natives and for-eign tourists rather liked, indeed preferred, what many of them still thought of as "the old country". In any case, rebranding was going on naturally all the time, and the government's efforts, although much publicized, seemed to have little to do with anything the general public cared much about. The "cool Britannia" project as a whole was soon quietly dropped.[40]

It left behind it, however, one concrete — or, more precisely, one fibre and steel-cable — memorial: the Millennium Dome, designed by Richard Rogers and erected on derelict land by the Thames in east London. Peter Mandelson, whose favourite project it was and who persuaded the Hinduja brothers to contribute to its "faith zone", declared before it opened: "The Dome will be like a gigantic mir-ror of the nation . . . I want the Dome to capture the spirit of modern Britain — a nation that is confident, excited, impatient for the future."[41] The nation may have been impatient for the future, but it showed no signs of being impatient for the Dome. The project cost far too much, the press condemned it, and, although the building itself won praise, its contents were generally adjudged mediocre — a theme park without a theme. Twelve million visitors were expected. In the end, only 6.5 million showed up, of whom nearly half paid less than the full price or were admitted free. The Dome never quite became a scandal — there were no allegations that people had their hands in the till — but it was a source of continu-ing embarrassment to the Blair government. Blair himself eventually admitted that the project should never have been proceeded with.

This sense of a certain fumbling, of having no clear sense of direction, mani-fested itself in another way. Tony Blair himself, probably more than most of his colleagues, seemed to yearn for some overarching, all-embracing moral and polit-ical philosophy, one that would both make sense of the political course on which he had embarked and, simultaneously, plot his and the government's course for the future. For Blair, pragmatism underpinned by moral values seemed some-how insufficient. He wanted an ideology, a faith. In opposition, he toyed with the concept of "the stakeholder society", but neither the phrase nor the concept caught on. Then, in government, he picked up the idea of "the third way", neither right, nor left, nor even centre, but a new way of combining capitalist economics with communitarian social values. The trouble with the third way was that, while it was clear what it was *not* (neither unbridled free-market economics nor old-fashioned state socialism), it was not entirely clear what it *was*: it did not tell one in precise terms, or even imprecise terms, what to *do*. Blair published a pamphlet on the third way and discussed the concept at a number of international conferences and seminars; Bill and Hillary Clinton were present at several of them.[42] But, like the idea of the stakeholder society, the idea of the third way never really caught on — except briefly as a phrase and latterly not even as that. By the time of the 2001 election, Blair's quest for an overarching philosophy seemed to have been given up, though whether temporarily or permanently no one could be sure.

Needless to say, it is doubtful whether more than a handful of ordinary voters, if that, either noticed Blair's ideological strivings or were in any way bothered by them; most people probably thought "the third way" was a rock band. But large numbers of voters almost certainly did notice that Blair often seemed to be espousing both of two opposing sets of values. He was not being devious or evasive or trying to be all things to all men; he was almost certainly trying to reconcile philosophical and emotional conflicts that existed in his own mind. But the effect could sometimes be faintly comic — and be portrayed as very comic. Simon Hoggart of the *Guardian* was bemused by Blair's first speech as prime minister to the annual Labour party conference:

> There were curious phrases.... There was the description of his mood when he won the election and we, the people, called on him to lead us into a new century. "That was your challenge to me. Proudly, humbly, I accepted it."
> Vainly, modestly, he set to work. Harshly, compassionately, he took the tough choices. Loudly, softly, he spoke to conference, and fascinated, bored, the audience gave him a standing ovation anyway.[43]

Whatever else Tony Blair had, and it was a great deal, he lacked Margaret Thatcher's unfathomable simplicity.

The Blair government was beset by another problem, one that made the government and, in particular, the cabinet appear considerably less united than they were. Although there were no deep ideological divisions within the government, and scarcely any important differences over policy, the government frequently gave the appearance of considerable disunity. The reason was simple: the absence of ideological differences was matched by the presence of personal differences among many of the government's most senior members. The personality tensions and clashes were real, and scarcely any effort was made to conceal them. On the contrary, they were widely and continually advertised, if not by the principals, then by their special advisers and press aides. The Blair cabinet was not, by modern standards, unduly leaky, but what it leaked was mainly spleen. In summary form, the position was this:

Blair feared Brown

Brown resented Blair

Prescott disliked Mandelson

Brown detested Mandelson

Cook disliked both Brown and Mandelson

Brown and almost everyone except Blair distrusted Campbell.

The effect — brilliantly conveyed and thoroughly documented by Andrew Rawnsley in *Servants of the People* — was that of a dysfunctional family. To take only the most extreme example, one of Tony Blair's inner circle — probably Alastair Campbell — contemptuously dismissed Gordon Brown, Blair's most powerful ministerial colleague, as a man with "psychological flaws".[44] Although only the Labour leadership's immediate neighbours in Whitehall and Westminster could actually hear the crockery smashing, echoes of the din could undoubtedly be heard, however faintly, across the land.

Most of this noise was in the background. More to the fore were the kinds of "events" that Harold Macmillan had had in mind. Two such events arose out of the Blair leadership's intense desire to control the Labour Party, not merely on the back benches in Parliament but outside in the country. As we shall see in the next chapter, the Blair government established a new parliament in Scotland, an assembly in Wales and both a directly elected mayoralty and an assembly in London. Not content, however, with establishing these new bodies and then letting the Labour parties in Scotland, Wales and London get on with the business of choosing their own leaders, Downing Street, in association with the Labour party headquarters at Millbank, sought to impose its preferred leadership candidates on the Scottish, Welsh and London organizations. Patrick Seyd in Chapter 4 describes how the internal party procedures worked.

In the short term, the national party's efforts at control were successful. Donald Dewar, the secretary of state for Scotland, became leader of the Scottish Labour Party and in due course Scotland's first minister. Alun Michael, the secretary of state for Wales, became leader of the Welsh Labour Party and in due course Welsh first secretary. Frank Dobson, the secretary of state for health, a London MP and the leadership's first choice, became the official Labour candidate for London mayor. But in the longer term — and, in the event, the longer term did not take long in coming — two of the three selections proved disastrous. It was not only "the message" that turned out to be uncontrollable.

Only in the case of Scotland was there unforced agreement that the man whom Number 10 wanted, Donald Dewar, and the man whom the Scottish Labour Party wanted were one and the same; when Dewar died unexpectedly in 2000, there was almost universal mourning. In Wales and London, matters took a different course. Although Alun Michael, Number 10's preferred candidate, did become leader of the Labour Party in Wales and did, to begin with, become the Principality's first secretary, Labour failed to win an outright majority in the first elections to the Welsh Assembly and found itself dependent on the votes of a small band of Liberal Democrats. After only a few months, the three Welsh opposition parties in the Assembly — Plaid Cymru (the Welsh national party), the Conservatives and the Liberal Democrats — combined to pass a vote of no-confidence in the minority Labour administration and Alun Michael was forced to resign. The man elected to succeed him, Rhodri Morgan, was, by a nice irony, the very person whom Number 10 had initially blocked in Michael's favour. It seemed that Wales's politicians, left to their own devices, were not prepared to accept Number 10's diktat.

Nor were the people of London — and their rebellion was far more cheeky than that of the Welsh Assembly members. A man called Ken Livingstone had been a thorn in the flesh of Labour's party hierarchy since anybody could remember. He was a contumacious left-winger, a brazen and successful publicity-seeker and a man Blair and his colleagues were convinced they could never work with. They were determined to prevent him becoming the official Labour candidate for the London mayoralty, and they persuaded the London Labour Party, with difficulty, to adopt Frank Dobson as Labour's candidate instead. The only trouble was that they could not prevent Livingstone from standing as an independent and they could certainly not prevent the people of London from voting for him. London was a Labour city; the party had won a substantial plurality of the city's vote at the 1997 general election. But, when Londoners went to the polls on May 4, 2000 to elect a mayor for the first time, they elected Livingstone by a comfortable majority. The Conservative candidate finished second. Dobson, who ought to have won, finished third. No one doubted that, while many of those who voted for Livingstone believed he would prove the most dynamic and effective in the office, at least as many were seizing the opportunity of making a rude two-fingered gesture in the government's direction. Tens of thousands of Londoners believed Tony Blair was trying to tell them who should be their mayor. They were not prepared to be told.

Further evidence of just how rebellious the mood of the country had become was provided by the widespread protests over the price of fuel that took place a few months later. Petroleum products have always been far more expensive in the United Kingdom than in the United States, but historically they have been somewhat cheaper in Britain than on the continent of Europe. However, successive British governments, both Conservative and Labour, had been continually ratcheting up the taxes on petrol (as the British call gasoline), partly to raise revenue, partly to try to protect the environment by reducing consumption of fossil fuels. By September 2000 these domestic tax increases, together with substantial increases in the world market price of oil, had had the effect both of sharply pushing up the price of petroleum products in the U.K. and also of causing British prices to rise to the high levels that people had hitherto associated with the Continent. Everyone in Britain was affected. Truckers who had to compete with continental haulage firms were especially so. Farmers and other country-dwellers were equally aggrieved.

Ministers knew perfectly well that fuel prices were a problem, and in his March 2000 budget the chancellor slowed the rate of increase in petrol and diesel taxes. But ministers, including the prime minister, were nevertheless caught completely off guard by the scale of, and the public support for, the protests that took place that autumn. Farmers and road hauliers picketed oil refineries and depots, and within forty-eight hours long queues appeared at petrol stations and supplies of fuel began to run short across the country. Members of the public might have been expected to turn against the protesters, who were subjecting them to such enormous inconvenience. But they did not. On the contrary, both protesters and public vented their wrath on the government for failing to keep petrol prices low. Tony Blair was shaken and on television appeared rattled; but, fortunately for him, the protesters appeared to sense that, if they prolonged their protest for too long, they would quickly lose public support. Within a few days, the pickets were withdrawn, and the government subsequently made a variety of concessions to motorists in general and the road hauliers in particular.

That particular crisis was soon over, but it had had, in its way, an existential quality. It showed how quickly the British people as a whole could be turned against their government as a whole: "us" against "them" — in political rather than class terms. It also showed how much political tinder there was out there in the country, just waiting to be ignited. At one level, the September 2000 protests were about the price of petrol, but at another level — and most people seemed to sense this — it was about the gap that increasingly yawned between governed and governors, between public and politicians. Blair and the people around him were accused of not "listening". In fact, they did listen, often intently, but seemed not to hear. Blair's biographer describes the fuel protests as "a burst of steam escaping from the boiler of anti-political rage".[45] This particular burst vanished with a hiss, but more seemed certain to come.

The fuel crisis came to an end on September 14, 2000. Almost exactly six months later, on February 20, 2001, officials from the Ministry of Agriculture confirmed an outbreak of foot and mouth disease on a pig farm in Essex. The disease spread rapidly, and by the end of April, only ten weeks later, some 1,500 cases had been confirmed across Great Britain and the government had ordered the slaughter of more than two million pigs, cattle and sheep. It was the worst crisis in the modern history of British agriculture. It was also a crisis for the British tourist industry. British tourists avoided the countryside, thousands choosing to take their holidays abroad instead. Large numbers of foreign tourists, having seen pictures of the burning pyres of animal carcasses on television, chose to avoid Britain altogether.

Fortunately for the government, little blame could be attached to it. Ministers had raised the price of petrol, but they had not infected the pigs. Moreover, they and their officials had detected the disease early and acted swiftly to prevent the epidemic from running out of control. Whatever else they did, the burning

pyres represented decisive action. Inevitably, the Conservative opposition criticized some details of the government's handling of the outbreak and some farmers
complained of delays, misinformation and the unnecessary slaughter of healthy
animals. But the National Farmers' Union supported the government throughout, and opinion polls indicated that most voters, while not over-impressed with
the government's performance, were nevertheless willing to give it the benefit of
the doubt. Few seemed to want to interpret the crisis in party-political terms.
Even so, the foot and mouth outbreak did have one direct political consequence:
the general election, which Blair had intended to hold on May 3, was, because
of the outbreak, postponed until June 7. The prime minister calculated that the
crisis would largely be over by late May and early June. He was right. It was.

NEW LABOUR'S OPPONENTS

From the above account, it should be clear by now that New Labour in office had
a mixed record and that, accordingly, large numbers of voters had mixed views
about it. On the one hand, a buoyant, well-managed economy, a broad-gauged
political appeal and some skilful crisis management; on the other hand, failure
to deliver on the public services, sleaze, a surfeit of spin and the lack of any clear
sense of direction. As the findings in Figure 1.2 (p. 19) suggest, most people did
not think ill of the government but they did not think very well of it either —
and both its standing and the personal standing of the prime minister showed a
distinct tendency to decline as time went on. By early 2001, any euphoria that
had attended New Labour's triumph in 1997 — and the extent of that euphoria
can easily be exaggerated — had long since evaporated. The Blair government
was a government in the doldrums.

On the basis of this information alone, any experienced observer of British
politics would have known exactly what to expect. He or she would have expected the Labour Party to lose a significant number of by-elections between 1997
and 2001, and he or she would also have expected Labour to fall well behind the
Conservatives in the opinion polls — at least until the immediate run-up to the
next election. Putting the same point another way, and irrespective of which party
eventually won the next election, he or she would have expected to see the government suffer a significant mid-term slump. He or she would also have expected
that, again irrespective of who eventually won the election, it would generally be
assumed that its outcome would be, to quote the Duke of Wellington, a "damned
near-run thing".[46]

But not a bit of it. This occasionally cack-handed, frequently hesitant and
not altogether honest administration, which also signally failed to improve the
quality of most of the public services, sailed through the whole of the 1997 parliament confident that, however choppy the political water might be at any given
moment, the chances of its actually losing the next general election approached
zero. Or, rather, it would have been thus confident had not a few of the officers on

the ship's bridge been, by nature, so nervous. The brute fact is that between 1997 and 2001 it was almost impossible to find anyone in Britain, of whatever political persuasion, who seriously believed that the Tory Party had any chance of winning the next election, whenever it came. There was, in that sense, no effective opposition either in Parliament or in the country.

Almost all British governments lose parliamentary by-elections (the equivalent of U.S. "special elections"). Every government in the nearly half-century between 1950 and 1997 lost at least one seat in the House of Commons in this way. Harold Wilson's Labour government between 1966 and 1970 lost fifteen. John Major's Conservative government between 1992 and 1997 lost eight. But Tony Blair's New Labour government lost none. Between 1997 and 2001 nine by-elections were held in previously Labour seats, and Labour won them all — the first time that had happened since Clement Attlee's administration immediately following the war. The only party to lose a by-election during the parliament was not Labour but the Conservatives, who lost Romsey in Hampshire to the Liberal Democrats in May 2000. It was the first time the main opposition party had lost a by-election since the 1980s.

However, far more important than by-elections in setting the political tone of the 1997 parliament were the findings of the monthly opinion polls. In the half-century between the end of the Second World War and 1997, every British government had at some stage fallen behind in the opinion polls, sometimes by small margins, often by large. The polls not only provided a measure of the relative popularity of the governing party and the main opposition party: they acted as a kind of *memento mori* to successive administrations: mend your ways, the polls seemed to say, or die. No such warnings, however, were issued in the case of Labour after 1997. Figure 1.3 covers the whole of the 1997 parliament and is based on data from a quarterly "poll of polls". As can be seen, apart from a brief downward blip at the time of the September 2000 fuel protests, Labour led the Conservatives comfortably during the whole of the four years. The polls never gave the slightest hint that the Conservatives might win the next election. More often than not, they gave the impression that there might actually be a swing in Labour's favour.

What can explain this strange state of affairs: a government that had disappointed so many expectations but was yet holding on in by-elections and riding high in the polls? The short answer is, of course, that, if people did not think much of Labour, they thought even less of the Tories. The Conservatives at the beginning of the twenty-first century were one of the most ill-regarded opposition parties in British history, rivalled in modern times only by the Labour Party under Michael Foot and Neil Kinnock in the early and mid 1980s. Labour might win only grudging applause, but a large majority of voters held the Conservatives in something approaching disdain and contempt.

Detailed explanations of why they did so and evidence for their having done

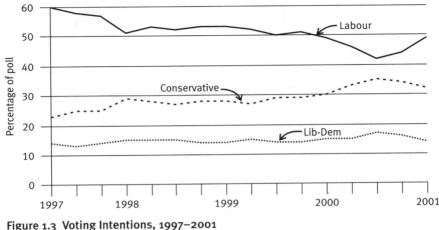

Figure 1.3 Voting Intentions, 1997–2001

Note: Average of findings of all published polls conducted between May 1997 and March 2001, a total of 189.

so, are provided by Philip Norton in Chapter 3 and John Bartle in Chapter 7. Suffice it to say here that large numbers of voters remembered the harshness of the Thatcher years and the ineptitude of the Major years, that they no longer trusted the Conservatives to manage the economy, that they feared the effect that a Conservative administration would have on the great public services, that they no longer had a clear idea of what the Conservatives stood for and that they had a low opinion of John Major's successor as Tory leader, William Hague. As a consequence, even when the Blair government ran into choppy water, which it frequently did, it never looked remotely like being sunk by enemy warships. Tony Blair had many assets, but his greatest single asset was the Conservative Party under the leadership of William Hague.

Beginning in Chapter 3, we shall explore these matters further, but it is time now to leave party politics for the moment and to consider the major changes to Britain's constitutional structure introduced by the Blair government, changes that are of immense long-term significance but have so far been scarcely referred to in these pages.

NOTES

1. Four full-length studies of Tony Blair's first term have already appeared (though, for obvious reasons, none of them touches on its last few months): John Rentoul, *Tony Blair: Prime Minister* (London: Little, Brown, 2001); Andrew Rawnsley, *Servants of the People: The Inside Story of New Labour* (London: Hamish Hamilton, 2000); Anthony Seldon, ed., *The Blair Effect* (London: Little, Brown, 2001); and Polly Toynbee and David Walker, *Did Things Get Better?* (London: Penguin, 2001). Rentoul's biography of Blair is well informed, thorough and detached. Rawnsley's *Servants of the People* is a rollicking account of the in-fighting within

the government. The volume edited by Seldon consists of 28 chapters by different authors analysing most aspects of the Blair government and its performance. Toynbee and Walker are journalists sympathetic to, but not uncritical of, the government. They seek to answer the question posed in their title *Did Things Get Better?* Their answer is a heavily qualified "yes". The factual material in this chapter draws heavily on all four of these books and also on contemporary newspaper accounts.

2. On Gordon Brown as a politician and human being, see Paul Routledge, *Gordon Brown: The Biography* (London: Simon & Schuster, 1998); and Hugh Pym and Nick Kochan, *Gordon Brown: The First Year in Power* (London: Bloomsbury, 1998). Insights into Brown's working methods are also provided by Geoffrey Robinson, *The Unconventional Minister: My Life Inside New Labour* (London: Michael Joseph, 2000). The many assessments of Brown's performance as chancellor of the exchequer include Andrew Glyn and Stewart Wood, "Economic Policy under New Labour: How Social Democratic is the Blair Government?" *Political Quarterly* 72 (January–March 2001), 50–66; Seldon, ed., *The Blair Effect,* section 2; and Toynbee and Walker, *Did Things Get Better?* chap. 5.

3. The Gallup Poll in most years since the war has asked on the occasion of each annual budget "Do you think that [name of the incumbent] is doing a good job or a bad job as chancellor of the exchequer?" By the time of the 2001 general election, Gordon Brown had achieved an average approval rating of 70 per cent. The average approval rating of his nearest postwar rival, R.A. Butler (1952–55), was 55 per cent. See Anthony King and Robert J. Wybrow, eds., *British Political Opinion 1937–2000: The Gallup Polls* (London: Politico's, 2001), 232–5; and *Gallup Political and Economic Index,* Report No. 487, March 2001, 19.

4. H.M. Treasury, *Building a Stronger Economic Future for Britain: Economic and Fiscal Strategy Report and Financial Statement and Budget Report March 1999,* House of Commons Paper HC 298 (London: Stationery Office, 1999), 15–6.

5. *United Kingdom: OECD Economic Surveys,* June 2001 (Paris: OECD, 2001), 15.

6. Calculations by Institute of Fiscal Studies reported in Toynbee and Walker, *Did Things Get Better?* 40.

7. H.M. Treasury, *Budget 2001,* quoted in Julian Glover, ed., *The Guardian Companion to the General Election 2001* (London: Atlantic, 2001), 73.

8. Labour manifesto reprinted in *The Times Guide to the House of Commons May 1997,* edited by Tim Austin (London: Times Books, 1997), 308.

9. Lincoln Steffens following a visit to the Soviet Union in 1919, quoted in Antony Jay, ed., *The Oxford Dictionary of Political Quotations* (Oxford: Oxford University Press, 1996), 349. Steffens, needless to say, was somewhat over-optimistic.

10. For a brief account of the New Deal, see Glyn and Wood, "Economic Policy under New Labour", 52–6.

11. A tally of the government's legislation on law and order is contained in Alan Travis, "Home Affairs" in *The Guardian Companion to the General Election 2001,* edited by Julian Glover, 95.

12. Home Office figures quoted in Toynbee and Walker, *Did Things Get Better?* 156.

13. Quoted in Peter Hennessy, *The Prime Minister: The Office and its Holders since 1945* (London: Allen Lane The Penguin Press, 2000), 478.

14. See Hennessy, *The Prime Minister,* chap. 18.

15. See "Labour MPs who rebelled against the government, 1997–2000" in Glover, ed., *Guardian Companion to the General Election,* 51–4.

16. Carl Emerson, Christine Frayne and Alissa Goodman, *Pressure in UK Healthcare: Challenges for the NHS* (London: Institute for Fiscal Studies, 2000), 57.

17. Toynbee and Walker, *Did Things Get Better?* 73.

18. Toynbee and Walker, *Did Things Get Better?* 75.

19. Toynbee and Walker, *Did Things Get Better?* 90.

20. Unusually for a politician, David Blunkett, while still in opposition, wrote a largely non-political autobiography, *On a Clear Day* (London: Michael O'Mara, 1995). The irony in the book's title is deliberate.

21. On the Hatfield rail crash, its causes and its aftermath, see Ian Jack, *The Crash that Stopped Britain* (London: Granta, 2001).

22. *The Times Guide to the House of Commons May 2001*, 309, 326.

23. Ecclestone quoted in Rentoul, *Tony Blair*, 368.

24. Robinson sets out his side of the story in *The Unconventional Minister*.

25. Quoted in Rawnsley, *Servants of the People*, 212. Blair used the phrase "purer than pure" on several other occasions.

26. On the first of what turned out to be the two Mandelson affairs, see Rentoul, *Tony Blair*, 461–4, 468–9, and Rawnsley, *Servants of the People*, chap. 12. Peter Mandelson was probably the most controversial single figure in the Blair administration — and also, in human terms, by far the most interesting — and, not surprisingly, there are already two biographies of him: Paul Routledge, *Mandy: The Unauthorised Biography of Peter Mandelson* (London: Simon & Schuster, 1999); and Donald Macintyre, *Mandelson: The Biography* (London: HarperCollins, 1999). The tone of the Routledge biography is overwhelmingly hostile, and the imminent publication of the book played a small part in Mandelson's resignation over the home-loan affair. The Macintyre biography is more balanced and sympathetic.

27. Anthony King, quoted in *Daily Telegraph*, January 2, 2000.

28. *Sunday Telegraph*, February 19, 2001.

29. Ibid.

30. For those unfamiliar with *Peter Pan*, Slightly Soiled is the name of one of Captain Hook's pirates in J.M. Barry's play.

31. A senior BBC political reporter, Nicholas Jones, has actually written two books devoted to the Blair government, its preoccupation with presentation and its practice of the black arts of spin: *Sultans of Spin* (London: Gollancz, 1999) and *The Control Freaks: How New Labour Gets Its Own Way* (London: Politico's, 2001).

32. Peter Oborne, *Alastair Campbell: New Labour and the Rise of the Media Class* (London: Aurum Press, 1999).

33. Philip Gould gives some account of his own role, but also describes the evolution of the whole New Labour project, in *The Unfinished Revolution: How the Modernisers Saved the Labour Party* (London: Little, Brown, 1998).

34. For example, in the index to Rentoul's *Tony Blair*, Campbell's entry runs to more than half a column, Mandelson's to three-quarters of a column and Gould's to a quarter of a column. Gould's is the shortest of the three but is still almost as long as Robin Cook's — and Cook was the foreign secretary throughout Blair's first term.

35. The issues of Britain's relations with Europe in general and whether the United Kingdom should join the euro in particular have scarcely been mentioned in this chapter because, although they featured prominently in the internal debate within the Conservative Party, they never featured in the electoral politics of the period. Europe and the euro were never high-priority issues for the great majority of voters, partly because the Blair government promised that, before the U.K. joined the euro, a national referendum on the issue would be held. Gordon Brown began by sounding enthusiastic for membership of the euro but managed to sound rather less enthusiastic as time went on. Tony Blair always sounded enthusiastic, but with qualifications. The two most outspoken euro-enthusiasts — and Euro-enthusiasts — in the government were Peter Mandelson, when he was in the government, and Robin Cook, the foreign secretary. In general, the government's line was "wait and see". It favoured membership of the euro in principle but said it did not want Britain to join until joining was clearly in the national interest. See Philip Stevens, "The Blair Government and Europe", *Political Quarterly* 72 (January–March 2001), 67–75; Anne Deighton, "European Union Policy" in Seldon, ed., *The Blair Effect*; Rentoul, *Tony Blair*, chap. 29; and David Baker, "Britain and Europe: The Argument Continues", *Parliamentary Affairs* 54 (April 2001), 276–88.

36. Blair announced on May 8 that the election would be held on June 7. The quotations in the text all appeared in the newspapers of May 9.

37. *Gallup Political and Economic Index*, Report No. 461, January 1999, 8.

38. *Daily Telegraph*, June 11, 2001.

39. The unnamed official's comments on Blair's handling of the Kosovo conflict are quoted in Hennessy, *The Prime Minister,* 507.

40. The manifesto of the "cool Britannia" movement (if it can be called that) was Mark Leonard, *Britain™: Renewing Our Identity* (London: Demos, 1997). "Britain", Leonard wrote, "is seen as a backward-looking has-been, a theme park world of royal pageantry and rolling green hills, where draughts blow through people's houses" (8). Under the heading, " 'Branding' Britain", he argued that there were "important lessons to be learned from businesses which have developed sophisticated techniques for managing their identity" (9).

41. Quoted in Robert Hewison, "Cultural Policy" in Seldon, ed., *The Blair Effect,* 548. Hewison provides a brief account of the whole Dome fiasco. See also Adam Nicolson, *Regeneration: The Story of the Dome* (London: HarperCollins, 1999), though Nicolson does not carry the story through to the end.

42. Much has been written about the third way. See, among many other things, Rentoul, *Tony Blair,* chap. 26; Tony Blair, *The Third Way: New Politics for the New Century* (London: Fabian Society, 1998); and Anthony Giddens, *The Third Way: The Renewal of Social Democracy* (Cambridge: Polity Press, 1998). Tony Blair and the German chancellor, Gerhard Schröder, also issued a joint statement entitled *The Third Way/Die Neue Mitte.* The difference in terminology — the "third way" versus the "new centre" — perhaps hints at the mushiness of the concept.

43. *Guardian,* October 11, 1997.

44. Rawnsley, *Servants of the People,* 150.

45. Rentoul, *Tony Blair,* 572.

46. The phrase in the text is what Wellington is usually supposed to have said about the battle of Waterloo. What he actually said was "It has been a damned nice thing — the nearest run thing you ever saw in your life." See *The Oxford Dictionary of Quotations,* 2nd edn (London: Oxford University Press, 1953), 564.

CHAPTER 2

Britain's Constitutional Revolution

Anthony King

THE BLAIR GOVERNMENT'S principal objective during its first term was — as the British say — "not to frighten the horses". However high-flown much of New Labour's rhetoric, its policy aims were limited, the targets that it set for itself modest. The Labour Party under Tony Blair set out to provide the country with old-fashioned good government rather than to bring about fundamental change. In so far as it was interested in fundamental change, its concerns were overwhelmingly with efficiency, delivery and something called "modernization" — a word that the prime minister repeated endlessly in the style of a Hindu mantra.

There was, however, one startling exception to the new government's safety-first approach. New Labour came to power committed to one of the most ambitious programmes of constitutional reform ever proposed by any political party. The programme did not constitute a coherent package. The various elements that it contained were not based on any fixed set of principles, and they had certainly not been conceived in relation to one another; they were, in that sense, a rag-bag. All the same, they were exceedingly radical in both form and content and they have already begun to affect profoundly the workings of the British political system. For that reason, they deserve a chapter to themselves even though — remarkably — they did not figure as major issues in the general elections of 1997 and 2001. They certainly had little or no effect on the outcome of either.[1]

Two central features of the British constitution have always been, first, the concentration of power in the hands of the executive branch of government and, second, the centralization of power in the hands of the national government in London. The first feature has meant that Parliament as a political institution has always been weak, certainly as compared with the United States Congress. It has also meant that historically the British judiciary has had neither the power nor the inclination to encroach on the authority of the executive branch (provided, of course, that that authority has been lawfully exercised). The second feature has meant not only that the United Kingdom is a unitary rather than a federal state but that there has never existed a powerful, autonomous or quasi-autonomous sub-national tier of government.[2] British government, in short, has been London government; and London government has been largely executive government. The significance of New Labour's constitutional reforms — not yet fully appreciated even by many people in Britain — is that the concentration and centralization of power are no longer features of the system to nearly the extent that they were. Thanks to the Blair government, power in the British system is now significantly more diffused than it was. The standard textbooks are, as a result, having to be rewritten.

THE HUMAN RIGHTS ACT

British politicians of all parties resisted for decades the idea that the U.K. should have a formal bill of rights. They believed that Britain's human rights record was a good one, better than that of many countries that did have bills of rights. They also believed that any abuses of human rights that occurred in Britain should be dealt with — and could be dealt with — through the normal democratic processes. They found the idea of judge-made law unattractive and were reluctant to see judges and lawyers becoming involved in what they regarded as essentially political matters. There was also the problem of what should be included in any British bill of rights. The list of rights included in the American Bill of Rights — the first ten amendments to the U.S. constitution — struck many Britons as distinctly odd. The right to "a speedy and public trial"? Of course. The right to "keep and bear arms"? Probably not.

Despite these and other reservations, the United Kingdom became a signatory to the European Convention on Human Rights shortly after the Second World War and in the 1960s went further, granting its citizens full legal access to the European Court of Human Rights in Strasbourg. When it granted British citizens access to the Strasbourg court, the British government was tacitly acknowledging that the United Kingdom would be bound by that court's judgments and that it would, if necessary, amend U.K. law to bring it into conformity with the court's rulings. As time went on, however, it seemed increasingly anomalous that U.K. citizens should have to go to a foreign court — or at least a court domiciled in a foreign country — to secure rights that the U.K. government itself had acknowledged were properly theirs. The Strasbourg procedures were complicated, long drawn out and expensive. Why not allow the people of Britain to defend their rights in British courts before British judges? In the end, there was no satisfactory answer to this question and Labour's 1997 election manifesto accordingly promised that a new Labour government would "by statute incorporate the European Convention on Human Rights into U.K. law".[3]

The Blair government acted on the pledge. The Human Rights Act 1998 came into force in Scotland in July 1999, in Northern Ireland in December 1999 and in England and Wales in October 2000. It incorporates the European Convention on Human Rights into U.K. domestic law for the first time, albeit with a few modifications. At the time of introducing any new legislation, British ministers are now required to certify that the proposed legislation is compatible with the terms of the convention. British judges are similarly required to give effect to the convention's provisions "so far as it is possible to do so". If the courts determine that actions of the central government, local authorities or other public bodies are in violation of the convention, they can strike them down. But Britain's courts — unlike those of the United States — are not empowered to strike down Acts of Parliament. Instead, the Human Rights Act gives the courts the power to declare that a specific piece of legislation violates the convention's terms. If a higher court does so declare, ministers can take advantage of a special fast-track procedure to amend the offending law.

At the time of the 2001 election, the Human Rights Act had been in force in England and Wales for only a few months — and in the rest of the U.K. for not much longer than that — and it was too early to say what its full political and constitutional ramifications would be. The Act's supporters were confident that the volume of litigation under it would be relatively small and that, even if it proved larger than expected, the courts would nevertheless exercise their usual judicial restraint. The Act's critics feared that there would a veritable explosion of litigation and that the British courts, like those in the U.S., would take it upon themselves to pronounce on great issues of policy. Whatever happens, there can be no doubt that the judiciary's potential role in the U.K. has been considerably expanded. British central government is no longer quite as executive-dominated as it once was. At the very least, ministers, both in drafting new legislation and in acting under existing laws, will have to bear constantly in mind the possible reactions of the courts to whatever they do.

DEVOLUTION

The Human Rights Act was a small step in the direction of de-concentrating power. Devolution to Scotland and Wales were much larger steps in the direction of decentralizing it. For the first time in its history, the U.K., following Labour's victory in the 1997 election, acquired sub-national governments with considerable statutory powers and a considerable measure of operational autonomy. The system by no means became federal; but parts of it began to look distinctly federalish.

Scotland

The United Kingdom is a strangely protean country. Foreigners are often unsure what to call it. First, there was only England. Then in the sixteenth century England incorporated Wales. Then, early in the eighteenth century, England formed a union with Scotland. By this time, the country was known as Great Britain.

Then, in the early nineteenth century, Great Britain incorporated Ireland to form the United Kingdom of Great Britain and Ireland. Finally, in the early twentieth century, Ireland broke in two, most of it becoming in time the Republic of Ireland, the rest of it Northern Ireland. The country now became, formally, the United Kingdom of Great Britain and Northern Ireland. To this day, the country is known variously to its inhabitants and others as "England", "Britain" and "the U.K."

The Scots, however, have been the Scots throughout. Although England and Scotland merged in 1707, with Scotland surrendering its right to a separate parliament, the Scottish people retained their own legal and educational systems and also their own churches, their own accents and their own customs and traditions. Most important, they retained their own sense of national identity. Scotland after 1707 might no longer be a nation-state, but Scotland never ceased to be a nation. In somewhat belated recognition of this fact, those laws of the United Kingdom that applied to Scotland were administered from the late nineteenth century onwards by the Scottish Office in Edinburgh. The Scottish Office was, in form, a U.K. government department like any other; in practice, it enjoyed considerable administrative autonomy. Successive secretaries of state for Scotland managed to ensure that levels of government spending north of the border remained considerably higher than those in the south.

Many Scots wanted to go further. Beginning in the 1930s, some sought complete independence. More sought "home rule" within the United Kingdom. The pro-independence Scottish National Party (SNP) began to chalk up electoral successes in the late 1960s and early 1970s — it won 30.4 per cent of the Scottish vote at the October 1974 general election — and, taking fright, the Labour Party, first under Harold Wilson, then under James Callaghan, took up the cause of home rule for Scotland, or "devolution" as it had become known by this time. During the late 1970s, enormous amounts of parliamentary time were taken up with passing bills providing for devolution to Scotland. However, in 1979 a referendum on the issue held in Scotland failed to carry by a sufficient majority and the whole devolution project was, for the time being, aborted. The Conservative governments of the 1980s and 1990s set their faces firmly against home rule in any form.[4]

Adamant Conservative opposition probably made large numbers of Scots even keener on devolution than before, and by the mid 1990s there was a widespread consensus north of the border that Scotland should again have its own parliament, with wide-ranging statutory powers. Scotland's union with the rest of the country was to remain intact, but on a new basis. Labour committed itself to devolution at the time of the 1992 election and again in 1997, and in September of that year, less than five months after the election of New Labour, the Scottish people were invited in a referendum to say whether they approved of the idea of devolution in principle and whether they wished any new Scottish parliament to have limited tax-varying powers. The referendum was held on September 11, 1997. The turnout was 60.2 per cent. Of those who voted, an overwhelming majority, 74.3 per cent, supported devolution. A smaller majority, but still a substantial one, 63.5 per cent, said they wanted the new Scottish parliament to have limited tax-varying powers.[5] The Blair government duly legislated along these lines, and the Scotland Act came into force in 1999.

The devolution of powers provided for by the Act is on a prodigious scale. Indeed there is probably no known case of any sovereign government voluntarily handing over a wider range of powers to any sub-national unit. Under the terms of the Act, the central government retains control over macroeconomic policy and the social security system. It also retains control over foreign and defence policy and over the Scotland-wide electoral system (though not over the electoral system for Scottish local authorities). But virtually everything else — that is, virtually the whole of domestic policy — is handed over to the new Scottish Parliament and Executive: education, including university education, health, transport, the environment, agriculture and fisheries, law and order, local government, economic development and personal social services. In all these areas, the writ of London now stops at the Scottish border.

The one anomaly in the new arrangements concerns money. Although the Scots now largely control their own domestic expenditure, they do not control their own revenue. The Scottish Parliament does have the power, confirmed by the September 1997 referendum, to raise or lower the standard rate of income tax north of the border by three pence in the pound; but otherwise the new Scottish institutions are wholly dependent on the central government for their revenue, which takes the form of a single, enormous block grant. It seems almost certain that at some time in the future — probably sooner rather than later — the size of this single block grant will become a source a friction between London and Edinburgh, especially if the government in London decides that Scotland's growing prosperity means that England no longer needs to subsidize Scotland on the same scale as in the past. The Scots may also decide in time that they wish to go further and achieve full fiscal autonomy, with the whole of Scotland's expenditures funded out of Scottish revenues.[6]

Scots went to the polls for the first time to elect their new Parliament on May 6, 1999. They voted under an electoral system that was new to the U.K.: the so-called additional member system, modelled on that of Germany. Each voter could cast two ballots. One was for a member of the Scottish Parliament (MSP) to represent his or her Scottish parliamentary constituency; that member was elected on the old-fashioned first-past-the-post, simple-plurality basis (with the candidate who secured the largest number of votes winning, even if the largest number fell short of 50 per cent). The other was for one of the party lists presented to voters in each of eight large Scottish regions. Seventy-three of the Parliament's 129 members were to represent old-fashioned parliamentary constituencies; the remaining 56 members, seven from each region, were to be drawn from the regional lists in such a way that each party was represented in the new Parliament roughly in proportion to the total share of the vote — both constituency and party list — cast for it in the region. The 56 members drawn from the regional party lists were known informally, for obvious reasons, as "top-up" members.[7] Given the nature of this new electoral system, given the fact that no party had won 50 per cent or more of the Scottish vote for nearly half a century and given the additional fact that four separate parties had each won 13 per cent of more of the vote at the 1997 general election, it was virtually certain that no single party would win an outright parliamentary majority in the elections and that either a minority administration or some kind of coalition would have to be formed.

And so it proved. The Scottish Labour Party won 38.8 per cent of the constituency vote, 34.0 per cent of the top-up vote and a total 56 seats, nine short of an overall majority. The SNP won 28.7 per cent of the constituency vote, 27.6 per cent of the top-up vote and a total of 35 seats, making it the second party in the Parliament. The Conservatives won almost the same proportions of the constituency and top-up votes — 15.6 per cent and 15.5 per cent respectively — and eighteen seats. The Liberal Democrats won 14.2 per cent of the constituency vote, not far behind the Conservatives, 12.6 per cent of the top-up vote and seventeen seats.[8] All the other parties were agreed that they did not want to form an administration with the SNP, and all the other parties were also agreed that they did not want to form an administration with the Conservatives. It therefore followed that Labour would either have to form a minority administration on its own or else enter a coalition with the Liberal Democrats. In the event, Labour and the Liberal Democrats, following a week of intense negotiations, formed a joint administration, with Donald Dewar, the Labour leader, as first minister and Jim Wallace, the Liberal Democrat leader, as his deputy. Following Dewar's sudden death in 2000, he was succeeded by another Labour politician, Henry McLeish. The Labour–Lib Dem coalition was still in place at the time of the general election, with the result that the country was treated to the novel spectacle of the two Scottish coalition partners in Scotland competing against each other for seats at Westminster.

The London-based Labour party leadership gave the impression of being surprised by the outcome of the May 1999 Scottish elections, though it clearly should not have been. It also gave the impression of being surprised when the new Scottish Parliament began to go its own way in policy terms. Far from simply adopting Westminster policy as Edinburgh policy and national Labour policy as Scottish Labour policy, the Labour Party in Scotland, under continuous pressure from the Liberal Democrats and conscious of having to respond to the wishes of the Scottish electorate, took a different approach from that of Westminster on a number of issues. The two most famous were university tuition fees and the method of paying for the care of the elderly in Scotland. The Westminster Parliament had imposed a £1,000 tuition fee on university students throughout the U.K.; the Scottish Parliament abolished the fee north of the border (substituting a form of graduate tax). The government in London sought to make the elderly and their families pay a higher proportion of the costs of their care; the Scottish Parliament and Executive — reluctantly, because the move was very expensive — moved in the direction of free care.

The creation of the Scottish Parliament inevitably created a new political dynamic north of the border, one with implications for the rest of the country. The new Scottish electoral system acted as a laboratory for possible changes to the U.K.-wide electoral system. The new Scottish electoral system also made it all but certain that coalitions and minority administrations would become the norm north of the border, a new development in the U.K.'s political history. Scotland and the rest of the U.K. also began to diverge in terms of what until very recently had been U.K.-wide areas of policy. Not least, Scotland came to have, for many purposes, its own political system: self-preoccupied, self-contained and increasingly inward looking. To an extent that surprised and even startled outsiders, the attention of Scottish politicians and the Scottish media came to be focused more and more on Scotland's internal affairs. Scotland increasingly felt like a separate country. It remained to be seen whether, in the fulness of time, it would actually become one.[9]

Wales

Parallel developments took place after 1997 in Wales. Pressure for home rule had always been much less intense and widespread in Wales than in Scotland, and there was a general acceptance that, if Wales did achieve a measure of home rule, its scope would have to be considerably more restricted than in Scotland. Nevertheless, New Labour in its 1997 manifesto promised that Wales would be offered a new directly elected assembly (as distinct from a fully fledged parliament) and that the people of Wales, like the people of Scotland, would be given a chance in a referendum to vote on the issue.

The referendum in Wales was held on the same day as the one in Scotland, on September 11, 1997, but it produced an infinitely closer result. Indeed the outcome in Wales remained seriously in doubt until the wee small hours of the next day. Whereas those who turned out to vote in Scotland opted for the creation of a new parliament by a margin of nearly three to one, those who bothered to turn out in Wales — only 50.1 per cent of the eligible electorate, a considerably smaller proportion than in Scotland — backed the creation of a Welsh assembly by a margin of only 50.3 per cent to 49.7 per cent. Predictably, support for the new assembly was greatest in Welsh-speaking mid and north Wales. The more

Anglicized and industrial parts of Wales — in south Wales and along the border with England — mostly voted "no".[10]

Although its proposals received only this tepid welcome, the government pressed ahead and the Government of Wales Act, like the Scotland Act, came into force in 1999. The Act provides for devolution, but only on a limited scale. The Welsh Assembly and its Executive Committee cannot, unlike the Scottish Parliament and Executive, pass primary legislation; it can only pass secondary legislation — that is, rules and regulations — under the terms of existing U.K. laws. Nor, again unlike the Scottish Parliament and Executive, do the Welsh Parliament and Executive Committee have any tax-raising or tax-varying powers. The whole of Wales's revenue comes from a central block grant. The main function of the new Welsh institutions is to perform the administrative functions hitherto performed by the London-appointed secretary of state for Wales and the Welsh Office in Cardiff.

However, despite the legal differences between the new Welsh and Scottish systems, the two countries' politics between 1997 and 2001 followed a similar trajectory. As in Scotland, the Labour Party failed to secure an overall majority in the first elections to the Welsh Assembly, which were held using the same additional member system as was used in Scotland. Labour won only 28 of 60 Assembly seats, three short of an overall majority. Plaid Cymru came second with seventeen seats, the Conservatives third with nine and the Liberal Democrats fourth with six.[11] In the case of Wales, Labour began by trying to govern alone, hoping to attract support from the other parties on a vote-by-vote basis. However, following the ouster of Alun Michael, the first Welsh first secretary, by the combined opposition parties in February 2000 and Alun Michael's replacement by Rhodri Morgan, the Welsh Labour Party followed the lead of its Scottish co-partisans and entered a coalition with the Liberal Democrats. This coalition, like the one in Scotland, survived to and through the 2001 general election.

Devolution to Wales was never going to have the same impact on British politics as devolution to Scotland. Wales was considerably smaller than Scotland — 2.9 million people compared with 5.1 million in Scotland — and the English and Welsh legal and administrative systems were inextricably intertwined in a way that England's and Scotland's never were. Even so, Wales after 1999, like Scotland after 1999, began to develop its own political subcultures and its own political style. Wales, too, was becoming a slightly more detached part of the United Kingdom.

LONDON

Between 1986 and 2000, London was the only major city in the world without its own city-wide government. Before 1986 London was governed first by the old London County Council, then by the Greater London Council. In 1986 Margaret Thatcher's government abolished the Greater London Council, and for the next decade and a half the city was administered partly by the central government, partly by ad hoc agencies like the London Fire Service, but mainly by the 32 London boroughs. Coordination and cooperation among the London boroughs, in so far as it existed, was largely voluntary. Labour, however, had long been committed to restoring a central authority to the city, and the party's 1997 manifesto contained a pledge along these lines. Once elected, the Blair government organized a referendum to determine whether or not the people of London wanted to see a new authority established. None of the political parties opposed the idea, and in May 1998, on an exceptionally low turnout, only 34.1 per cent, 72.0 per cent of the minority who bothered to turn out voted "yes".[12]

The new Greater London Authority, established two years later, in 2000, is a modest affair, with powers far more limited in scope than were those of either the old London County Council or the Greater London Council. The 32 London boroughs remain London's principal executive agencies, with the Greater London Authority largely restricted to devising strategic plans in such fields as transport, economic development, air quality, waste disposal and culture and the arts. The new authority also has a substantial input into the activities of a number of specialized agencies covering such fields as transport, economic development, land-use planning, fire and emergency services and, not least, the Metropolitan Police (which, for the first time since 1829, is now controlled by a local police authority rather than by the central government).

Yet to emphasize the new authority's restricted powers is to miss a large part of the point. In the first place, London, the largest city in Britain and one of the largest in Europe, can now speak with a single voice for the first time since 1986. In the second place, that single voice will, in practice, be the voice of the mayor. The new mayor of London (not to be confused with the Lord Mayor of the City of London, a purely ceremonial officer) is the first directly elected chief executive in British history. The monarch is not directly elected. The prime minister is not directly elected. The leaders of Britain's big cities have not, until now, been directly elected. But the mayor of London is. And he or she is the voice of 7 million people, many more than in Denmark, Norway or, for that matter, Scotland. Across Europe, only the president of France, also directly elected, has a larger constituency. The mayor of London can scarcely avoid becoming the personal embodiment of Londoners' aspirations and grievances. With skill and luck, he or she can translate influence — which is really all that the Greater London Authority Act provides — into effective power.

Moreover, it happens that, as we saw in the last chapter, the first mayor of London, in office until at least 2004, is Ken Livingstone, an assertive and wily politician, with a large personal following, much loved by the media. Livingstone resembles in style, not one of Britain's traditional big-city politicians — typically a rather grey figure, a committee man and behind-the-scenes wheeler-dealer — but, rather, one of New York city's more flamboyant mayors, a Fiorello

La Guardia or a Rudy Giuliani. It actually strengthens Livingstone's position that he was elected as an independent, as his own man. Had he been elected as the official Labour candidate, he would be seen as a Labour politician and be subject to the vicissitudes of Labour's electoral fortunes nationally. As it is, he can claim to be genuinely independent and to speak for the whole of London. One of his first actions as mayor was to establish an all-party local administration. The importance of the London mayoralty is likely to have been strengthened by the mere fact of Ken Livingstone's having been the office's first holder.

It is also worth noting that, in establishing the new Greater London Authority, New Labour added two further systems to Britain's already fast-growing array of electoral systems. The traditional first-past-the-post system continues to operate in most local authorities and for elections to the Westminster Parliament. The single transferable vote is used in some Northern Ireland elections. Britain's members of the European Parliament at Strasbourg are now elected by means of regional party lists. The additional member system, as we have just seen, has been adopted for elections to both the Scottish Parliament and the Welsh Assembly. Two other systems are used in London. The mayor is elected by means of the so-called supplementary vote. Some members of the Greater London Assembly — essentially a body that advises the mayor — are elected on the basis of first-past-the-post; but others are "top-up" members, elected by means of the additional member system except that, unlike in Scotland and Wales, the top-up members are chosen on the basis of the total number of votes cast London-wide and not on the basis of Scottish-type or Welsh-type regions. Once upon a time, the only electoral system that Britons knew was first-past-the-post. Now at least five, possibly six, different systems operate within the confines of a single country. Many voters appear bewildered. It is hardly surprising.[13]

NORTHERN IRELAND

No subject preoccupied Tony Blair more completely or more continuously during his first term as prime minister than the future of Northern Ireland. There were no votes in it. On the contrary, Blair and his government stood to lose far more from failing in Northern Ireland than they could possibly hope to gain by succeeding. Success would mean that Northern Ireland and its problems would simply fade away; people would forget about them. Failure might mean loss of prestige, the appearance of ineptitude and possibly the renewal of terrorist activity by the Irish Republican Army (IRA) on the British mainland. The stakes were high — far higher than in any other field of British politics. People's lives were at risk. Like John Major, his Conservative predecessor, Tony Blair applied his mind, his energies and his considerable negotiating skills to trying to bring peace to the unhappy province.

One of the ironies of the situation is that Great Britain has no stake in Northern Ireland. Apart from the long-established constitutional and political links between Great Britain and Northern Ireland, there is no reason for the British to be there. Ireland's strategic importance to Great Britain, once overwhelming, has long since vanished; no one in Britain any longer fears invasion by France or Spain. Northern Ireland is a considerable drain on Britain's financial resources. Maintaining a military presence in the province costs money and diverts British soldiers from performing other, and arguably more important, tasks. Not least, Britain's continuing presence in Northern Ireland complicates Britain's relations with the United States, notably with that country's large Irish-American community. Most people in Great Britain do not, in a visceral way, regard Northern Ireland as part of "their" country. They view television pictures of riots and disturbances in Northern Ireland with incredulity, dismay and a certain detachment. If Northern Ireland declared itself independent, or decided to join the Republic of Ireland, most people in Britain would not mind. They would heave a sigh of relief.

The fact is, however, that the six counties that make up Northern Ireland have been a part of the United Kingdom for at least two hundred years (and, in reality, for considerably longer than that). The majority of the people of Northern Ireland, more than 60 per cent, feel themselves to be British and desperately want Northern Ireland to remain part of the United Kingdom. Ulstermen fought in their tens of thousands for Britain in both of two World Wars; thousands of them died for Britain on the Somme and at Ypres. The British cannot simply turn their backs on them. Furthermore, if they did, there is every chance that a full-scale civil war would break out in Northern Ireland, with immense casualties on both sides. The British security forces in Northern Ireland are thus, in essence, peace-keeping forces, engaged in peace-keeping operations. The politics of Northern Ireland is best understood in terms of the conflicts in the Balkans and the Middle East.

The core problem is easily stated. There are two peoples in Northern Ireland, and they do not want to live together. Each wishes the other would go away. The majority are Unionist and overwhelmingly Protestant. The minority are Republican and overwhelmingly Roman Catholic. The Unionists, as their name implies, want to maintain Northern Ireland's union with Great Britain. The Republicans, as their name implies, want Northern Ireland to unite with the Republic of Ireland. The differences between the two peoples go far behind politics in any conventional sense. They send their children to different schools, worship in different churches, drink in different pubs and even drink different brands of beer and whisky. They seldom intermarry. They seldom live together in the same neighbourhoods. They hate each other and, even when they do not hate each other, they fear each other. Much blood has been spilt — over a period of eighty years, far more than most people outside Northern Ireland realize. There has also been ethnic cleansing on a large scale — again, on a far larger scale than most people outside the province realize.[14]

The British government finds itself in an ambiguous position. On the one hand, it is the sovereign power in Northern Ireland, responsible for the government of the province and therefore also responsible for attempting to maintain law and order in the province. On the other hand, the British government is at the same time a totally disinterested party, concerned solely with maintaining the peace; Britain is prepared to accept any settlement — maintenance of the existing union, union with the Republic, complete independence, anything — provided only that the two warring peoples of Northern Ireland can agree. And, from the British point of view, the sooner they agree the better. Facilitating agreement is the sole purpose of British policy, a fact that, among other things, enables the British and Irish governments to work closely together. But, of course, the ambiguity of the British government's position creates difficulties. The Unionists fear that, because the British government is ultimately disinterested, it will sooner or later sell them out; at the very least, it will be "soft" on the Republicans. The Republicans believe that, because Britain remains the sovereign power in Northern Ireland, it is not in fact ultimately disinterested and will always, in the end, side with the Unionists. In other words, the Unionists distrust the Republicans, the Republicans distrust the Unionists, and both distrust the British. Hence the desire of successive British governments to involve outsiders in the attempt to bring peace to Northern Ireland: the Irish government, the United States government, President Bill Clinton, former U.S. Senator George J. Mitchell, retired Canadian General Jean de Chastelain — anyone who it is thought can help.

Against this background and determined to secure a permanent peace if he could, Tony Blair during his first year in office devoted a large proportion of his time and energy to trying to broker a comprehensive settlement. The culmination, if by no means the end, of his efforts came on April 10, 1998, when the British and Irish governments and the main Unionist and Republican parties signed the Belfast Agreement, soon known as the Good Friday Agreement.[15] The agreement represented a significant step — indeed probably the most significant step ever taken — towards bringing peace to Northern Ireland; but it also represented, in the context of the United Kingdom as a whole, constitutional innovation on a massive scale. The central principle of the British constitution has always been "winner take all": political parties compete in a general election, one of them wins, the winner forms the government, the losers play no part in the government (beyond forming the opposition in Parliament). The terms of the Good Friday Agreement embody exactly the opposite principle: the principle of "power sharing", with all or most of the political parties in Northern Ireland expected to participate directly in the province's administration.[16]

The Good Friday Agreement establishes a new devolved administration in the province, with extensive powers akin to those of the Scottish Parliament and Executive; but it is the way in which the new administration is to operate that is remarkable. Those who negotiated the Good Friday Agreement had two problems to solve, not just one. In the first place, they had to find some means of enabling the Unionists and Republicans to work together politically in the province. In the second place, given that the Unionists were in a permanent majority and the Republicans in a permanent minority, they also had to find some means of ensuring that the Unionists could not take advantage of their majority status to impose their will on the Republicans.

Accordingly, the new Northern Ireland Assembly is large, consisting of 108 members, in order to ensure that almost every political grouping in the province can find a place within it. Its members are elected by means of the single transferable vote, a highly proportional electoral system. Ministerial portfolios, the chairmanships of Assembly committees and also the memberships of those committees are allocated in strict proportion to the parties' numerical strength in the Assembly. The first minister presides over a multi-party cabinet which he is in no conceivable position to dominate (except perhaps, rarely, by sheer force of personality). Moreover, the multi-party Northern Ireland cabinet is "over-sized" in the sense of comprising representatives of more parties than are absolutely necessary for purposes of commanding an overall majority in the Assembly.

The new system embodies, in addition, procedures designed to ensure that the minority community is in a position effectively to protect its interests. These procedures include both the device of "parallel consent", with majorities of the Unionist and Republican delegations in the Assembly both having to vote in favour of certain designated measures, and the device of "weighted majorities", with 60 per cent of members having to vote in favour of other measures, the 60 per cent having to include at least 40 per cent of each of the two delegations. The terms of the agreement also ensure that, in practice, the deputy first minister will always be from the minority community and that the Northern Ireland cabinet will not merely be over-sized but will comprise Republican as well as Unionist ministers. In the Good Friday Agreement's own words, the aim is to put in place "safeguards to ensure that all sections of the community can participate and work together successfully in the operation of these institutions and that all sections of the community are protected".[17]

Referendums on the Good Friday Agreement were held in both Northern Ireland and the Republic on May 22, 1998. In the Republic, a massive 94.4 per cent of voters supported the proposal, contained in the agreement, that Ireland should drop its constitutional claim to incorporate the six counties of the north. In Northern Ireland, on a turnout of 81.0 per cent, the result was closer, with 71.1 per cent voting "yes" to the agreement as a whole and 28.9 per cent voting "no".[18] To the relief of politicians on both sides of the Irish Sea, opinion polls indicated that a majority of Unionists, as well as a (larger) majority of Republicans, had voted "yes". Elections to the new Assembly were held only a month later, on June 25, 1998, with pro–Good Friday Agreement parties winning roughly two-thirds of the vote.[19] David Trimble, the leader of the pro-agreement Ulster Unionist Party, became first minister, Seamus Mallon, the deputy leader of the pro-agreement Social Democratic and Labour Party, becoming his deputy. Sinn Féin representatives took their places in the new multi-party cabinet even though Sinn Féin continued to have close links with the IRA (so close that Unionists insisted on referring to the two organizations as though they were one, as in "Sinn Féin/IRA").

Because of Unionists' and Republicans' mutual fears and suspicions, which have shown few signs of abating, and because of deep divisions within each of the two communities, the Good Friday Agreement has proved extraordinarily difficult to implement, and Tony Blair and successive secretaries of state for Northern Ireland — Mo Mowlam, Peter Mandelson and John Reid — have been forced to go on investing vast amounts of time and energy (nervous energy as well as physical) into trying to make it work. Mandelson was forced to suspend the workings of the Assembly for three months in 2000, and violence on the streets of the province has continued. At the time of the 2001 U.K. general election, it was by no means certain that either Northern Ireland's new devolved institutions or the Good Friday Agreement on which they are based would survive.

THE HOUSE OF LORDS

The British House of Lords is one of the world's oldest legislative assemblies, dating back to at least the thirteenth century. Its membership for many centuries consisted exclusively of peers of the realm — dukes (including royal dukes), marquesses, earls, viscounts and barons — together with archbishops and bishops of the Church of England and a number of senior judges. Its membership for many centuries also consisted exclusively of men, mainly because only men and boys could inherit their father's titles. Change, however, came in 1958. The hereditary peers retained their peerages and therefore their places in the House of Lords (apart from a few who later chose to renounce their peerages), but a new class of life peers was created. Life peers could be women as well as men, and they did not bequeath to their children either their titles or their places in the upper house. By the time the Blair government came to power in 1997, there were approximately 1,300 members of the House of Lords, of whom roughly two-thirds were hereditary peers and one-third life peers.[20]

Until 1911 the legislative powers of the House of Lords and the House of Commons were coextensive. Each of the two houses of Parliament had an absolute veto over legislation passed by the other. The House of Lords lost that power in 1911 and for most of the past hundred years has had only a suspensory veto. In addition, the tradition developed, especially after 1945, that the House of Lords would not block major government legislation, especially legislation that had been mentioned explicitly in the governing party's election manifesto. Partly as a result, although clashes between the House of Lords and the House of Commons continued to be frequent, the Lords usually in the end deferred to the Commons. Total deadlocks were few. By the time of the 1997 election, it was generally accepted — including by the House of Lords — that their lordships' functions were to advise, encourage and warn the democratically elected government of the day but not to obstruct its business. The once mighty House of Lords had become a secondary and ancillary body.

Almost everyone in the Labour Party, however, still disliked the Lords. They did so for three reasons. First, they saw the House of Lords — stuffed full, as it was, with dukes, marquesses, earls and such like — as a bastion of hereditary class privilege. Second, they saw no reason why an unelected chamber like the House of Lords should have any substantial power, even if it was only a delaying power, over the democratically elected House of Commons. Third, they objected to the fact that the House of Lords was stuffed full not merely with hereditary peers but, largely for that reason, with people who were also capital-C Conservatives. One would expect a body like the House of Lords to be a conservative institution, but it was also a Conservative institution. Even when the Conservative Party did not have an overall majority in the Lords, it was invariably, by a wide margin, the largest single party in the chamber. Whatever the Lords' defenders might say, the upper house consistently gave Labour governments a harder time than Tory governments.

Labour governments prior to 1997 had, rather surprisingly, left the House of Lords largely alone. The Attlee government between 1945 and 1951 went no further than to reduce the Lords' suspensory veto to one year and two parliamentary sessions. It was actually a Conservative government that introduced life peers in 1958. The Wilson government in the 1960s sought to reform the Lords but abandoned the attempt in the face of sustained opposition, including from within its own ranks. The Wilson and Callaghan governments of the 1970s had too many other things on their minds. Tony Blair and his senior colleagues were determined to be bolder. New Labour's election manifesto announced that "the House of Lords must be reformed." It went on:

> As an initial, self-contained reform, not dependent on further reform in the future, the right of hereditary peers to sit and vote in the House of Lords will be ended by statute. This will be the first stage in a process of reform to make the House of Lords more democratic and representative. The legislative powers of the House of Lords will remain unaltered.[21]

True to its word, the Blair government proceeded almost immediately to remove the hereditary peers from the House of Lords, and by the end of 1999 the great majority of them had gone, halving the House of Lords' size at a stroke from roughly 1,300 to roughly 650. The number of Conservative peers fell by more than half, though the Conservatives remained for the time being the largest single party. As the result of a compromise reached between the government and the Conservative leadership in the Lords, 92 hereditary peers were permitted to remain until the second stage of Lords reform, promised in the Labour manifesto, had been completed. The hereditary peers who were expelled from the Lords disappeared overnight: they were not even allowed to retain so-called "club" privileges. Long-serving House of Lords' employees were heard to complain that the hereditaries' departure had "lowered the whole tone of the place."

The government was clear that it wanted to expel the hereditary peers; but it had no very clear idea of what it wanted to do next. The Labour manifesto was noticeably vague about stage two of the reform. Some ministers wanted the reformed upper house to contain an elected element; some did not. Some wanted any elected element to be large; others did not. Most ministers had probably given little thought to the matter one way or the other. Unsure how to proceed, the Blair government did what most British governments do under such circumstances: it appointed a royal commission, including members of all the main political parties, to enquire into the matter.[22] The government hoped that the commission would produce recommendations acceptable to it. It also hoped that there would be broad cross-party support for the commission's recommendations, whatever they were.

The royal commission reported in January 2000.[23] Many of its recommendations were radical: the new upper house was to move rapidly towards gender equality; no one party, not even the governing party, was ever to have a majority in the upper house; the prime minister was to be deprived totally of his patronage power in respect of the upper house; the reformed house's appointed members were to be nominated by an independent appointments commission; and the links between the upper house and the peerage were to be completely severed (so that, just as hereditary peers as well as commoners could now sit in the House of Commons, so commoners as well as both hereditary and life peers would be enabled to sit in House of Lords, if indeed it continued to be called that).[24] But some of the commission's recommendations were less radical. In particular, the commission declined to recommend a wholly elected second chamber, as many reformers wished, and instead recommended that the new body should contain only a minority of elected members. The commission's members were unable to agree among themselves on the detail of this recommendation, and their report, *A House for the Future,* went no further than to list three possible "models". The three ranged from the indirect election of 65 of the new house's members (via a system of "complementary voting") to the direct election of 195 of its members (via a party-list system of proportional representation).[25]

The Blair government at once accepted the principle that the new upper house should contain at least a small elected element, but between the publication of the royal commission's report in January 2000 and the election in June 2001 matters were not taken significantly further. The government had a crowded legislative timetable and was not in any great hurry. It was also clear, following extensive consultations with the other parties, that all-party agreement on House of Lords reform was going to be difficult, if not impossible, to achieve. The government contented itself with giving the royal commission's report a generalized welcome and with promising in its 2001 election manifesto that stage two of Lords reform would indeed be proceeded with (there had been fears that the whole matter would simply be shelved) and that the reform would follow the broad lines of the royal commission's recommendations.

The results of the 2001 election left it unclear when the government would proceed to reform the House of Lords and what precise form any changes to the upper house would take. There is certainly no intention on the Blair government's part either to augment the House of Lords' formal powers or to strengthen significantly the Lords' position in political terms. That said, it seems clear that, if a new upper house is created, and especially if it contains a directly elected element, it will have considerably greater democratic legitimacy than the unreformed House of Lords and is likely, therefore, to become considerably more assertive than the old House was. Any reformed second chamber will contribute to the further dispersal of power in the British system.

THE PARTY SYSTEM

A country's party system is not normally considered part of its constitution, but the British party system over the past hundred years has been at the heart of the way in which the British constitutional and political order has functioned. For most (though not all) of the past hundred years, there have been two and only two major political parties in Britain. The overwhelming majority of voters have voted for one or other of them. The two major parties' have dominated the membership of the House of Commons. One or other of them has consistently provided the government of the day. Not only that, but the same two major parties have competed across the whole country. To be sure, there have always been individual constituencies — many — that were safe for one party or the other, but in the past the overall pattern of party competition varied but little from one part of the country to another.

At the beginning of the twenty-first century, that position has changed significantly. Table 2.1 (p. 62) illustrates the scale of the changes by setting out a simple comparison between the results of the 1970 general election — the election that might be regarded, in retrospect, as having been the last "normal" British election — and the results of the June 2001 general election. Northern Ireland has been omitted from the table because the party system there has been so completely transformed that it is impossible to make any sensible comparisons. In 1970 Ulster Unionism was still largely aligned with the mainland Conservative Party; now it is split into two main parties — the Ulster Unionist Party and the Democratic Unionist Party — and a number of smaller ones. In 1970 one of the

Table 2.1 Comparing 1970 and 2001

	1970	2001
United Kingdom		
Conservative percentage of vote	47	32
Labour percentage of vote	44	41
Liberal (Democrat) percentage of vote	14	18
Other parties' percentage of vote	11	9
Conservative seats	330	166
Labour seats	287	412
Liberal (Democrat) seats	6	52
Other parties' seats	7	29
Parties' rank order in percentage of vote:	Conservative	Labour
	Labour	Conservative
	Liberal	Liberal Democrat
	Other	Other
England		
Conservative percentage of vote	48	35
Labour percentage of vote	43	41
Liberal (Democrat) percentage of vote	14	19
Other parties' percentage of vote	4	4
Conservative seats	292	165
Labour seats	216	323
Liberal (Democrat) seats	2	40
Other parties' seats	1	1
Parties' rank order in percentage of vote:	Conservative	Labour
	Labour	Conservative
	Liberal	Liberal Democrat
	Other	Other
Scotland		
Conservative percentage of vote	39	16
Labour percentage of vote	45	43
Liberal (Democrat) percentage of vote	15	16
SNP percentage of vote	11	20
Conservative seats	23	1
Labour seats	44	56
Liberal (Democrat) seats	3	10
SNP seats	1	5
Parties' rank order in percentage of vote:	Labour	Labour
	Conservative	SNP
	Liberal	Liberal Democrat
	SNP	Conservative
Wales		
Conservative percentage of vote	28	21
Labour percentage of vote	52	49
Liberal (Democrat) percentage of vote	13	14
Plaid Cymru percentage of vote	14	14
Conservative seats	7	0
Labour seats	27	34
Liberal (Democrat) seats	1	2
Plaid Cymru seats	1	4
Parties' rank order in percentage of vote	Labour	Labour
	Conservative	Conservative
	PC	PC
	Liberal	Liberal Democrat

Sources: David Butler and Michael Pinto-Duschinsky, *The British General Election of 1970* (London: Macmillan, 1971), 356; House of Commons Library Research Paper 01/54, June 18, 2001.

two main Republican parties of recent years, the Social Democratic and Labour Party, had not yet come into existence. The party system of Northern Ireland in 1970 was still a semi-detached part of the mainland system. It has now completely come adrift.

The four parts of Table 2.1 are worth examining separately and then together. With regard to the United Kingdom as a whole, it is worth noting that the Conservative and Labour parties between them secured 91 per cent of the popular vote in 1970 but only 73 per cent in 2001—a decline in the two parties' share of the vote of nearly a fifth. In 1970 all the other parties, apart from the Conservatives and the Labour Party, won only thirteen seats in the House of Commons. In 2001 they won a total of 81. The fact that the parties' rank order, in terms of their share of the vote, has not changed a great deal serves only to mask the scale of the other changes that have been taking place. It is also worth noting, in passing, that Labour's share of the popular vote winning a landslide victory over the Conservatives in 2001 was actually smaller than its share of the vote losing to Tories three decades earlier. As John Bartle points out in Chapter 7, Labour's victory in 2001 is in many ways better characterized as a Conservative defeat.

The part of the table relating to England closely resembles the part relating to the U.K. as a whole—not surprisingly, since England alone accounts for more than four-fifths of the U.K. electorate. The parts of the table relating to Scotland and Wales, however, tell quite different stories. The positions of the Scottish Labour Party and the Scottish Liberal Democrats have changed relatively little over the past thirty years, but the Scottish National Party has nearly doubled its share of the popular vote and increased the number of its seats in the House of Commons from one to five. In terms of its share of the vote, it is now the second party north of the border, having been only the fourth party three decades ago. But it is the Conservatives' position that has changed most dramatically. Thirty years ago the Conservatives, in terms of both their share of the vote in Scotland and the number of Scottish seats they held at Westminster, lagged not far behind the Labour Party. Now they have been virtually eliminated from the Scottish political scene. In terms of their share of the vote, they fell into fourth place in 2001. And they won only one Scottish seat (having won none at all in 1997).

The picture in Wales is not dissimilar. Labour remains the dominant party in the Principality, with roughly half the vote and practically all the seats. The Liberal Democrats' position likewise remains virtually unchanged. But, as the figures in the table show, the Conservatives have lost nearly a third of their vote and, whereas they held seven of Wales's 36 seats in 1970, they now hold none (and did not hold any in 1997). Meanwhile, Plaid Cymru has gained seats although its share of the popular vote has remained more or less static.

However, it is when one comes to compare the three sub-national parts of the table that the scale of the changes over the past three decades emerges most clearly. In 1970 the Conservative and Labour parties were the top two parties in all of England, Scotland and Wales. In all three parts of Great Britain, they were the principal, indeed almost the only, contenders for power. In England the Conservatives were ahead. In Scotland and Wales they were behind, but within hailing distance of Labour. Now each of Great Britain's three nations has, in effect, its own separate, distinct party system. The principal contenders in Scotland are Labour and the SNP, with the Conservatives nowhere. In Wales the Conservatives are still in second place, but the gap between them and the Labour Party has widened substantially and the gap between the Conservatives and Plaid Cymru has closed. It is just possible to imagine Plaid overtaking the Conservatives in Wales in a few years' time.[26]

The implications of these changes for the future of British electoral politics, and for the functioning of the British political system as a whole, are considerable. One of the most important has been scarcely noticed, even in Britain. There are currently 659 seats in the United Kingdom House of Commons, and the number is unlikely to change much in the coming decades although Scotland's representation at Westminster is planned to decline as a consequence of the setting up of the Scottish Parliament. Of these 659 seats, eighteen are in Northern Ireland; the remaining 641 are in Great Britain. Of these 641 British seats, 72 are currently in Scotland and 40 in Wales — a total of 112. The Conservative Party at the moment holds only one of these 112 seats and seems unlikely to gain more than a handful, if that, at any general election in the foreseeable future. That means that, at least for the foreseeable future, the Conservatives will go into every general election carrying a handicap of some 100–110 seats. Putting the same point another way, if the Conservatives win only, say, ten seats in Scotland and Wales at any election, they will have to win no fewer than 320 of England's 528 seats — more than 60 per cent — to gain an outright majority in Parliament. That is a formidable task. Only four times since the war has any party done so well (the Conservatives under Margaret Thatcher in 1983 and again in 1987 and Labour in 1997 and again in 2001).[27]

The growth in the number of seats held by parties other than the Conservative and Labour parties has an additional, obvious implication. If any party has to win 330 seats in order to win an outright majority in Parliament, and if the non-Conservative, non-Labour parties continue to win somewhere between 40 and 60 seats, then either the Conservative Party or the Labour Party must establish a formidable lead over its principal rival, at least in terms of seats, if it is to form a majority government. The growth of third-party strength in the House of Commons means that, as a matter of simple arithmetic, the chances of no one party's obtaining an overall majority in the House have increased. For the time being, Labour is so far ahead of the Conservatives that the matter does not arise. But there is no reason to suppose that Labour's overwhelming predominance will last forever.

Scotland raises another issue. Labour looks like remaining the dominant party in Scotland for the foreseeable future (it has been the dominant party since 1959), and, even if it is eventually displaced, it is more likely to be displaced by the SNP than by either the Liberal Democrats or the Conservatives. It follows that the Edinburgh Parliament is likely to be dominated for many years, perhaps even decades to come, by non-Conservative, indeed anti-Conservative political forces. As the Conservatives, despite their electoral handicap, are bound sooner or later to regain power at Westminster, it seems highly probable that an incoming Conservative government will find itself confronting some kind of anti-Conservative administration in Edinburgh. If and when that happens, there will exist great potential for friction between London and Edinburgh, over money but not only over money. The union between England and Scotland, first established in 1707, may not be dissolved, but it could come under unprecedented strain.

The constitutional and other political changes described in this chapter have not occurred one at a time. They have all occurred at the same time. They mean, in effect, that the simple, elegant political structures that characterized the British political system during the quarter-century after the war have become markedly less simple and less elegant. They have become more complex and much harder to predict in their operations. To that extent, Britain in 2001 has come to resemble, far more than in the past, the United States, Canada or one of the countries on the European continent. The British political system, like American society as a whole, used to be described in terms of its "exceptionalism". With a bill of rights, a new sub-national tier of government, a directly elected mayor in the country's largest city and an increasingly fragmented party system, the British political system today is no longer nearly as exceptional as it was.

NOTES

1. For more or less detailed accounts of the post–1997 constitutional revolution, see Anthony King, *Does the United Kingdom Still Have a Constitution?* (London: Sweet & Maxwell, 2001); John Morrison, *Reforming Britain: New Labour, New Constitution?* (London: Reuters, 2001); Vernon Bogdanor, "Constitutional Reform", in Anthony Seldon, ed., *The Blair Effect: The Blair Government 1997–2001* (London: Little, Brown, 2001), 139–56; and Robert Hazell, "Reforming the Constitution", *Political Quarterly* 72 (January–March 2001), 39–49.

2. The only exception to this general rule was Northern Ireland, which was covered semi-autonomously between 1922, when Ireland was partitioned, and 1972, when the United Kingdom government reimposed direct rule. The head of the Northern Ireland government during this period was even accorded the title of prime minister.

3. Labour manifesto reprinted in Tim Austin, ed., *The Times Guide to the House of Commons May 1997* (London: Times Books, 1997), 328.

4. For an account of the Scottish and U.K.-wide debates on devolution between the 1960s and the 1990s, see Andrew Marr, *The Battle for Scotland* (London: Penguin, 1992).

5. For the detailed results of the 1997 Scottish referendum, see Colin Rallings and Michael Thrasher, *New Britain, New Elections: The Media Guide to the New Political Map of Britain* (London: Vacher Dod, 1999), 51–2.

6. There are other potential sources of friction. The most important is the role that Scotland's 72 members of Parliament are to play at Westminster. Why, it is asked, should Scotland's Westminster MPs be able to vote on exclusively English and Welsh legislation when English

and Welsh MPs cannot vote on Scottish legislation, which now falls within the province of the Scottish Parliament? There is no obvious answer to this question — except to try, as the Blair government is doing, not to answer it. For brief discussions of what is often referred to as "the West Lothian question" (after the constituency of the Scottish MP who first raised it in modern times), see King, *Does the United Kingdom Still Have a Constitution?* 86–7, and Iain McLean, "The National Question", in Seldon, ed., *The Blair Effect,* 429–47. The McLean chapter contains an excellent discussion of a wide variety of aspects of the whole devolution issue.

7. The Scottish electoral system is described in detail in Rallings and Thrasher, *New Britain, New Elections,* 55–8.

8. David Butler and Gareth Butler, *Twentieth-Century British Political Facts 1900–2000,* 8th edn (Basingstoke, Hants.: Macmillan, 2000), 459. Detailed results are reported in Gerry Hassan and Peter Lynch, *The Almanac of Scottish Politics* (London: Politico's, 2001).

9. On post–1997 developments in Scottish politics, see Hassan and Lynch, *The Almanac of British Politics;* Alice Brown, David McCrone, Lindsay Patterson and Paula Surridge, *The Scottish Electorate: The 1997 General Election and Beyond* (Basingstoke, Hants.: Macmillan, 1999); and Bridget Taylor and Katarina Thomson, eds., *Scotland and Wales: Nations Again?* (Cardiff: University of Wales Press, 1999).

10. Rallings and Thrasher, *New Britain, New Elections,* 91.

11. Butler and Butler, *Twentieth-Century British Political Facts,* 460.

12. Rallings and Thrasher, *New Britain, New Elections,* 149.

13. Of course not all British voters vote under all of these systems. In particular, English and Welsh voters outside London experience only first-past-the-post and the regional party list system used for elections to the European Parliament. Even so, voters in London, for example, vote under four different systems (which four can be worked out from the text).

14. For accounts of the sad, bleak history of Northern Ireland since 1922 and especially since 1969, see, among many other things, John McGarry, *Explaining Northern Ireland: Broken Images* (Oxford: Blackwell, 1995); Tom Wilson, *Ulster: Conflict and Consent* (Oxford: Blackwell, 1989); Paul Arthur and Keith Jeffrey, *Northern Ireland since 1968* (Oxford: Blackwell, 1988); James Loughlin, *The Ulster Question since 1945* (Basingstoke, Hants.: Macmillan, 1998); and Cathal McCall, *Identity in Northern Ireland: Communities, Politics and Change* (Basingstoke, Hants.: Macmillan, 1999).

15. For a brief history of the negotiations leading up to the Good Friday Agreement, see John Rentoul, *Tony Blair: Prime Minister* (London: Little, Brown, 2001), chap. 24.

16. The Good Friday Agreement, "a principled compromise" as Senator Mitchell called it, is worth reading in full: *The Belfast Agreement: An Agreement Reached at the Multi-Party Talks on Northern Ireland,* Cm. 3883 (London: Stationery Office, 1998).

17. *The Belfast Agreement,* 5.

18. Rallings and Thrasher, *New Britain, New Elections,* 121.

19. Rallings and Thrasher, *New Britain, New Elections,* 127.

20. Butler and Butler, *Twentieth-Century British Political Facts,* 224.

21. *The Times Guide to the House of Commons May 1997,* 326.

22. Formally, the royal commission was entitled the Royal Commission on the Reform of the House of Lords. Informally, it was known as the Wakeham commission after the name of its chairman, Lord Wakeham, a former Conservative cabinet minister. The present writer needs to declare an interest at this point: he was a member of the royal commission.

23. Royal Commission on the Reform of the House of Lords, *A House for the Future,* Cm. 4534 (London: Stationery Office, 2000).

24. The Act of Parliament that removed the hereditary peers from the House of Lords gave them the right, which they had not hitherto enjoyed, to vote for and sit in the House of Commons. On June 7, 2001, a hereditary peer, Viscount Thurso, was elected to sit for the Commons constituency of Caithness, Sutherland and Easter Ross. As it happened, he was not a Conservative but a Liberal Democrat. The royal commission was agnostic on whether or not

the House of Lords should continue to be called that (given that not all of its members would be lords); see *A House for the Future*, chap. 18.

25. *A House for the Future*, 122–7.
26. Plaid Cyrmu actually did overtake the Conservatives in the first elections to the Welsh Assembly. Labour won 37.6 per cent of the direct vote, Plaid Cymru 28.4 per cent and the Conservatives only 15.8 per cent, with the Liberal Democrats trailing in fourth place on 13.5 per cent. The percentages of the top-up vote were similar. The results are reported in Butler and Butler, *Twentieth-Century British Political Facts*, 460.
27. The Conservatives won 362 English seats in 1983 and 358 in 1987. Labour won 329 English seats in 1997 and 323 in 2001.

CHAPTER 3

The Conservative Party: Is There Anyone Out There?

Philip Norton

IN THE YEARS following its defeat in the 1997 general election, leading figures in the Conservative Party called for the party to unite behind the leader. One member of the shadow cabinet, Gary Streeter, said that the party had still to find its voice.[1] Though the press reported divisions within the party's ranks, calls for a united voice missed the essential truth. Whether the party spoke with one voice or several did not really matter because no one was listening. The party was the "out" party in British politics and, however loud it shouted or whatever its leader did, there was little chance of it reclaiming the attention, let alone the voting support, of the electorate.

The Conservative Party lost the 2001 general election nearly nine years before it took place. The withdrawal from the Exchange Rate Mechanism (ERM) in September 1992 triggered a collapse in support for the Conservative Party.[2] The public no longer saw the party as a party of governance — a party that was not only competent in handling the affairs, especially the economic affairs, of the nation, but also a party that was more competent than its opponents in handling those affairs. Support for the party collapsed. Other variables — such as "sleaze" and divisions over European integration — reinforced, but were not the cause of, the party's unpopularity.[3] The electors swept the party from power in 1997 and thereafter the party failed to reclaim its status as a party of governance — a task that may be considered near impossible while in the first parliament of opposition. The Labour government did not do enough to lose the 2001 election. There was, in consequence, little that the Conservative Party could do to win it. However good or bad an election campaign it conducted, it was not going to win the election. All that the campaign and all that William Hague's leadership of the party could do was to affect the size of Labour's overall majority in the House of Commons.

In the event, the party failed to dent Labour's massive parliamentary majority. Though the party set the agenda on some issues and was reasonably well prepared, the election campaign replicated the approach of the party in the preceding years. It adopted a strident tone in order to be heard. Desperate to garner attention and support, it switched from one issue to another. If there was a message, it was not a coherent one.

EXPLANATIONS OF FAILURE

The twentieth century was characterized as the "Conservative century".[4] Various reasons have been advanced for Conservative success. Some (the psychological, sociological and the ideological) explain the core support the party enjoyed. Some (the political, instrumental and the coincidental) explain why it won more elections than its opponents.[5] I have argued that Conservative success — the reason why it was the "in" party for much of the century — derives from a combination of the political and the instrumental. In essence, the Conservative Party succeeded because it managed to convey that it was an effective party of governance. This idea has four essential components: competence in handling the affairs of the nation (especially its public finances), unity, strong leadership and public service.[6] There has also been a fifth variable, independent of the party: that is, it has been fortunate in its opponents, which have often split at times opportune to the Tories.

These variables were present for much of the twentieth century; in combination, they delivered substantial victory. However, in the 1990s they were lost. None was present by the time of the 1997 general election, and the party went down to its worst defeat for nearly a century. The problem in 1997 was not only that none of the essential components was present but also that all four were now features of its opponents. New Labour was open to the accusation of stealing the Conservative Party's clothes in terms of policy: it could also be said to have acquired the distinguishing features that had made the Conservative Party the essential party of governance. New Labour appeared competent in handling the affairs of the nation, it appeared (relatively) united, it had an apparently firm leader, and it appeared more attuned to the ideals of public service than its opponents. It also now appeared to benefit from *its* opponents: it could berate the years of Tory government and, as we shall see, berate an opposition that appeared divided and uncertain. The Conservative Party had to overcome a party that had invaded "their" territory.

After the initial, and traumatic, shock of losing so badly in 1997, the party appeared to be adapting to the new situation and, under a new leader, to be setting out on a new path. The party achieved some successes in electoral contests. However, as the parliament progressed and a general election came nearer — with Labour still riding high in the opinion polls — old problems began to emerge and the leadership adopted a more reactive strategy. The party was beset by problems that had undermined it in government: it was riven by divisions, occasionally by scandal, and by a failure to articulate a coherent message. Voters were offered a disparate array of policies, many articulated in an apparently populist response to issues as they came on the political agenda. The party leader moved from playing it long to playing it very short. It was a strategy that not only failed but failed quite spectacularly.

New Beginnings

In the wake of the 1997 defeat, the members of the diminished parliamentary Conservative Party were shell-shocked. The terminology is appropriate. Not only had the party lost the election but re-elected members of Parliament had also lost many close friends in the electoral rout. The defeat created a shock in personal as well as political terms. The Conservative front bench took some time to get its act together. Many Tory MPs had difficulty in adjusting to life in opposition. For some, it took most or even all of the parliament. There was the problem not only of coming to terms, after eighteen years of Tory rule, with being in opposition, but also of coming to terms with the fact that there appeared to be little prospect of returning to office at the next election.

The scale of the defeat was staggering. The parliamentary party was halved in size. The loss was qualitative as well as quantitative. Seven cabinet members, including defence secretary Michael Portillo and foreign secretary Malcolm Rifkind, lost their seats. The scale of the defeat took many, though not all, Tory MPs by surprise. The scale, though, was such as to lead many to believe that any Tory who had survived the carnage of the election was virtually guaranteed re-election at the next election. The belief was that, with such a massive swing, the party — with its worst result since 1906 — was at rock bottom and could only improve on its performance. The party began, somewhat shakily, to look to the future.

The first opportunity to begin the march back to victory occurred in the immediate wake of the election. John Major announced his resignation as party leader. The parliamentary party elected a new leader. That leader immediately embarked on a new strategy, in terms of both organization and policy. He reorganized the party. He initiated a policy review, disavowing some of the policies of the previous Conservative government, and he listened to party members. He enunciated a policy of inclusion, bringing disaffected sections of society within the Conservative fold. His approach appeared to bear electoral reward in both European and local elections. The party appeared to be on the road to recovery.

New Leader

John Major announced his resignation on May 2. Six MPs, drawn from different strands in the party, announced their intention to seek election as his successor. The political composition of the parliamentary party favoured candidates

Table 3.1 Classification of the Parliamentary Conservative Party, May 1997

Eurosceptic right		30%
Party faithful		50%
of which:		
Eurosceptic leaning	29%	
Agnostic/don't know	17%	
Pro-European leaning	4%	
Pro-European left		21%

Source: Philip Norton, "Electing the Leader", *Politics Review* 7, April 1998: 13.

Note: Total exceeds 100 per cent because of rounding up. N=165.

from the party's centre and centre-right. An analysis of the 165 Tory MPs revealed that most MPs were sceptical on the issue of further European integration (Table 3.1). The MPs on the party's right, almost wholly sceptical of further European integration, were more numerous than those on the party's pro-European left wing.

One candidate, former health secretary Stephen Dorrell, from the party's pro-European left, dropped out when his candidature attracted little support. Another, former Welsh secretary William Hague, decided to stand after initially promising to support the bid of former home secretary Michael Howard. On Tuesday, June 10, 1997, Conservative MPs trooped into Committee Room 14 of the House of Commons to vote for one of five candidates. In the first ballot, former chancellor of the exchequer, Kenneth Clarke, topped the poll (see Table 3.2). William Hague came second. Clarke failed to meet the requirements to be declared elected (absolute majority, plus a majority representing 15 per cent of the parliamentary party). A second ballot was necessary. Given their disappointing performances, the two candidates who came bottom of the poll — Peter Lilley

Table 3.2 Election of the Conservative Leader, 1997

First Ballot (June 10, 1997)	
Clarke	49
Hague	41
Redwood	27
Lilley	24
Howard	23
Second Ballot (June 17, 1997)	
Clarke	64
Hague	62
Redwood	38
Third Ballot (June 19, 1997)	
Hague	92
Clarke	70

and Michael Howard — dropped out voluntarily. In the second ballot, Clarke still led, but only just, obtaining 64 votes to 62 for Hague. As no candidate had an absolute majority, it went to a third ballot. Under the rules, only the top two candidates went forward. Clarke and Redwood formed an alliance, but it failed to prevent (some would suggest it encouraged) a Hague victory. Hague won 90 votes to Clarke's 70 and he was duly declared elected as leader.

Hague had achieved a remarkable victory. He was 36 years old, had entered Parliament at a by-election only in 1989 and had spent just two years as a cabinet minister. He had attracted national attention when, at the age of 16, he made a barnstorming speech to the annual party conference. He had gone on to be a gifted student at Oxford University (first class honours in politics, philosophy and economics, president of the Oxford Union) and then, after gaining an MBA, had worked for the management consultancy firm of McKinsey and Company, before entering Parliament at the age of 28. He was recognized from the beginning as a high flyer, and he entered government as a junior minister in 1992. John Major brought him into the cabinet three years later, at age 34, to replace John Redwood, who had resigned as secretary of state for Wales in order to challenge Major (unsuccessfully) for the party leadership. Hague was a good parliamentary debater and widely tipped as a future party leader.

In emerging victorious, Hague had defeated senior figures in the party. Clarke was the strongest candidate in terms of cabinet experience and electoral appeal. Hague, however, won because he was more ideologically acceptable to Tory MPs than Clarke.[7] Clarke was a noted supporter of further European integration and appealed to the Europhile left within the party. Redwood was an ardent opponent of further European integration and appealed especially to the Eurosceptic right wing. Howard and Lilley drew their support also predominantly from MPs wary of further European integration. The bulk of Hague's support came from the "party faithful".

Analysis of the voting in the three rounds shows that the candidates appealed to their natural constituencies in the first round.[8] In the second ballot, Redwood continued to draw his support from his natural constituency, picking up support from former Lilley and Howard supporters. Clarke also attracted some support from Eurosceptic MPs (not so much because of his views, but because he was seen as a potential electoral asset), while Hague started to make some inroads into the votes of the Eurosceptic right. However, only in the third ballot did most MPs on the Eurosceptic right vote for Hague and even then their support was not overwhelming. He carried the Eurosceptic right by a margin of two to one. Clarke carried the Europhile left by a margin of three to one.

Hague was victorious, but his support was neither broad nor deep. He was not the first choice of most Tory MPs. Only a quarter had voted for him in the first ballot. He had difficulty attracting support from the party's left and right wings. He picked up the support of the Eurosceptic right because he was not

Kenneth Clarke and also because Redwood had done a deal with Clarke that many on the right treated with contempt. Both Clarke and Redwood had committed supporters, but they also had MPs who were opposed to them. Hague had supporters but few committed opponents. For Tory MPs, he was the least objectionable candidate.

Hague thus started out with something to prove. He had little political capital in the bank. He did not have the status of a former prime minister. He had to prove his worth to a demoralized parliamentary party that appeared supportive but not overly enthusiastic and to an electorate to whom he was largely unknown and which had just decisively rejected his party. It is perhaps not surprising that he had hesitated for a time before joining the race.

New Strategy

Hague recognized that the party needed a new start. In marketing terms, the party needed rebranding. There were essentially two stages to this rebranding. The first was recognizing the mistakes the party had made in the past and drawing a line under those mistakes. The second was embarking on a new strategy of organizational and policy renewal.

Apologising for past mistakes. Hague acknowledged that the party in government had been seen as arrogant, had made mistakes and had become too detached from the people. Addressing the party's first post-election conference in Blackpool in October 1997, he declared "Our parliamentary party came to be seen as divided, arrogant, selfish and conceited." He conceded that, on some policies, the party had been wrong. He told the conference that the decision to go into the Exchange Rate Mechanism "was a great mistake, and I'm sorry we did it. We should have the courage and confidence to say so. It did enormous damage to the credibility of our party."[9]

Returning to the theme the following March, when addressing a party rally in Reading, he declared that the party should be proud of its record in government but let go of "arguments that it had lost". "Our party", he declared, "can be trapped in the past, or it can choose to be free to face the future. We must choose to be free, free of old structures, free of old habits, free of old thinking."[10] He stressed that he was not asking the party to spend the next three years in mumbling apologies, but Tories should admit "that for all our successes, we made some mistakes". He announced the reversal of some of the previous government's policies, not least in relation to local government finance, and committed the party to greater independence for local government.

Organizational and policy renewal. The second stage of the process was organizational and policy renewal. Hague made clear his intentions shortly after becoming leader. However, the most cogent intellectual case for such renewal was put by one of the party's leading thinkers, David Willetts. Analysing past defeats, he concluded that the party had to accept the need for change in terms of organization and policy.[11] The party, he wrote, was "the western world's most successful political party precisely because it has been able to respond to such challenges and can do so again". He argued that the party had to unite and find policies that it could advance on a united front. "The party cannot afford to parade its divisions before the electorate". Organizational reform was one way of showing the electorate that the party had changed. Addressing ideas was also essential. The party had to look at the big picture and advance ideas and not simply detailed policy proposals. It had to convey what the party had conveyed when it had been in opposition before: re-birth, not fighting old battles.

Organizational reform began shortly after Hague took up the reins of leadership. He immediately sought the endorsement of party members. He had promised to submit himself for endorsement as leader by party members and — in a novel departure — a postal ballot was conducted. Members were asked to vote yes or no on the question, "Do you endorse William Hague as leader of the Conservative Party and support the principles of reform which he has outlined?" The results were announced at the party conference on October 7, 1997: 142,299 (81 per cent) voted yes and only 34,092 (19 per cent) voted no.

Following the vote, Hague moved ahead with reform. A consultation paper, *Our Party: Blueprint for Change,* was published immediately. The following spring, the recommendations for reform were published under the title of *The Fresh Future.* Under the new structure, the three elements of the party (professional, voluntary and parliamentary) were integrated into one. At the head of the organization was a governing board, with most of its members elected, drawn from the three parts of the party. In addition to the annual party conference, a national convention, meeting twice a year, was to be created to act as a link between party leaders and members. At local level, each constituency party was to have a chair, plus one deputy chair responsible for political activity and campaigning and another for finance and membership.

An ethics and integrity committee, chaired by a leading lawyer, was to investigate cases of misconduct by party members. The party had suffered from long-drawn out scandals affecting various Conservative MPs in the previous parliament, and there was a recognition that the party had been damaged by the media attention they attracted. However, perhaps the two most radical departures were the creation of a national membership and the involvement of the party membership in the election of the leader. Previously, supporters did not join the national party: there was no national party, but simply a collective of constituency parties. Now a national party membership was created. That membership was also to be consulted on the next manifesto and to be involved in the election of the party leader. Under the rules proposed by Hague, the party leader would in future be elected by a two-stage process. In the first stage, Conservative MPs would vote for their preferred candidates, in a manner not dissimilar to the existing arrangements; there would be a ballot or a series of eliminating ballots until only two candidates remained. Then the names of those two candidates would be placed before the party membership and the membership would choose between them, members voting on the basis of one member, one vote. The winning candidate would become the party leader. The new procedure came into effect in 1998.

Policy renewal was also signalled early in Hague's leadership. At the 1997 party conference, he declared that the party had embarked on reform and renewal. At the heart of his policy renewal — the "idea" rather than the detailed policy — was the establishment of the party as a national party, drawing together different sections of British society. It was Disraeli who had moulded the Conservative Party into a national rather than a sectional party, recognizing that it was, in his words, national or it was nothing. Hague sought to re-create what he later termed — in a speech to mark the twentieth anniversary of Margaret Thatcher's election as prime minister — a "bond of understanding with the British people".[12] This entailed a free enterprise revolution but also a commitment to public services. There were "limits to the role of the free market," he said. It also entailed, in what was the most significant feature of Hague's rebranding of the party, a more inclusive approach to different sections of society.

At the 1997 conference, Hague sought to portray the party as a party of tolerance. Though he expressed his support for the traditional family, he also told the activists that the party had to accept that social attitudes had changed and that they should be tolerant of individual lifestyles such as lone mothers, unmarried couples and, by implication, gay couples. The party, he said early in 1999, must be seen as "open, inclusive and compassionate",[13] a theme he reiterated a few weeks later addressing Welsh Conservatives. "We're going to be an open party that represents all of us, that stands for fair play for all."[14] In April 1999, repeating that he wanted the party to be "open, inclusive and tolerant", he said that "In the future, there will be no no-go areas for Conservatives. The party that truly understands and embraces the concept of One Nation will be truly representative of One Nation."[15] He envisaged a day when the party would be led by one of Britain's Asian community. Later in the year, he stressed that the party was committed to diversity. In the first of a series of campaigning speeches in 2000, he said that the party was reaching out to all sectors. He spoke of the need to accept that Britain was "a nation of immigrants" and said that the party needed to "respect people of different sexual orientation".[16]

These expressions were accompanied on occasion by concrete action. Early in 1998, Hague held talks with leaders of the Trades Union Congress. The following year he established a new unit to help recruit more party members from ethnic communities. There were also other actions that reflected his views. He and his fiancée, Ffion Jenkins, lived together before getting married: during the

1997 party conference they famously shared a hotel suite. A body calling itself the Conservative Family Institute, noted primarily for the homophobic views of its leader, Dr Adrian Rogers, disbanded after reports that the party chairman, Michael Ancram, was seeking ways of getting the organization to drop the name Conservative from its title. Rogers later resigned from the party.[17]

Hague embarked on a series of lectures, setting out his views on a range of issues. The Centre for Policy Studies, the think tank established by Margaret Thatcher and Sir Keith Joseph in 1975, provided a regular platform for his views. He also began a process of consulting party members and people outside the party. In July 1998, he launched "Listening to Britain", an exercise in which meetings were held around the country at which party members and others could feed in their views on public policy. Within a year, 40,000 people had attended over 1,400 meetings. The conclusions from these meetings were published in a document, *Listening to Britain,* in 1999.[18] The document summarized the concerns expressed and what people said they wanted from the party. A review of policy was also begun, under the direction the party's deputy leader, Peter Lilley. In October 1999, the fruits of the review were published under the title, *The Common Sense Revolution,* and placed before the party conference.

The document sought to establish the main priorities of the next Conservative government. These were to give more power to communities, families and independent institutions; to build a more secure society; to release the potential of the country; to protect the integrity and independence of the country; and to restore faith in politics. "All this", it stated, "is plain common sense. Making it happen in the world of politics would be a Common Sense Revolution."[19] The 43–page document included a range of policy commitments, including five guarantees. These included a tax guarantee: "We guarantee that taxes will fall as a share of the nation's income over the term of the next Parliament." There was also a sterling guarantee: "We will oppose entry into the Single Currency at the next election."

A further document, *Believing in Britain,* was published a year later.[20] This was intended to develop policy proposals based on the principles enunciated in *The Common Sense Revolution.* The document comprised 29 pages of dense text. It stressed the need for lower taxes and for giving power back to local communities and parents. Though, by its own admission, not a comprehensive document, it nonetheless was intended to form the basis for the party's manifesto at the next election and party members were asked to endorse it as such. They did so in a postal ballot by an overwhelming majority.

Other policy statements were made during Hague's leadership. At his instigation, the shadow cabinet appointed commissions to report on reform of the House of Lords, the single European currency and parliamentary reform. Conducted at an arm's length relationship from the party, the commissions were able to put in the public domain proposals that the party could draw on although they did not constitute party policy.

Having sought to draw a line under past mistakes, Hague also sought to move on from what the Labour government was doing. Though the party opposed the government's measures to devolve powers to elected bodies in Scotland and Wales, he accepted that, once in place, the new bodies were there to stay and that the party should work to make a success of them. He accepted the case for an elected mayor for London. In a speech to the Centre for Policy Studies in February 1998, he accepted that the party could not put the clock back on constitutional issues and would need to engage in fresh thinking. He also came to accept that the national minimum wage and the independence of the Monetary Policy Committee of the Bank of England were here to stay.

Hague thus set out to create a "New" Conservative Party, in both organization and its approach to contemporary society. He was not afraid to lead from the front and, if necessary, to exercise his powers as party leader. At various points in the parliament, he could claim that his approach was bringing electoral rewards.

Electoral Successes

In various electoral contests during the parliament, the Conservative Party either won or put up a creditable performance. It held some seats in by-elections, it gained a presence in the new Scottish Parliament and Welsh Assembly, it made advances in local elections, and — most spectacularly of all — it emerged the victor in the elections to the European Parliament in 1999.

The first test of the party came shortly after the general election. The MP for Uxbridge, Sir Michael Shersby, suffered a fatal heart attack. His seat was highly marginal. The party selected a local candidate and he retained the seat — the first seat to be retained by the party since the Richmond by-election of 1989 (which returned William Hague to Parliament). The party was to retain three more seats — Beckenham (1997), Eddisbury (1999) and Kensington and Chelsea (1999) — following the resignation of the incumbents in the first two and the death of the incumbent (diarist and former minister Alan Clark) in the third. The Kensington and Chelsea by-election enabled Michael Portillo to return to the House of Commons. Though retaining seats was not exactly a spectacular achievement — and, as we shall see, it was not be sustained — it was regarded at least as demonstrating that the party's base of support was not being further eroded.

The party also made gains in local elections. It made advances in 1998 (making a net gain of more than 250 council seats and two councils), 1999 (1,340 more seats and 48 councils) and 2000 (592 more seats and 16 councils). It won seats in both the Scottish Parliament and the Welsh Assembly in 1998, in both cases behind the nationalist party but ahead of the Liberal Democrats. Early in 2000, in a by-election in Ayr, it won its first directly elected seat in the Scottish Parliament (its other members having been elected as list members under the regional list system). In the election of a London mayor in 2000, the independent candidate, Ken Livingstone, won easily but the Conservative candidate, Steven Norris, came second, pushing the official Labour candidate into third place.

However, the party's biggest electoral success came in the European Parliament elections in 1999. The party published its manifesto for the election and campaigned on the slogan "In Europe, Not Run by Europe". The party opposed entry into the single European currency. Though it was expected to increase its number of members of the European Parliament (MEPs) because of a switch from the first-past-the-post system of election to that of a closed list system, the party's performance exceeded even its own expectations. On the lowest turnout achieved to date in elections to the European Parliament (24 per cent), the party won 36 seats, seven more than the number won by Labour. In the 1994 elections, Labour had won 62 seats and the Conservatives 18. Labour recorded its lowest share of the poll since the disastrous leadership of Michael Foot. It was calculated that, if the results were repeated in a general election, the Conservatives would have a majority of 96 seats. Hague welcomed the result as a "major breakthrough" for the party.

The results of the European elections, combined with advances in the local elections, led some in the Tory party to believe that the party had turned the corner. In the event, the breakthrough was to prove a chimera.

OLD PROBLEMS

Viewed in isolation, Hague's attempt to rebrand the party might be seen to be bearing fruit. However, the successes in local elections and the European Parliament elections took place against a backcloth of a poor standing in the opinion polls and of survey evidence that electors rated Labour as having the better policies for dealing with the nation's problems. The Conservative Party was achieving some improvements on its disastrous electoral performances in the mid 1990s, but it was not making inroads where it mattered: electors' voting intentions for the next general election. The gap in the opinion polls between Labour and the Conservative parties hardly shifted during most of the parliament. The Labour Party regularly stood at 50 per cent or just below in the opinion polls. The Conservative Party had difficulty getting much above 30 per cent. The party appeared to be as or almost as unpopular throughout the parliament as it had been in 1997. If the party was doing some things right, it must also have been doing some things wrong.

What the party appeared to be doing wrong was repeating its mistakes of the previous parliament. Far from demonstrating that it was a party of governance, it was doing the opposite. It failed to convey that it had a clear sense of direction, it was divided, its leader failed to engage popular support, and some of its members were mired in scandal.

Lack of Direction

The party could not be accused of failing to put forward policies. However, they failed to attract popular support. There were essentially five reasons for this failure.

First, there was no fresh thinking that allowed the party to claim the intellectual high ground. In some previous periods of opposition, the party had managed to convey that it had new ideas that set it apart. Under Hague's leadership, it appeared initially as though he were indulging in such fresh thinking. His lectures on different areas of policy suggested that he was moving in this direction, but the end result was a raft of specific policy proposals which, however individually relevant they might be, failed to convey new ideas, certainly ideas that captured the imagination. As the political journalist Peter Riddell was to observe: "The Tories seem afraid of thinking boldly about the size of the state."[21] Instead, he noted, their proposals had been timid. "Even when originally bold, they have often been toned down and modified in response to focus group research, as has happened with David Willetts's sensible ideas on pensions." When in April 1998 Peter Lilley said that the free market had its limits and, in effect, that the party had to embark on a new direction, he attracted criticism within the parliamentary party and was subsequently dropped as deputy leader. Under Margaret Thatcher's leadership, the party in the period after 1975 engaged in a radical re-think — the party "became the party of intellectual debate and philosophical argument"[22] — and the leader sought to set the tone rather than present a finished product. Under William Hague, the party engaged in a re-think, but it was not radical and it failed to set a tone. In David Willetts's terminology, the party failed to identify "the big picture". Instead, there was too much emphasis on the detail.

Second, there was a failure to link ideas to policies. In so far as the party embraced a new approach, it was not clearly connected to the policy detail. Hague embraced the approach championed by the then governor of Texas, George W. Bush: that of "compassionate conservatism". As we have seen, he gave voice to this approach at his first party conference as leader. However, there were few specific policies that flowed from the new approach. Some of the policies adopted by the party leader even appeared at odds with it. His advocacy of inclusiveness in respect of gays created controversy within the party and he found no resonance to his stance on gay rights. Though he personally favoured lowering the age of consent for gay sex from 18 to 16, this remained — as it had in the past — an issue to be decided on a free vote in the House of Commons. Most Tory MPs voted against lowering the age. He supported the retention of Section 28 of the 1988 Local Government Act, prohibiting local authorities from "promoting" homosexuality. Section 28 was a target of gay rights campaigners, who saw it as a potent symbol of discrimination. When the government attempted to repeal the provision, Hague imposed a three-line whip in support of its retention. His stance resulted in one front-bench MP, Shaun Woodward, leaving the front bench; Woodward subsequently defected to the Labour Party. A prominent gay millionaire, Ivan Massow, also defected to Labour. The party's stance on asylum seekers, involving detention while their claims were assessed, also appeared to send out signals that were not encouraging to Britain's ethnic communities. In March 2001, Hague claimed that four more years of a Labour government would turn Britain into "a foreign land".[23] The new approach taken by the leader thus appeared indistinct and unrelated to the specific policies that the party was putting forward. Internal conflict contributed to the lack of clarity.

Third, there was an excess of policy proposals. Hague recognized that the party had to put forward proposals to show that the party was again ready for government. However, he tried too hard. Various policy documents were, as we have seen, put in the public domain. But the more that were published, the more confused the picture became. Electors were not overly interested in the detail. The party continued to publish more detail. The problem was inadvertently well summarized in an opening statement in *Believing in Britain.* The document, it said, "is not a comprehensive list of Conservative policies, nor does it draw a line under Conservative policy making. We have made many policy announcements in the past year and we will go on doing so."[24] The more it carried on doing so, the less clear was the basic message that it wished to convey. In a newspaper article in January 2000, former chancellor of the exchequer, Geoffrey Howe (Lord Howe of Aberavon), said the party needed fresh policy positions: "That certainly doesn't require another bible of detail on everything under the sun, such as the *Common Sense Revolution* document."[25]

Also, the more it published, the more ammunition the party handed to its critics. They were able to draw attention to inconsistencies or changes. Various policies attracted serious criticism, outside as well as within the party, and were abandoned. "The Tories", wrote Tom Baldwin in *The Times,* "have published any number of pre-manifesto documents only to rip them up and start all over again in the manner of a panic-stricken student sitting an exam that he knows he will fail."[26] The tax guarantee that appeared in *The Common Sense Revolution* had been dropped by the time that *Believing in Britain* was published: now the party said that "in all normal circumstances" it would reduce the burden of taxation. By early 2001, there had been eleven significant changes in policy.[27]

Furthermore, the more policies that there were, the more the party's opponents could be selective in drawing out and emphasizing those that made the party look bad. Critics were especially effective in labelling the party as "extreme". Though most of the party's policies were not that far removed from the government's, its policies on the single currency and on asylum seekers were picked on as examples of a party that was operating at the political extreme. The Conservatives were derided as an excessively right-wing party. The claim of extremism was also levelled by some within the party. A number, including defecting MP

Shaun Woodward, used it as a basis for leaving. During the election campaign in 2001, two ex-MPs, both former ministers (John Lee and Anthony Nelson), also defected to Labour, claiming that the party had become too right-wing.

Fourth, the proposals seemed too reactive. Some policies were dropped when they attracted flak, whether from inside or outside the party. Michael Portillo, brought in as shadow chancellor following his return to the Commons, persuaded Hague to drop the tax guarantee because it was unrealistic. Other policies appeared to be introduced in response to issues as they appeared on the agenda. When there was a public protest over fuel prices, resulting in a blockading of petrol depots, Hague said initially that he would not cave in to the protests but then announced a policy of a 3p a litre cut in fuel duty. When the number of people seeking asylum in the United Kingdom showed a dramatic rise, the party brought in a tough policy on detention for asylum seekers. The effect was to convey the impression that the party was opportunistic, ready to jump on any passing populist bandwagon. By seeking to harness popular sentiment on these issues, the party served to undermine its own popularity. It also alarmed some within the party who feared that a more populist stance would undermine the moves towards a more inclusive approach. In October 2000, the former leader, John Major, addressing a fringe meeting at the party conference, felt compelled to warn that the party must continue to reach out to the disadvantaged and pursue a One Nation approach.[28]

Fifth, the party appeared divided on many issues. Not only could the party not convey a consistent message, it could not convey a united message. The party not only continued to be split on the issue of European integration, it also found a new fissure. Whereas before the 1990s, electors regularly perceived the Labour Party as more divided than the Conservatives, the position was reversed in the 1990s. The Conservatives were viewed as a divided party under John Major. They continued to be viewed as a divided party under William Hague — as John Bartle shows in detail in Chapter 7.

A Divided Party

The party had been badly divided over the issue of European integration during John Major's premiership. Indeed, it was one of the few issues on which the parliamentary party was divided. During that period, Labour MPs were actually more rebellious.[29] But under William Hague's leadership the issue of Europe was, in many respects, even more divisive, producing more resignations from the front bench. It was compounded by new divisions, especially on social policy. There was a growing divide between those who favoured a policy of inclusion and those who favoured a hard-line moral agenda.

European integration has long been the fault line of British politics, essentially since negotiations took place in the late 1940s leading to the Treaty of Paris. Under William Hague's leadership, the issue at the heart of dispute within the party was that of a single European currency. Hague was opposed to joining. On October 23, 1997 the shadow cabinet agreed to rule out membership of the single currency in both the current and the next parliament, in effect ruling out membership for the next ten years. Shadow agriculture secretary David Curry, a leading pro-European, resigned from the shadow cabinet. A spokesman on Northern Ireland, Ian Taylor, also resigned from the front bench. The party's policy on the single currency was variously criticized by former senior cabinet members, notably Michael Heseltine (Major's deputy prime minister), Chris Patten (a former party chairman), Douglas Hurd (a former foreign secretary), European commissioner Sir Leon Brittan and former prime minister Sir Edward Heath. In November 1997, Hague suspended from the party a leading pro-European MP, Peter Temple-Morris, who was critical of the party's stance on a range of issues. Temple-Morris promptly resigned from the party, sat as an Independent Conservative and the following June crossed the floor to join the Labour Party. (A Conservative peer, Lord Hacking, did the same in the House of Lords.) In January 1998, the *Independent* published a letter from Chris Patten and eleven other senior Conservatives supporting the government's stance on the single currency.[30] In July Kenneth Clarke told journalists that Hague had got it wrong on the single currency. The stance taken, he said, was unsustainable.[31]

As attacks on the party's stance continued from within the party, Hague decided to ballot the party membership on the issue. The move was criticized by the leading Europhiles. Ballot papers were sent to the party's 300,000 members in September 1998. The result was declared on October 5, just before the party conference. On the policy on the single currency, 170,558 (84.4 per cent) voted in support and 31,000 (15.6 per cent) voted against. Patten and others continued to make clear that the issue would not go away because of the ballot.

Dissent from the party line continued, especially from within the ranks of the party's members of the European Parliament (MEPs). Immediately after the ballot, one MEP, James Moorhouse, defected to the Liberal Democrats. In January 1999, two MEPs, John Stevens and Brendan Donnelly, resigned from the party and in the following month formed a new Pro-Euro Conservative Party. The party contested the European Parliament elections. On June 8, *The Times* carried a supportive letter from ten former MPs and MEPs. However, no senior figure in the party switched to support the new party and it gained only 1.4 per cent of the vote. The 1999 elections, though, did not produce a wholly supportive parliamentary party in the European Parliament. Some Tory MEPs were supportive of a single currency, and in 2000 a longstanding MEP, Bill Newton-Dunn, a former leader of the party in the parliament, defected to the Liberal Democrats. He was the seventh MEP to defect in the previous four years.

The issue of the single currency continued to split the party. Though many leading advocates of a single currency were less vocal following the 1998 ballot, dissenting voices continued to be heard. Both Heseltine and Clarke shared a pro-European platform with prime minister Tony Blair. Dissenting voices were not exclusive to the pro-European wing of the party. Some opponents of a single currency wanted Hague to go further in his opposition and to rule out membership in principle. One multi-millionaire member of the party, Paul Sykes, resigned in order to give financial support to candidates opposed in principle to the single currency. A former MP, Roger Knapman, defected to the United Kingdom Independence Party, and there were persistent rumours that a sitting MP would also do so. The MP most frequently mentioned, Teresa Gorman, did not; but another did. Christopher Gill, the MP for Ludlow, who had announced he would be stepping down at the next election, resigned from the party in March 2001, just before the general election, saying that he would be addressing meetings of the United Kingdom Independence Party.

Hague was thus buffeted by critics on both sides of the issue. The party remained divided up to, and during, the election campaign in 2001. However, Europe was not the only area in which the party was divided. A fissure emerged on social policies. Hague, as we have seen, signalled a more "inclusive" approach in his 1997 conference speech. It was a theme taken up by Michael Portillo following his return to the House of Commons in 1999. Prior to his return, he had gone through a very public agonizing over the problems facing the party and had also admitted in a newspaper interview that he had had a homosexual relationship prior to his marriage. Appointed shadow chancellor of the exchequer early in 2000, Portillo spoke out on issues extending beyond his economic portfolio. He spoke in support of inclusiveness, especially in a wide-ranging and personal speech to the party conference in 2000.[32] His embrace of an inclusive approach did not endear him to all party members. Some emphasized the need to uphold "traditional family values". One leading proponent of such values, former cabinet minister Lord Tebbit, who had criticized Portillo for not being more candid in his admission of a homosexual past,[33] attacked the "touchy feely" stance that the shadow chancellor was taking.[34]

The issue polarized opinion, not least in the shadow cabinet. Some members lined up behind Portillo, others behind Tebbit and shadow home secretary Ann Widdecombe in subscribing to a hardline conservative approach. Though still emphasizing that he wanted a compassionate and inclusive party, Hague appeared increasingly to side more with the hard-line approach. He gave speeches on morality and the family, he espoused a tax break for certain married couples with young children ("to signal the support of the state for the institution of marriage"),[35] and he sought to exploit what he saw as popular opposition to the government's attempts to abolish Section 28. The more he made an issue of Section 28, the more confused the message became.

Conflict within the party on social issues was not confined to homosexuality. In 2000, the issue of drugs came to the fore, and in 2001, just as the election campaign was getting under way, there was a particularly bitter conflict over the issue of race. Both conflicts left the party looking divided and Hague's leadership uncertain.

At the party conference in 2000, Widdecombe made a rousing speech, announcing a "zero tolerance" approach to those caught taking drugs, including soft drugs. Those caught in possession of drugs would be treated as criminals.[36] She got an enthusiastic ovation. However, within a matter of days the policy was unravelling. The police indicated that they thought the policy was unworkable. Seven members of the shadow cabinet, contacted by members of the press, admitted that they had at some point tried cannabis. They included the shadow foreign secretary, Francis Maude, as well as the party's leader in the House of Lords, Lord Strathclyde. One of the seven said: "The policy will have to be redefined. We are all furious with Ann."[37] Hague initially stood by Widdecombe's position but then distanced himself from it. The following Monday, he abandoned it, announcing that the policy would be subject to further consultation.[38]

The party's stance on asylum seekers and immigration also upset some members of the party who felt it conveyed that the party was uncaring and possibly xenophobic. Hague's speech claiming that there was a danger that Britain could become "a foreign land" seemed to confirm those fears and was taken by critics as confirming the right-ward drift within the party. The issue hit the headlines shortly before the general election in 2001 when a Conservative MP, John Townend, claimed that immigration had undermined Britain's "homogeneous Anglo-Saxon culture". His comments drew immediate criticism and demands that Hague expel Townend from the party.

Hague initially declined to take action, arguing that there was no point as Townend was standing down at the general election. Townend's comments, and Hague's refusal to take disciplinary action, drew condemnation from a black Conservative peer, Lord Taylor of Warwick, a former adviser to Conservative Home Office ministers.[39] Taylor agonized publicly over whether to resign from the party. Under pressure from senior members of the shadow cabinet, such as Portillo and Maude, Hague told Townend that he had to apologize or be expelled from the party. Townend issued an apology. The situation was not helped when another Conservative MP, Laurence Robertson, expressed sympathy for Townend's position and yet another, Christopher Gill — shortly to leave the party — compared asylum seekers to "rats in a bucket".[40] The dispute served to reinforce the sense of a divided party, one open to claims of extremism and led by a leader who failed to act decisively and, in Peter Riddell's words, "ended up with the worst of all worlds".[41]

The divisions on social policy, coming on top of those on European integration, not only conveyed a picture of a divided party but also left journalists confused as to the ideological configurations that were developing in the party.

Portillo was portrayed as having moved from the right of the party to a more lib-eral, but not well-defined, position. He was accused of turning his back on his ideological heroine, Margaret Thatcher, and her eponymous philosophy. Along with shadow foreign secretary Francis Maude, he resigned from the Thatcherite No Turning Back group. Some writers, as we have seen, portrayed him as leading an "inclusive" tendency within the shadow cabinet and Widdecombe as leading an "exclusive" tendency. Various terms were drawn on, such as "mods" and "rock-ers",[42] to convey the stance of, and the conflict between, the two tendencies. There was a perception that the party was undergoing something of a realign-ment and, although the line-up of the members in the opposing camps could be identified, the exact nature of that realignment was difficult to describe in terms of Conservative philosophy. To many commentators, it appeared that the new line-up bore little relationship to previous philosophical divisions within the party.

Though the public portrayal of the stance taken by different leading mem-bers of the party was a confused one, there was actually some coherence in what was happening. It is possible to identify changes within the framework of existing strands within the party. In an analysis, based on research of every Conservative MP in 1989, I identified seven strands within the party: neo-liberal, Thatcherite, Tory right, populist, party faithful, damps and wets.[43] It has since been possible to refine these categories and they remain useful for understanding what was hap-pening in the parliamentary party under Hague. The categories are shown in Table 3.3 (p. 86).

Neo-liberals adopt a liberal stance on economic and social issues. They want to see the individual free from encroachment by the state. On social issues, this extends to supporting liberalization of the laws on homosexuality and can en-compass opposition to the death penalty. Those on the Tory right tend not to be too concerned with economic issues and take a conservative stance on social issues. They are strong supporters of maintaining moral standards and will sup-port legislation necessary to maintain those standards. They support strongly the reintroduction of the death penalty and are opposed to liberalization of the law on such issues as homosexuality. The genius of Margaret Thatcher was to weld together economic liberalism with social conservatism. Thatcherism was never the dominant strand within the parliamentary party,[44] but it did attract a body of committed adherents, among them Michael Portillo. Populists will tend to give preference to spending on public services (what I have termed economic statism) over the fiscal prudence of the Treasury and to support a conservative position on social issues. Like neo-liberals, Thatcherites and the Tory right, they are opposed to further European integration. These strands are grouped together in Table 3.1, in our earlier section analysing the 1997 leadership contest, as the Eurosceptic right.

The party faithful comprises those members who will give priority in their

Table 3.3 Taxonomy of the Parliamentary Conservative Party, May 2001

Category	Stance	Examples of MPs in the category
Neo-liberal	Economic liberal Social liberal Eurosceptic	*Michael Portillo* *Francis Maude* *Alan Duncan* *John Bercow* *Nigel Evans* *Bernard Jenkin* *David Prior*
Thatcherite	Economic liberal Social conservative Eurosceptic	*John Redwood* *Iain Duncan Smith* *John Townend* *David Davis* *Oliver Letwin*
Tory right	Economic agnostic Social conservative Eurosceptic	*Ann Widdecombe* *Julian Brazier* *James Cran*
Populist	Economic statist Social conservative Anti-Europe	*Nicholas Winterton* *Ann Winterton* *Sir Teddy Taylor* *Teresa Gorman*
Party faithful	Put party interest ahead of ideological preferences	*Michael Ancram* *John Major*
Damp	Moderately economic statist Social liberal Pro-Europe	*Steven Norris* *Tim Yeo* *Peter Bottomley* *David Curry*
Wet	Economic statist Social conservative Pro-Europe	*Michael Heseltine* *John Gummer* *Virginia Bottomley* *Tony Baldry*

actions to what they see as being in the best interests of the party. They may hold views on a range of issues and support intellectually or instinctively a particular strand of thought, but they do not let their particular views dictate their public actions. They will tend to follow the lead of the party leader, usually giving the leader the benefit of the doubt. Only when the leader appears to be jeopardizing the future success of the party will the party faithful withdraw its support.

The damps adopt a moderately statist position on economic issues, being willing to support state spending on fairly pragmatic grounds. They are social liberals. Wets — the terminology derives from Thatcher's castigation of some of her colleagues as "wet" — have a greater commitment than damps to state intervention. They tend to be social conservatives in respect of contemporary social issues, such as gay rights. Both damps and wets are supporters of greater European integration. The damps and wets are grouped together in Table 3.1 as the pro-European left.

The broad headings employed earlier in Table 3.1 are useful for understanding the party at the beginning of the parliament, when Europe was still (as it remained) a divisive issue. However, for explaining what happened in the party during the parliament we have to separate the strands that form those groupings (Table 3.3). What happened was that Thatcherism started to unravel. Economic liberals had been drawn to Thatcherism by its intellectual appeal, the Tory right by its instinctive support of traditional values. They were uneasy partners. The scale of the defeat in 1997 forced some who had been drawn to Thatcherism because of its advocacy of the free market to reflect more deeply on the reasons for the defeat than those who were instinctively wedded to the maintenance of traditional social standards. Michael Portillo was in the van of those Thatcherites engaging in fresh thinking. His background is instructive. He had been converted to the economic liberal brand of Conservatism as an undergraduate (he had previously supported Labour). He had lost his previously safe seat in the 1997 landslide. He spent his time outside parliament reflecting, rather publicly, on the reasons for the party's disastrous performance. Rather than some dramatic Damascus-like conversion, he appears to have moved from the Thatcherite camp to the neo-liberal camp. In so doing, he joined another Thatcherite, Francis Maude, and they began to influence the thinking of others. Among those in the shadow cabinet siding with their views were David Willetts and Archie Norman. Willetts — known as "two-brains Willetts" — was an intellectual who had headed a think tank. Norman had made his name as a business man heading a national supermarket chain. They were opposed by shadow defence secretary Iain Duncan Smith, a Thatcherite former army officer, and Ann Widdecombe, a leading exponent of the values of the Tory right.

This move by economic liberals away from the social conservatism of Thatcherism thus created some new alliances. The old dividing line between Eurosceptics and pro-Europeans remained, but people's stance on social issues cut across this division. Damps made common cause on social issues with the neo-liberals. The party faithful, essentially agnostic on European integration, followed the leadership in their attitude to the single currency. However, on the new social division within the party, the leadership was sending out confused signals. Portillo, for his part, was clearly moving towards a new approach but had not articulated a stance that was well honed and coherent.

What was happening within the parliamentary party can thus be explained in terms of the taxonomy of strands within the party. It helps us understand a dynamic and complex process. It thus has intellectual value. However, two caveats are necessary. The first is that the categories identified in Table 3.3 are ideal types. Each category permits variation and none has an immutable border. Some Conservatives straddle categories and some cannot easily be placed within any category. For example, Kenneth Clarke oscillated between the wet and damp category, being a liberal on some social issues and highly conservative on others;

in his conservative stance, he exhibited some of the instinctive features associated with the Tory right. Second, and linked, all the public saw during the parliament was the apparently confusing shifts of view and the conflicts that those shifts engendered within the party and especially in the shadow cabinet. Widdecombe was seen to be at odds with Portillo. Portillo's public ruminations were interpreted as an attempt to re-position himself in order to challenge for the leadership. The pronouncements of the party leader seemed to favour both inclusiveness and adherence to traditional family values. There was, of course, little incentive for members of the public to try to cut through the media portrayal of divisions and confusion within the party in order to make sense of what has happening.

Leader

William Hague was thrust into the leadership of the Conservative Party at a very early stage, not only in his own life but in the life of the parliament. As we have seen, he hesitated before contesting the leadership election and he won because he was the least objectionable candidate. He set about reforming the party. However, as the parliament progressed, his leadership appeared to become part of the party's problem rather than part of its solution. Hague failed to make a mark (at least a positive one) with the public and antagonized part of his party.

He initially sought to convey the image of someone in touch with young people. He and his fiancée attended the multi-racial Notting Hill Carnival. His presence, in denim shirt and jeans, conveyed "the overwhelming impression of a man trying too hard to be 'young and in touch' and it was difficult to suppress a laugh."[45] He visited a theme park wearing a baseball cap emblazoned with his surname, in so doing attracting ridicule from the media. This attempt to craft a youthful and fashionable image clashed with perceptions of him as a traditional, albeit very effective, parliamentarian. He was a skilful parliamentary debater, often getting the better of the prime minister at Prime Minister's Question Time, but the image of him at the dispatch box failed to impress voters as much as it impressed his own supporters in the Commons and some commentators.

He failed to boost his popularity ratings. After five months, only 19 per cent of the public were satisfied with his leadership. His support among Conservative supporters fell. In October, 41 per cent were satisfied with his leadership; in November the figure was only 29 per cent. To try to improve his ratings, he underwent various re-launches. In April 1999, one party source was quoted as saying: "We need to demonstrate that the real William Hague is not just a one-dimensional parliamentary performer."[46] There was an attempt to portray him as a family man (he married in December 1997 and his wife was photogenic) in touch with the concerns of ordinary voters. The various re-launches all failed. He failed to convey that he was an experienced and effective leader. His ratings remained low, trailing the popularity of the party. He continued to trail behind the other party leaders in most of fourteen attributes tested in MORI's monthly image poll. After nearly four years in the leadership, a third of those questioned considered him "rather inexperienced" (as against a mere 11 per cent giving the same answer for Tony Blair) and only 5 per cent thought he had "a lot of personality". Only 6 per cent thought that he would be "good in a crisis".[47] Throughout the parliament, popular approval of his leadership remained negative, more people expressing dissatisfaction with his leadership than expressing satisfaction. According to MORI polls carried out every month during his leadership, the proportion of those satisfied with it never reached 30 per cent.[48]

Hague sought to convey an impression of strong leadership. He made clear that he was not prepared to tolerate the lack of discipline that had marked the party before 1997. As we have seen, he called a ballot of party members in order to silence pro-European critics. He suspended Peter Temple-Morris from the party. He sacked Shaun Woodward from the front bench because of his refusal to accept the party line on Section 28. At the end of the parliament, the whip was withdrawn from Charles Wardle, a disaffected Conservative MP who was standing down, because it was thought he would be supporting an independent candidate. However, the smack of firm leadership was criticized for being applied to only one section of the party. Hague failed to expel or suspend John Townend or Christopher Gill in 2001 following their comments on race, despite various calls for him to do so. This attracted criticism from some on the left of the party. According to one former cabinet minister, "The problem is that William will not pick a fight with the Right, that is why we are being dragged to the Right."[49]

Hague thus alienated some on the party's left. He also managed for a time to alienate Conservative members of the House of Lords. At the beginning of December 1998, it emerged that the Conservative leader in the Lords, Viscount Cranborne, had — unknown to Hague and other members of the shadow cabinet — done a deal with the Lord Chancellor, Lord Irvine, on reform of the upper house. Hague discovered that talks had taken place, raised the matter at Prime Minister's Question Time, only to be told by the prime minister that a deal had been done. An infuriated Hague stormed over to the Lords, interrupted Cranborne in a meeting of Conservative peers and then, in a stormy private meeting, dismissed him. Hague said Cranborne had been sacked for being "duplicitous". The party's deputy leader in the Lords resigned in protest at Cranborne's sacking and all the members of the front bench in the Lords offered to resign. After frantic negotiations, they were dissuaded and the party's chief whip in the Lords, Lord Strathclyde, was appointed leader. Two women peers resigned the Conservative whip in protest at Cranborne's dismissal; one later returned to the fold — the other did not.

Hague's stance on policies also undermined his position. As we have seen, he sent out conflicting signals. There was no clear statement of philosophy. There was a mismatch between rhetoric and action. "Mr Hague has talked big about a slimmer State and lower taxes, but he has thought small."[50] As the parliament progressed and the next election came nearer, any attempt at long-term thinking appeared to give way to reactive, short-term policy initiatives. The initiatives failed to make an impact on the party's support, resulting in Hague looking for more policy avenues to explore. Some of the stances taken smacked of exasperation and, to his critics, of extremism. He tried to exploit those issues that resonated with the public and that he believed would allow him to play to the party's strengths. He emphasized the issues of the single currency and asylum. This emphasis was marked as the party entered the election campaign in 2001. However, the party continued to trail Labour by about 20 points in the polls. The position taken by Hague allowed opponents to paint the party as right-wing and it attracted criticism from some within the party.[51] Hague then ratcheted up the campaign by claiming that the election was the voters' last chance to "save the pound", even though the government was committed to a referendum on entry to the single currency. He then backed away from the claim and sought to move on to other issues. The problem for Hague was that, although he was having success in attracting attention to the issues he was pushing, they were not the issues at the top of voters' concerns. The health service and education headed voter concerns, and the party was not seen as addressing either.

Not only did the strategy fail in respect of policy, it also failed to live up to expectations in terms of party organization. Some of the reforms initially promised were not implemented because of lack of resources. Hague had set a target of doubling the membership within two years and achieving a membership of one million in the new millennium. However, membership was reported never to have moved much beyond the 350,000 mark and in 2000 to be actually falling. One estimate put it at 325,000, though some suspected it was much lower. Attempts to persuade local associations to select more women and ethnic candidates resulted in little action. The party was also criticized for remaining heavily dependent on generous benefactors, the more so as contributions from big business declined. Donations to the party declined, from £9.7 million in 1998 to £6.4 million in 1999.[52] The party's treasurer, multi-millionaire business man Michael Ashcroft, was also the party's biggest donor, giving large donations and loans; in 1998–99 he gave £750,000 in cash donations and £400,00 in loans. At the beginning of 2001, another business man, Stuart Wheeler, gave a £5 million donation to the party.

During his leadership, Hague attracted criticism from friends as well as enemies. Some of the criticism from his supporters got into the public domain. In May 1999, one of his closest supporters, frontbencher Alan Duncan, referred in an interview to Hague's "confusion of tactics, strategy and belief". He issued a public apology.[53] A parliamentary candidate, Nigel Hastilow, conceded on his website at the beginning of 2001 that the party's "leader is not popular, its policies have been aped by New Labour, and its personalities are still mired in sleaze".[54] Hague's Yorkshire accent and his fairly static tone of delivery went down badly with the public. The influence of his coterie of close aides went down badly with leading party members. There was criticism that he had no heavyweight figure close to him to advise him, akin to William Whitelaw under Margaret Thatcher or Michael Heseltine under John Major. His chief of staff was former athlete and ex-MP Sebastian Coe (sent to the Lords by Hague), and his political secretary, George Osborne, was still in his twenties. Hague was also criticized for moving his office from the House of Commons to Conservative Central Office. He was seen as too detached from the parliamentary party, with access to him controlled too tightly by Coe.

"You can praise his intellect. You can admire his rhetorical skills. You can be impressed by him at the dispatch box," wrote Mary Ann Sieghart in *The Times* in February 2001. "But there is no getting away from it: William Hague is a ball and chain around the ankle of the Tory Party."[55] Commentators were sometimes perplexed as to why he was such a ball and chain, but few if any would challenge the conclusion. Parallels were drawn with Neil Kinnock, who improved Labour's performance in the 1980s but failed to make it to the premiership. However, as Sieghart noted, Hague's satisfaction ratings were closer to those of Kinnock's hapless predecessor, Michael Foot, than they were to Kinnock's. The Conservative Party entered the general election in 2001 with their leader as their leading champion (he dominated the campaign) and one of their liabilities, if not by any means their greatest.

Scandal

The Conservative Party had suffered from "sleaze" in the previous parliament, various figures in the party having been the subject of sexual, financial or political scandals. Their actions undermined the claim of the party to be a party of probity, with members operating in the public interest rather than for personal gain. As the extract from Nigel Hastilow's website reveals, the issue did not disappear during Hague's leadership.

During the parliament, scandals surrounding two well-known names continued. Neil Hamilton, who had lost one of the safest seats in the country in 1997 to independent candidate Martin Bell, pursued a case for libel against the man who brought him down, Harrod's owner Mohammed Al Fayed. (Al Fayed had alleged that he had paid money to Hamilton to table parliamentary questions.) The case served to keep the name of Hamilton to the fore, reminding people of the scandal that had engulfed the party during John Major's premiership. Hamilton lost. Former cabinet minister Jonathan Aitken also went to prison after being convicted of committing perjury during a libel case he had brought against the *Guardian*. The libel trial had begun in 1995 and collapsed in June 1997. Aitken was imprisoned in June 1999 and released early the following year. However, a number of fresh scandals occurred during Hague's tenure of the leadership. One, as he was to acknowledge, reflected badly on his own judgement.

In October 1997 — five months after the general election — the Conservative MP for Beckenham, Piers Merchant, who was married with two children, resigned after it was revealed that he had renewed an affair with a teenage girl. In January 1999, a Conservative MEP, Tom Spencer, was suspended from the Tory whip in the European Parliament after he was caught by customs officials at Heathrow airport with soft drugs and gay pornography; he subsequently withdrew from contesting the European Parliament elections in May. In August 1999 the leader of the Conservatives in the Welsh Assembly, Rod Richards, a former MP, resigned after allegations of assault had been made against him by a young woman. Controversy also surrounded party treasurer Michael Ashcroft, because of his business dealings in Belize. He spent more time in Belize than in Britain. When he was nominated for a peerage by Hague, the move was delayed until he gave assurances that he would take up residence in the United Kingdom.

However, by far the biggest scandal erupted in November 1998. Lord Archer of Weston-super-Mare — better known as the novelist Jeffrey Archer — had been selected by party members in London to contest the election for mayor of London. However, a former friend of Archer's alleged that Archer had asked him to lie for him during a famous libel trial (which Archer had won) in 1987, when Archer was deputy chairman of the party. The allegations led to Archer withdrawing from the race. He was then expelled from the party for five years. In 2001 Archer was arrested and tried for attempting to pervert the course of justice.

Archer's withdrawal from the mayoral race raised questions about Hague's judgement. Hague had been warned by a former MP, Sir Timothy Kitson, as well as by a biographer of Archer, Michael Crick, that Archer's background was suspect. Hague, after being assured by Archer that there was nothing in his background that was a liability to the party, declined to refer the matter to the party's ethics and integrity committee. Hague later conceded that his failure to act was probably the worst mistake he had made. Archer's withdrawal from the race created a crisis for the party and a new candidate was hastily selected. Steven Norris, an ex-MP with a colourful past (he had weathered media coverage of his five mistresses), fought a lively and not unsuccessful campaign.

The Archer affair, along with the other scandals, undermined Hague's attempt to clean up the party after the "sleaze" years of the 1990s. The stories served to reinforce the image of a party that had not changed all that much since the days when it was in power.

CONCLUSION

Women seeking to reach the top in their careers face a glass ceiling. Conservatives seeking to win the 2001 general election faced a brick wall. Scaling that wall always looked an impossible task. As the election approached, it looked as if it might become an even more substantial wall than in 1997. The Conservative

Party at the beginning of the new parliament in 1997 was in disarray and, in many respects, it was still so at the end of it.

The actions of the party during the parliament allowed its opponents to portray it as becoming even more reactive — jumping on every passing band-wagon — and extremist as the next election came ever closer. William Hague was accused of abandoning attempts to reach out to new voters and concentrating in-stead on retaining the party's core vote as a way of bolstering his position in the party in the event of another bad defeat. Such analyses suggest a coherence in ac-tions that is probably not justified. The stance of the party was more confused than it was coherent. Voters had difficulty comprehending what the party stood for — or rather what it now stood for that it had not stood for during eighteen years in power. There was little evidence that they were, in any event, particu-larly interested. The harder the party tried to have an impact on public opinion, the greater the "interference" encountered by voters in hearing what was being said. The party stood no realistic chance of winning the election in 2001. What it could have done was to reduce substantially Labour's parliamentary majority, cre-ating the potential for a Tory victory at the next election. In that, it failed. It was, in essence, a standstill election. William Hague emulated his predecessor and im-mediately resigned the leadership of the party. Party activists in June 2001 could be forgiven for experiencing a sense of *déjà vu*.

NOTES

1. "Tories need a voice — Streeter", BBC News Online: UK Politics, December 1, 2000.
2. See Ivor Crewe, "Electoral Behaviour", in Dennis Kavanagh and Anthony Seldon, eds., *The Major Effect* (London: Macmillan, 1994), 109.
3. Philip Norton, "The Conservative Party: 'In Office but Not in Power'", in Anthony King *et al., New Labour Triumphs: Britain at the Polls* (Chatham, N.J.: Chatham House, 1998).
4. Anthony Seldon and Stuart Ball, eds., *Conservative Century* (Oxford: Oxford University Press, 1994).
5. See Philip Norton, "Introduction: The Party in Perspective", in Philip Norton, ed., *The Conservative Party* (London: Prentice-Hall/Harvester Wheatsheaf, 1996), 1–14.
6. See Norton, "The Conservative Party: 'In Office but Not in Power'", 76–9.
7. Philip Norton, "Electing the Leader: The Conservative Leadership Contest 1997", *Politics Review* 7, April 1998: 10–14.
8. Philip Cowley, "Beyond our Ken: The Conservative Leadership Contest of 1997", paper presented at the Elections, Public Opinion and Parties (EPOP) Conference, University of Essex, September 1997.
9. George Jones, "Hague gives the Tories fresh heart", *Daily Telegraph,* October 11, 1997.
10. "Hague calls for new agenda", BBC News Online: UK Politics, March 13, 1999.
11. David Willetts and Richard Forsdyke, *After the Landslide: Learning the Lessons of 1906 and 1945* (London: Centre for Policy Studies, 1999).
12. "William Hague: 'No giant is greater than Margaret Thatcher'", *Guardian,* April 20, 1999.
13. "Hague: Compassion key to Tory revival", BBC News Online: UK Politics, February 12, 1999.
14. "Tories a changed party — Hague", BBC News Online: UK Politics, March 19, 1999.
15. "Hague wants Asian Tory leader", BBC News Online: UK Politics, April 22, 1999.
16. "Hague tries to square the circle", BBC News Online: UK Politics, October 17, 2000.
17. Rogers, a former parliamentary candidate, resigned under threat of expulsion. He later joined the United Kingdom Independence Party.

18. *Listening to Britain* (London: The Conservative Party, 1999).
19. *The Common Sense Revolution* (London: The Conservative Party, 1999), 5.
20. *Believing in Britain* (London: The Conservative Party, 2000).
21. Peter Riddell, "Who do you think you are kidding, Mr Hague?" *The Times,* February 19, 2001.
22. Philip Norton and Arthur Aughey, *Conservatives and Conservatism* (London: Temple Smith, 1981), 157.
23. "Last-chance election for Britain, Hague says", *The Times,* March 5, 2001.
24. *Believing in Britain,* 2.
25. Lord Howe of Aberavon, *Independent,* January 4, 2000.
26. Tom Baldwin, "The polished prose that is written by many and read by few", *The Times,* February 24, 2001.
27. Nicholas Watt, "Hague's policy reversals take another turn", *Guardian,* February 22, 2001.
28. James Landale, "Major warns Hague he must reach out to all", *The Times,* October 3, 2000.
29. Philip Cowley and Philip Norton, with Mark Stuart and Matthew Bailey, *Blair's Bastards: Discontent within the Parliamentary Labour Party,* Research Paper 1/96 (Hull: University of Hull Centre for Legislative Studies, 1996), 17–24.
30. *Independent,* January 5, 1998.
31. "Former chancellor turns up heat on Hague", BBC News Online: UK Politics, July 9, 1998.
32. George Jones, " 'Caring' Portillo back on leadership stage", *Daily Telegraph,* October 4, 2000.
33. Andrew Sparrow, "Portillo failed to give us the whole truth, says Tebbit", *Daily Telegraph,* September 24, 1999; Robert Shrimsley and George Jones, "Portillo less than honest", *Daily Telegraph,* October 6, 1999.
34. George Jones, "Tebbit attacks the new Portillo", *Daily Telegraph,* November 24, 2000.
35. Tom Baldwin, "Hague reduces claim for marriage tax plan", *The Times,* February 22, 2001.
36. George Jones, "Tory crackdown on cannabis", *Daily Telegraph,* October 4, 2000.
37. Joe Murphy, "Top Tories admit to smoking cannabis", *Sunday Telegraph,* October 8, 2000.
38. George Jones, "Hague signals retreat on drugs", *Daily Telegraph,* October 10, 2000.
39. John Taylor, "The Conservative Party cannot contain Townend and people like me", *The Times,* April 30, 2001.
40. Tom Baldwin, Philip Webster and Roland Watson, "Tory divisions on race expose Hague weakness", *The Times,* May 1, 2001.
41. Peter Riddell, " 'Firm action' ends in worst of all worlds", *The Times,* May 1, 2001.
42. The terms derive from trendy scooter-riding "mods" and more macho motorcycle-riding "rockers" in the 1960s. Mods and rockers occasionally clashed.
43. Philip Norton, " 'The Lady's Not for Turning': But What About the Rest of the Party? Margaret Thatcher and the Conservative Party, 1979–89", *Parliamentary Affairs* 43 (1990): 41–58.
44. Norton, " 'The Lady's Not for Turning' ".
45. "Hague fails to make an impact with voters", BBC News Online: June 19, 1998.
46. "The all new William Hague", BBC News Online: UK Politics, April 13, 1999.
47. "Leader image", *The Times,* April 27, 2001.
48. MORI polls. www.mori.com.
49. Tom Baldwin, Philip Webster and Roland Watson, "Tory divisions on race expose Hague weakness", *The Times,* May 1, 2001.
50. Peter Riddell, "Who do you think you are kidding, Mr Hague?" *The Times,* February 19, 2001.
51. James Landale and Philip Webster, "Tory grandee shatters Europe truce", *The Times,* May 21, 2001; Rachel Sylvester, "Hague faces party backlash over euro campaign", *Daily Telegraph,* May 31, 2001.
52. Tom Baldwin, "Tory accounts reveal £2m. Ashcroft loans", *The Times,* December 18, 1999.
53. "Hague aide apologises after interview", BBC News Online: UK Politics, May 7, 1999.
54. "Tory candidate 'right over poll gloom' ", BBC News Online: UK Politics, January 16, 2001.
55. Mary Ann Sieghart, "Why Hague will be a one-election wonder", *The Times,* February 23, 2001.

CHAPTER 4

Labour Government–Party Relationships: Maturity or Marginalization?

Patrick Seyd

> I take pride in the fact that this is the first Labour government in history where the party in the country and in government have stayed together.
> — Tony Blair, *Guardian*, February 19, 2001

SOME OF THE CLAIMS made by Tony Blair regarding his New Labour project, especially those that describe the party's past, have been tendentious and inaccurate. However, the one quoted above is credible. Previous Labour governments in the 1960s and 1970s, led by Harold Wilson and James Callaghan, experienced considerable intra-party strife and during their times as prime minister both men felt the need to assert their obligations to govern on behalf of a broader constituency than the party's activists. Between 1964 and 1970 Wilson suffered numerous defeats at the party's annual conferences. Furthermore, he was forced to modify a major government initiative on industrial relations reforms because of opposition from the trade unions and the Parliamentary Labour Party (PLP). Again between 1974 and 1979 the relationships between government and party were fraught and hostile. Callaghan was confronted by the party's National Executive Committee (NEC) acting almost as an opposition party as it passed critical motions regarding the government and supported demonstrations organized against the government's policies. Such open warfare between party and government did not prevail during the first Blair government: instead a truce operated, albeit uneasy at times, and only minor skirmishes broke out.

To give just one example of the striking contrast between the past and the present of government–party relationships, and a measure of the transformation that has taken place within the Labour Party, the formal approval of the party's 1979 and 2001 election manifestos is worth comparing. The approval process is embedded in constitutional regulation. The party constitution stipulates that a joint meeting of the members of the cabinet and the NEC has to approve the election manifesto, and this meeting is an important symbolic affirmation of the fusion of the parliamentary and extra-parliamentary wings of the party. The meeting to approve the 1979 election manifesto lasted eight hours and involved furious arguments, disagreements, amendments, votes and ultimately the use of a prime ministerial veto to ensure the acceptance of a document of which Callaghan approved.[1] By contrast, the meeting to approve the 2001 manifesto was more a formal ritual, keeping to the letter of the constitution. There was none of the antagonism of the previous meeting. It lasted less than two hours, there were no votes, and there was very strong pressure on all present to agree the document quickly because it had all been previously discussed in meetings of the National Policy Forum. The contrast between what happened in 1979 and what happened in 2001 neatly epitomizes the changes that have taken place within the party.

From its inception the New Labour project has been about more than just policies; it has also been about the nature of the Labour Party itself. In addition to making clear that Labour was no longer a party committed to the trade unions, state ownership, centralized planning and high taxes and public expenditure, those closely associated with New Labour also emphasized that the party was no longer dominated by its activists.[2] Furthermore, from the moment that Blair entered 10 Downing Street as prime minister, he made clear his intention that Labour should become *the* governing party in Britain and that the twenty-first century should be the "progressive century". The party was intended to play its part in fulfilling his ambition by being disciplined and united and by not being an institutional critic of his government.[3]

Inevitably the party leadership after 1997 became more concerned with government and governing than with the party and its structures. In opposition the leadership had devoted a considerable amount of time and energy to party matters, but its attention in government was concentrated more on policy outputs. Nevertheless, although the leadership therefore became more reliant upon the party's general secretaries — first Tom Sawyer and then Margaret McDonagh[4] — and the political office staff at 10 Downing Street, headed by Sally Morgan,[5] it was impossible for Blair and his colleagues to ignore party matters completely. The creation of new devolved bodies in Scotland and Wales, elections to the European Parliament in 1999 by a new, proportional system and the establishment of an elected mayor and authority for London, necessitated the selection and election of new party personnel in which the party leadership felt impelled to intervene. Its interventions were generally disastrous. Furthermore, new party policy-making procedures were initiated immediately after the general election in 1997 and the party leadership could not afford to ignore them completely.

By the time that the Labour government was elected in 1997 many fundamental, organizational changes to the party had already been implemented, thanks to the efforts of the two previous leaders, Neil Kinnock and John Smith.

The central thrust of the entire reform programme has been to replace the party's hydra-headed decision-making apparatus with a single-centred source of power and then to reduce the influence of the activists at the party's grassroots. First, the trade unions' collective role in the party had been reduced. Some had intimated that a more fundamental reform of the trade union–party link was necessary,[6] but this would have required as difficult and extensive a campaign as had occurred over the reform of Clause 4, which was deemed inappropriate at the time. Second, the NEC now possessed the power to control candidate selections in parliamentary by-elections. Thirdly, the NEC's role in policy making had been reduced relative to the parliamentary leadership. Finally, individual members had been directly balloted over both policy matters, such as reform of Clause 4 of the party's constitution and approval of the 1997 election manifesto, and also the choice of party personnel, including the leader, parliamentary candidates and members of the NEC, thereby by-passing and undermining the influence of the meeting-attending activists.

Only two major innovations concerning party structures and rules were implemented after 1997. New policy-making and candidate-selection procedures were introduced, both of which further strengthened the leadership's powers to control the extra-parliamentary party. These two innovations will be considered first in this chapter before we move on to discuss trends in individual party membership, the management of the PLP, the relationship with the trade unions and, finally, the decline and marginalization of the Labour left. In conclusion, we will consider the extent to which Labour government–party relations between 1997 and 2001 suggest a mature relationship of mutual respect and trust between the leadership and membership or a complete marginalization of the membership such that the notion of a mass party, epitomized traditionally by the Labour Party, is now a relic of the past.

POLICY MAKING IN THE PARTY

> The National Policy Forum...will give the membership of this party an opportunity for participation and involvement the likes of which they have never seen before.
> —Tom Sawyer, speaking at the Labour Party Annual Conference, 1997

We have already referred to the strained relationships that existed between previous Labour governments and the party. The party's structures and procedures provided numerous opportunities for government critics to voice their opposition. Upon assuming the party leadership in 1994, Blair displayed little initial enthusiasm for any attempts to modify the party's policy-making procedures.[7] But his awareness that an unpredictable annual conference could cause him problems as leader led to his approval of Sawyer's initiative in 1996 to establish four NEC task forces to examine how the party should behave with a Labour government in office.[8] The task force reports formed the basis of *Labour into Power:*

A Framework for Partnership (1997), which, after consultations within the party, became *Partnership in Power* (1997). *Partnership in Power* was approved by the first party conference after Labour had been elected to government and laid the basis for new policy-making procedures which substituted the annual, public, confrontational displays with a continuous, private, negotiatory exercise.

The party's century-long policy-making tradition, organized around NEC policy documents and annual conference resolutions, was now replaced by a joint policy committee, responsible for "strategic oversight of policy development",[9] a national policy forum (NPF), responsible for overseeing "the systematic and continuous development of policy in the rolling programme"[10] and eight policy commissions responsible for "preparing reports on the areas of policy under review".[11] Formally, the policies emerging from these policy commissions, debated at the NPF and approved by the joint policy committee, still required the final endorsement of the annual conference. *Partnership in Power* reaffirmed that the annual conference "remains the sovereign policy- and decision-making body of the Labour Party" and therefore "no statement would become party policy without being approved by Conference".[12] In practice, however, the annual conference was being relegated to a subordinate role in policy making and would instead take on the role of "main showcase for the Prime Minister, other members of the Government and for a review of progress and achievements".[13]

Instead of resolutions from local parties and affiliated bodies such as the trade unions going to the NEC or forming the basis of debates at annual conferences, they would now go to policy commissions. All local parties and affiliated bodies would have the right to submit one resolution to the annual conference on a topic not being covered by the policy commissions, and conference delegates would ballot to decide which should be discussed. However, since the policy commissions covered an extensive range of topics in their on-going discussions, the new arrangement severely limited what could be discussed and the important role of the conference as an immediate "bellwether" of grassroots' opinions had been significantly modified.

Seasoned participants and observers of Labour's annual conferences are conscious of the considerable changes to the proceedings that have taken place in recent years. Passionate debate, disputation and disagreement, intrigue and leadership manipulation were all features of past proceedings.[14] Today, by contrast, conferences are relatively lifeless. On occasions the annual conference still becomes the venue for set-piece confrontations between government and its critics as, for example, in 2000 over the question of linking pensions to average earnings; but such events are now a rarity. Now the real debate takes place, if at all, at the fringe meetings off the conference floor.

Here is not the place to examine the intricate internal politics from which these massive and fundamental changes to the basic structure of the party occurred. The key personnel involved in the reform process had differing political agendas and objectives, including the wish to encourage a more participative and educative politics like that to be found in some European and Scandinavian social democratic parties, to introduce a more efficient process of political communication, to develop a new form of stakeholder managerialism and, finally, to create an alternative power base to Blair and New Labour. The reform proposals generated suspicion at the party's grassroots, but outright opposition was compromised by a general recognition that existing procedures required overhaul. There were enough in the party satisfied by the promises that the annual party conference and the NEC would remain important institutions in policy development to support the proposed changes. Furthermore, the traditional left in the party, which was opposed to many aspects of New Labour, had by 1997 become marginalized as a political force within the party.

We have already quoted the claim by the party's general secretary, Tom Sawyer, prior to their implementation, that these new structures would empower the individual member. After the first cycle of policy making had been almost completed, the vice-chair of the NPF, Ian McCartney, claimed at its meeting in July 2000 that "never before have members had such a direct input into policy making".[15] To what extent are Sawyer and McCartney's claims accurate? Have the new structures empowered the membership or further strengthened the leadership? A definitive answer is difficult to give since the structures are still in their infancy. Nevertheless, all the policy commissions have completed their first cycle of policy making and an election manifesto has been produced, so it is possible to draw some immediate conclusions about the new process.[16]

We should remember that the new structures and procedures were intended to manage disagreement and facilitate consensus.[17] Debate and disagreement have not been totally eliminated, but they now go on in a more subdued and limited fashion. The small size of the NPF (175 members), and the fact that when it meets two or three times a year it meets in private, reduces the chances of adversarial confrontations and encourages a more consensual atmosphere. But privacy provides greater scope for manipulation: reports, agendas, minutes and debates, all in public, do not eliminate manipulation but they make it more difficult. For example, the workshop discussions at the NPF are guided by facilitators, who then produce summary reports of the proceedings, which are the basis for the final NPF statement. This gives considerable interpretative powers to facilitators who are often full-time personnel working in the party organization. Furthermore, a large part of the discussions at the NPF regarding amendments to commission reports are between ministerial teams and individual members of the NPF and in such an environment the individual members are at a disadvantage.

The brokerage and collective bargaining process that previously went on in the party, especially in the run up to and at the party conference, still goes on at NPF amendment sessions. The privacy of NPF deliberations enables concessions to be made by the leadership with little likelihood of media accusations of weakness, defeat and climb-down. However, NPF privacy means that much of the party membership is unaware of its existence and of its deliberations. This reduces the likelihood of members having any sense of ownership of party policies. As Sawyer notes, "It still only involves a small number of party activists, and those who are not involved feel distanced from the process."[18] At least open and public disputes at party conferences ensured that members were more likely to be aware of the party's policies even if, on occasions, they disapproved of them.[19]

Under the previous structures, the bargaining process was particularly associated with key trade-union leaders and their delegations. Now that there are no bloc or weighted votes in the NPF and one person, one vote prevails, trade-union general secretaries cast one single vote as does a rank-and-file constituency party representative. There is none of the inbuilt weighting of votes in favour of the trade unions that prevailed in the past. In that sense, the power of the trade unions in relation to the constituency parties has been reduced quite dramatically. Nevertheless, trade unionists have access to resources — research expertise and information in particular — and they also organize collectively, so that their position within the NPF is strong.[20] Trade unions therefore possess a considerable potential to influence outcomes. For example, at the National Policy Forum held in July 1999, when concern had been expressed within the party about the government's welfare policies in general and about cuts to some benefits and the need to link the rise in pensions to the rise in average earnings in particular, agreement between the party leadership and a few senior trade unionists to establish an enquiry into welfare provision resulted in trade unionists supporting none of the critical amendments that had been tabled. As a consequence, none of these critical amendments received the level of NPF support required to guarantee their discussion at the subsequent annual conference. So subjects of critical concern for a significant part of the membership had been eliminated from debate at the 1999 party conference.[21]

In this new process, resources, particularly expertise, time and information, are distributed very unevenly. The party leadership, with its policy knowledge, has a huge advantage in meetings of the policy commissions, in NPF workshops, amendment and plenary sessions. Ministerial input to NPF deliberations is very considerable, and ministers, with their advisers, inevitably dominate discussions and proceedings. In the preliminary discussions of policy documents at the NPF, the imbalance of power between the well-resourced ministerial team and others has been very apparent. To some extent trade-union and local government representatives can call upon their own professional staff for support. But the constituency party representatives lack such resources and lack even the knowledge amassed through collective organization. It is also difficult for them even to acquire information: for example, NPF members do not see the submissions coming into the eight policy commissions from constituency parties and other affiliated bodies.

One final thought on these more consensual policy-making procedures is that they can produce blandness and a fudging of issues. Sir Jeremy Beecham, a prominent local government leader, has argued that disagreement and conflict is sometimes worthwhile as it helps to clarify policies and make them more meaningful. He comments on the NPF meeting held in July 2000 that "the pressure to find consensus at the Forum was intense and I believe that we run the danger of producing muddled and unworkable policies in some cases — it would be better to resolve those arguments and for those who lose to accept the outcome."[22]

After four years of the new policy-making structures, involving hundreds of local policy forums, a vast number of submissions to the policy commissions from local parties and trade unions and numerous meetings of the NPF and the policy commissions, the dominance of the party leadership has become even greater. While there were specific proposals in NPF policy documents that found their way into the 2001 election manifesto, some of the party's key commitments during the election campaign, such as a greater involvement for the private sector in public service provision or the downgrading of comprehensive secondary education in favour of specialist and faith-based schools, had not been discussed and approved by this process. It would appear that these new procedures provide the leadership with an important means of gauging the activists' views on particular issues but are of very limited relevance in developing Labour's programme in government.

In conclusion, it appears that four key principles of the party's policy-making procedures have been undermined. First, the principle of equity has been compromised to the extent that the articulate professionals and the well resourced are likely to have greatest impact. Second, transparency is now less apparent because very few have knowledge of what happens to submissions coming into the policy commissions. Third, accountability has been reduced because the scope for manipulation is enormous. Finally, autonomy has been undermined by the tight control of the NPF's activities by the party centre.[23]

Although *Partnership in Power* was predominantly about reforming the party's policy-making procedures, the document also contained proposals regarding the role and structure of the NEC. The report asserted that the NEC should represent "all the key stakeholders in the party" and this was implemented.[24] In practice, the NEC has become completely devalued in importance and is now nothing more than the administrative arm of the leadership. Nevertheless, the annual election of the six constituency representatives on the NEC continues to offer an opening for the party's "awkward squad", although the new rules prohibiting MPs from this section reduces its impact. The "grassroots alliance", a loose grouping of organizations committed to greater internal party democracy,[25] each year managed to secure the election of some of the members of their slate of candidates.[26] However, their impact has been more symbolic than real since they have had nothing like the influence of the Bevanites in the 1950s or the Bennites in the 1970s. Nevertheless, their symbolic importance has been to reveal that the party's individual members cannot be directed to behave just as the leadership wishes. It is evidence of an alternative voice within the party. To what extent those who vote in NEC elections (and the numbers are rapidly diminishing) are representative of the entire membership is a question we shall address later in this chapter.

We now turn to the second major innovation that occurred within the party after 1997, concerning candidate-selection procedures.

CANDIDATE-SELECTION PROCEDURES

The power of local Labour parties to select their parliamentary candidates has been critically important in determining the political composition of the parliamentary party and ultimately, therefore, of its leadership. Only through the NEC's final approval and endorsement of the local choice was the party leadership able to exercise any control, and it used this power on occasions to refuse to sanction a local choice where the person's political beliefs or behaviour were deemed to be unacceptable. We have already noted that the power of local parties to select their parliamentary candidates was modified slightly when the NEC assumed responsibility for drawing up the short list of candidates in by-elections. Now, however, local parties have had their freedom to select candidates further restricted.

Because new rules were required for the selection of candidates for the European Parliament and the new devolved bodies in Scotland, Wales and London, and the party leadership believed that existing candidate-selection procedures had not produced people of sufficient calibre or representativeness as MPs, a complete overhaul was introduced in 1998. The new rules and procedures covered the selection of party representatives at European, national and devolved parliamentary levels. Here the rules and procedures for the selection of Westminster candidates will be examined, although the general principles are similar throughout.

Would-be parliamentary candidates can now apply personally to be placed on an NEC-approved list of names from whom local parties will almost always make their choice of candidates. Applicants have to outline their experience, their reasons for wanting to represent the party and their communication and campaigning skills. After an initial assessment and sifting procedure carried out by a panel made up of NEC members, MPs and professional external assessors, the would-be candidates are required to make presentations, answer questions and be interviewed by a hostile journalist in front of a selection panel. Those who succeed in passing successfully through these tests are then added to the list of NEC-approved candidates. Although it remains possible for a local party to nominate and select someone not on this list, such a candidate would still require the approval of the NEC. And, in fact, the overwhelming majority of candidates have been chosen from the approved list.

David Gardner, the party's assistant general secretary at the time of the change, and in charge of these new procedures, claimed that they had produced "quality candidates... [who] have met minimum criteria".[27] The procedures, however, raise two questions. First, the qualities deemed appropriate may discriminate against particular applicants who lack what are perceived as the necessary communication and strategic-thinking skills. The skills criteria may advantage the young professional, university-educated applicant. One trade union, the AEEU, has become so concerned at recruitment trends among Labour MPs that it resources training for its members to ensure that they satisfy the new recruitment criteria and will therefore be stronger candidates for selection. Second, the procedures provide an opportunity for the selectors to reject candidates on political grounds. Suggestions were made that the list of candidates for the Scottish and London devolved bodies excluded critics of New Labour. Eric Shaw's analysis of the new procedures leads him to conclude that the practice varied. While some of those deemed politically undesirable by the party leadership had been excluded, others made it onto the lists. However, he goes on to add that the circumstances between 1997 and 2001 were such as not to require a comprehensive weeding mechanism, though similar circumstances may not prevail in the future.[28]

In addition to these new procedures for creating an approved list of candidates, new electoral systems for the European and Scottish parliaments, and the Welsh and London assemblies, required nominees to be ranked on the party lists. The rank positioning on the list was crucial in affecting a person's chances of election. Whereas the selection of candidates remained in the hands of local members, the ranking was determined neither by voters nor by members but by NEC-composed panels. The particular composition of these panels varied but was made up of NEC personnel, MPs and party and trade-union regional executives. The importance of the rank ordering of candidates was seen in the European parliamentary elections. The adoption of the new additional member (AMS) electoral system meant that Labour would not secure as large a number of MEPs as had been elected in 1994. Previously the European Parliamentary Labour Party had contained many critics of Blair, yet, as Shaw notes, few of these critics remained after the European elections in 1999.[29]

The creation of new devolved institutions in Scotland and Wales, and a mayor of London, necessitated the selection of party leaders and nominees respectively. In Scotland there was no controversy regarding Donald Dewar's election as first minister and leader, but in Wales the resignation of the incumbent leader, Ron Davies, prompted a conflict between Blair and the membership. Blair made clear his antagonism towards the heir-apparent, Rhodri Morgan, and he eventually persuaded Alun Michael, his own secretary of state for Wales, to stand as candidate. An electoral college composed of equal proportions of individual members, affiliated organizations and Welsh Assembly candidates decided marginally in favour of Michael. But Morgan won the majority of votes of individual Welsh members and also of union levy-payers in those unions that conducted ballots. It required the votes of three trade unions to be cast for Michael without ballots of their levy-paying members to ensure his victory. The leadership's imposition of a person against the wishes of the majority of the members in Wales by means of a trade-union bloc vote damaged it among the membership, among Welsh voters and also way beyond the Welsh boundaries.[30]

A similar attempt by Blair to impose his preferred candidate as mayor of London spectacularly backfired. Many senior figures within the party, including some of Ken Livingstone's previous colleagues on the left of the party, were determined to stop Livingstone being the party's London nominee. Again, as in Wales, rather than a ballot of individual members and union levy-payers being the means of electing the candidate, an electoral college composed of (1) members, (2) affiliated organizations and (3) London MPs, MEPs and Assembly candidates was devised. The equal weighting of the votes of these three components reduced the relative strength of Livingstone's support among the members. Even after Blair and Kinnock had campaigned hard against Livingstone and in favour of the leadership-supported candidate, Frank Dobson, and the party headquarter's staff at Millbank had provided strong support for Dobson, Livingstone still secured a majority of individual members' votes. It required the relative overweighting of MPs', MEPs' and Assembly candidates' votes, the votes of non-balloting, affiliated organizations and the vote of one MEP, who had in fact already resigned her post, for Dobson to win the party nomination. Again as in Wales, this "fix" disaffected both party members and voters.[31]

As far as the selection of personnel was concerned, New Labour had, first, established strict parameters for the recruitment of its candidates and, second, created electoral colleges to choose its leading standard bearers in order to reduce the influence of individual members.[32] Both the election of the party leader in Wales and the selection of the mayoral candidate in London reveal individual members at variance with Blair. To what extent was this general among the membership?

THE MEMBERS

When Blair became party leader he invested considerable personal energy and party resources in the recruitment of new members. New members helped to legitimize New Labour by enabling Blair to reject accusations that Old Labour was still lurking in the woodshed. Second, new members helped him to substantiate his claims to be a modernizer intent on eliminating the *ancien régime* in Britain. After he became prime minister he continued to make statements reiterating the importance of party members in contrast with his prime ministerial

Table 4.1 Labour Party Individual Membership, 1993–99

1993	266,270
1994	305,189
1995	365,110
1996	400,465
1997	405,238
1998	387,776
1999	361,000

Source: Labour Party National Executive Committee Reports, 1994–2000.

predecessors, Wilson and Callaghan, who took little interest in party membership while in government.[33] However, Blair's rhetoric and his practice were contradictory. After 1997 only limited resources were directed towards recruiting and maintaining a membership, and the day-to-day administration of membership matters was handed over to a private agency. Furthermore, some of the signals coming from the party leadership, such as those during the leadership election in Wales and the mayoral selection in London, suggested that it attached little importance to members' opinions.

After the surge in the number of members that occurred between the time when Blair first became leader and his becoming prime minister, the party has faced the problem of declining numbers, as can be seen in Table 4.1.

Countervailing factors were at work with regard to membership recruitment and retention. As the party in government, on one hand, Labour could no longer exploit anti-Conservative sentiment as an inducement to join the party. In addition, particular government policies such as the bombing of Kosovo, the maintenance of sanctions on Iraq, the introduction of student tuition fees, the cutting of lone parent and disability benefits and the expansion of selective secondary schools prompted individual resignations. On the other hand, now that Labour was the governing party, at least a few individuals were undoubtedly attracted by the potential collective benefits, namely influence on policy outcomes, or by the potential selective benefits, notably the chance to develop a personal political career.

To what extent were the members supportive of Blair and New Labour when the party took office in 1997, and did they continue to maintain that level of support? Earlier we noted that New Labour at the top was no longer committed to the trade unions, state ownership, centralized planning and high taxes and public expenditure. We are able to use surveys of the party membership to see whether this was also the case at the grassroots.[34] In Tables 4.2–4.5 we distinguish the percentage responses of all members to a series of questions and Likert-scale statements in 1990, 1997 and 1999 and also the responses of long-standing members, namely those recruited before Blair became party leader in 1994, and newly recruited members, namely those recruited between 1994 and 1997.

Table 4.2 Labour Party Members' Attitudes to Public Ownership, 1990–99

(a) Question: "Are you generally in favour of . . ."

	1990	1997	1997 Old	1997 New	1999
More nationalization of companies by government	71	49	52	44	44
More privatization of companies by government	2	4	4	5	5
Things should be left as they are now	27	47	44	51	51

(b) Statement: "The public enterprises privatized by the Tory government [by the Conservative party, 1999] should be returned to the public sector."

	Strongly agree	Agree	Neither agree nor disagree	Disagree	Strongly disagree
1990	45	37	10	7	1
1997	22	28	22	21	7
1997 Old	23	29	22	10	6
1997 New	20	41	22	14	3
1999	18	32	23	23	4

Note: In this table and all the following ones, 1997 Old and 1997 New is using data from our 1997 survey to distinguish the members who joined the party before 1994 (Old), and those who joined between 1994 and 1997 (New).

We see in Table 4.2 that between 1990 and 1999 members' views of nationalization in general changed dramatically. Whereas almost three-quarters of them in 1990 had believed in more nationalization of companies, by 1999 those holding this view were in a minority. The majority preferred to maintain the existing ownership structure. Similarly, a dramatic drop in members' support for renationalizing the privatized utilities occurred, with the number of members "strongly" agreeing with this position dropping by more than half; however, a majority of members still preferred public ownership of these utilities.

If members have become less enamoured of the virtues of nationalization as a general principle, they are by no means, however, enthusiasts of the free market. In Table 4.3 it is clear that throughout the 1990s a majority of members remained sceptical of the values of the free market.

Table 4.3 Labour Party Members' Attitudes to Centralized Planning, 1990–99

Statement: "The production of goods and services is best left to the free market."

	Strongly agree	Agree	Neither agree nor disagree	Disagree	Strongly disagree
1990	5	20	17	34	24
1997	4	23	22	39	13
1997 Old	3	20	20	41	16
1997 New	4	28	24	36	8
1999	3	24	19	39	15

Table 4.4 Labour Party Members' Attitudes to Taxation and Public Expenditure, 1990–99

(a) Question: "Suppose the government had to choose between the following three options. Which do you think it should choose?"

	1990	1997	1997 Old	1997 New	1999
Reduce taxes and spend less on health, education and social benefits	2	1	1	1	1
Keep taxes and spending on these services at the same level as now	6	13	11	16	24
Increase taxes and spend more on health, education and social benefits	92	87	89	83	75

(b) Statement: "Please indicate whether you think the government should or should not do the following things, or doesn't it matter either way: Reduce government spending generally..."

	Definitely should	Probably should	Doesn't matter	Probably should not	Definitely should not
1990	6	15	6	29	44
1997	5	26	10	37	23
1997 Old	4	22	9	38	27
1997 New	6	30	11	36	17
1999	3	20	12	38	27

A specific New Labour challenge to Old Labour concerned the party's traditional attachment to high taxation and public expenditure. In Table 4.4 it is clear that members' views on taxation have certainly shifted from an almost unanimous view that taxes should be increased to provide better services in health, education and social welfare; however, three-quarters of the members still believe that taxes should be raised. Further, in response to a question asking whether government spending should be reduced, two-thirds are opposed, only a slight reduction from 1990. So attempts by Tony Blair and Gordon Brown before the 1997 general election to move the party away from a "tax and spend" position did not have the support of members. Brown's lavish public spending commitments undertaken before the 2001 general election were more in accord with the members' point of view. New Labour also wanted to distance itself from the trade unions. However, as we see in Table 4.5, members remain resolutely committed to their belief in strong trade unionism.

Our answer, therefore, to the question posed earlier — to what extent have members adapted to the Blairite political agenda? — is that they shared the leadership's critical views of public ownership in general but did not share its views on central planning, taxes and public expenditure or the trade unions. Furthermore, although there is evidence that the members recruited after Blair became party leader in 1994 were less attached to the four canons of old party orthodoxy, the differences between the long-standing and newly recruited members

Table 4.5 Labour Party Members' Attitudes to the Trade Unions, 1990–99

Statement: "It is better for Britain when trade unions have little power."

	Strongly agree	Agree	Neither agree nor disagree	Disagree	Strongly disagree
1990	4	10	13	45	29
1997	3	11	16	49	21
1997 Old	3	10	14	49	25
1997 New	4	13	19	48	17
1999	2	11	14	46	28

are not so great as to suggest that a distinctively new party is developing at the grassroots. The implications of members', old and new, stubborn commitment to many of the traditional values of social democracy could be considerable when the party leadership returns to the question of the future role of its membership during the second term of this New Labour government.

In addition to the decline in the number of members since Labour came to office in 1997, a further point of importance is that those who remained as members became less active in the party. In Table 4.6 we first compare the number of hours members devoted to party activities and, second, their perceptions of their own levels of activism. We see that declining activism was a continuous trend during the 1990s, which the election of a Labour government did nothing to halt; rather the reverse, with a serious haemorrhaging of activists since 1997. Activism is broadly defined here to encompass attendance at meetings, distributing party literature, contacting voters and standing for elected office. Whatever the activity, there has been a decline.

This decline creates a problem for the party in fighting election campaigns. Legal restrictions on the amount of money that parties can spend in elections, both locally and nationally, necessitate a minimum level of human resources to

Table 4.6 Labour Party Members' Activism, 1990–99

Question (a): "How much time do you devote to party activities in the average month?"

	1990	1997	1999
Number of hours			
None	51	63	65
Up to 5	30	25	22
5 and under 20	16	10	10
20 and over	4	3	4

Question (b): "Are you more or less active within the party than you were five years ago (or when you joined if less than five years ago), or about the same?"

	1990	1997	1999
Levels of activism			
More active	20	18	9
Less active	43	29	48
About the same	38	53	43

Table 4.7 Number of Labour Back-bench Rebellions, 1964–2000

Years	Number of back-bench rebellions
1964–70	110
1974–79	317
1997–2000	83

Source: Philip Cowley and Mark Stuart, "Parliament", *Parliamentary Affairs* 54 (2001), 238–56.

provide the campaigning essentials. Research suggests that constituency campaigning can have a significant impact on election outcomes.[35] One of the reasons why the party performed badly in the Scottish, Welsh, European, London and local government elections in 1999 and 2000 was because of its lack of active campaigners. Stories abound of moribund parties, inquorate meetings and limited campaigns, and the survey evidence confirms that the de-energizing process within the party has picked up speed.

THE PARLIAMENTARY LABOUR PARTY[36]

Conventional wisdom has always suggested that governments with large parliamentary majorities have difficulties managing their backbenchers. This assertion is strikingly disproved by this Labour government. Even though the size of Labour's 1997 majority was its biggest ever, the party whips' task was not onerous. We see in Table 4.7 that rebellious back-bench behaviour was nothing like as bad as during the Wilson and Callaghan governments. The back-bench rebellions that did succeed in attracting a large number of Labour MPs occurred over the government's withdrawal of disability and lone parents' benefits, its linking of pension increases to prices rather than earnings, its privatization of air traffic control, its refusal to divulge information provided to ministers by civil servants and its charging of student tuition fees.

What are the explanations of this low level of parliamentary dissent between 1997 and 2001? One suggestion is that backbenchers were ruthlessly kept "on message" by the whips. There is no doubt that the Labour whips worked hard to preserve party unity, but this does not seem convincing as a sole reason. Another suggestion is that the new intake of MPs in 1997 had been carefully chosen in the party's key winnable seats as New Labour loyalists. The problem with this explanation is that not all the new Labour MPs selected in key seats were loyalists, and, furthermore, the party won 56 seats in addition to those that had been selected by party headquarters as key ones, and in these contests less concern had been shown with the candidate-selection outcomes. A third explanation is that the large cohort of new female Labour MPs were particularly loyal. There is some evidence showing that female backbenchers were less prone to rebellion than their male colleagues, possibly because women prefer private negotiation to public gestures. Maybe, however, the major underlying reasons for the high degree of unity within the parliamentary party was that the majority of backbenchers shared the government's general objectives, desired more than a one-term government, hoped for personal preferment and promotion, associated public rebellion with the previous bad times in opposition and believed that there were better ways of achieving their objectives than by rebellion. Furthermore, the structural "fault lines" that Hugh Berrington had identified in the PLP in the 1940s and 1950s no longer existed.[37]

THE TRADE UNIONS

We have already noted that a major feature of New Labour was its desire to distance the party from the trade unions. The historic and formal links between the party and the unions were regarded as an electoral weakness.[38] Blair spelled out clearly what his government's strategy would be towards the unions in a speech to the 1996 party conference in which he promised them "fairness, not favours". As Anthony King notes in Chapter 1, notwithstanding the government's pro-business stance, the trade unions did relatively well out of the new government. Both of the previous Labour prime ministers, Wilson and Callaghan, had stressed close party–union links as an important potential source of electoral support before being elected to government, but then the relationship between the two had soured by the time they left office. By contrast, Blair questioned the relationship before election, yet — paradoxically — by 2001 it was in better shape than it had been four years earlier. The reasons were that there were more pluses than minuses in the government's policies as far as the trade unions were concerned and more pluses than minuses in the unions' behaviour as far as the party leadership was concerned.

For a start, the government had managed an economy in which economic growth and low unemployment prevailed, and such an economic environment strengthened trade unions' shop-floor bargaining powers. In addition, the Employment Relations Act guaranteed both automatic trade-union recognition where unions had recruited over 50 per cent of the workforce and the right of a worker to have union representation in any disciplinary dispute. Furthermore, the statutory protection of individual workers' rights with regard to overall working time, part-time work and employment disputes was instituted. For the first time ever, a national minimum wage was introduced, and, even though many unions were unhappy at the rate of pay and the existence of a lower youth rate for those up to the age of 21, these were issues upon which the trade unions could bargain in the future. Finally, on the credit side, the government had encouraged and funded union participation in workplace learning initiatives.

On the debit side for the unions were the government's limits on the impact of the European social chapter and its failure in the Employment Relations Act to allow the right to strike in support of other workers involved in disputes. Furthermore, the government blocked the implementation of the EU Information and Consultation of Employers' directive and declined to introduce a statutory obligation on employers to conduct equal-pay reviews of their labour forces. Finally, the trade unions opposed the government's private finance initiative strategy for funding many public projects and would also much have preferred retirement pensions to be indexed to earnings rather than prices.

As compared with the previous Labour governments of the 1960s and 1970s, the role of the trade unions within the party has been drastically reduced. Formal structural affiliation remains, but the unions no longer dominate party institutions and procedures and they no longer formally sponsor Labour MPs (although they informally maintain their links by continuing to provide financial support to many constituency Labour parties). In addition, the party has diversified its regular annual income sources to the extent that it is no longer almost totally reliant upon union money (although trade-union funds remained critically important in helping to fund the party's 2001 general election campaign). Nevertheless, despite these changes, the unions continued to play an important role, one that was broadly supportive of the party leadership. We have already noted the support that particular unions accorded Blair in the ballots to choose the party leader in Wales and the party nominee in the London mayoral election. Further, the trade-union representatives on the NEC were loyal supporters of the party leadership even when, on occasions, their support was contrary to union policy.[39] Finally, the unions and, in particular, the Transport and General Workers' Union, played a major role in assisting the government to defuse the fuel crisis in the autumn of 2000. We conclude, therefore, our examination of the party–union relationship by noting that, whereas there were those among the party leadership quite willing to consider breaking the formal attachment between the party and the unions before Labour came to office in 1997, by 2001 that idea had disappeared from the New Labour agenda.

Finally, we turn to the question of factionalism within the party.

FACTIONALISM

All previous postwar Labour governments had faced the problem of a critical and vociferous Labour left. Both the Keep Left group in the late 1940s and the Tribune group in the 1960s and 1970s had demanded more left-wing government policies. We have already noted that the PLP was far more united under Blair's leadership than during previous Labour governments. Although a small number of Labour MPs, identified with the Campaign group, voiced their criticisms of the government, their impact was minimal. But in earlier times the left's influence and organization extended well beyond the PLP into the constituency parties and the trade unions. By the 1990s, however, left factionalism was almost non-existent throughout the party. As Anthony King points out in Chapter 1, the left of the party had all but disappeared as a consequence of external political developments such as the collapse of communism, the increasing importance of global economic forces and the powerful impact of right-wing ideas on the British voter. The marginalization of the Labour left was given further impetus by Kinnock's strategy of programmatic adaptation and organizational transformation from 1983 onwards. The Labour left's last gasp had been to defend, unsuccessfully, the party's constitutional commitment to the "common ownership of the means of production, distribution and exchange" in 1994. But the ease with which Blair succeeded in rewriting Clause 4, this symbolic socialist totem, revealed the extent to which there was a desperate desire at all levels of the party to abandon the past in search of power. By 1994 the loss of four consecutive general elections had taken its toll on the "socialist generation".[40] It is paradoxical that after 1997 the most powerful and consistent critic of the Labour government — on the grounds that it was abandoning the party's socialist ideals — was Roy Hattersley, previously closely identified with the party's right wing. By contrast, formerly prominent left-wing critics of the leadership, such as Dennis Skinner and Ken Livingstone, were relatively silent. Even the traditional house journal of the Labour left, *Tribune,* was no longer the Rottweiler at the throat of the party leadership. Individual voices from the left could now and then still be heard, but the heart had gone out of the organized awkward squad. A combination of intellectual uncertainty, a desperate desire to win elections and deference to an increasingly powerful and authoritarian party leadership contributed to the absence of an organized left for the first time in the party's history since the 1920s.

CONCLUSION

This chapter has outlined some of the very considerable changes to the Labour Party that have occurred over the past ten years, changes involving its constitution, programme, personnel and ethos that together justify the distinction between New and Old. These changes can be categorized as either institutional, involving alterations to rules and procedures, or behavioural, involving modifications of people's attitudes and actions. The institutional changes are primarily the result of the many years that the party spent out of power. Reforms were required to re-establish the party's electoral attractiveness and then, once it was back in power, to ensure that it became a more permanent governing party than in the past. An explanation of both institutional and behavioural change is the recruitment of a new party elite less enamoured of the labour movement's traditional institutions. Back in the late 1970s the rise of the Labour left was explained in part by the recruitment of a new urban left. Now the significant alterations to behaviour within the party are a consequence, in part, of the recruitment of young middle-class professionals intent on political careers. More than twenty years ago Henry Drucker defined the ethos of the Labour Party — attitudes to leaders and money and a reverence for formal procedures — as rooted in a strong sense of the party's past.[41] But that past has now been written off and discarded as symptomatic of electoral failure, and many of the essential features of the ethos that Drucker was writing about no longer exist.

Two final points are worth emphasizing. First, there has been a tendency in the past for scholars to treat the Labour Party as a single entity. The weakness of such an interpretation was that it ignored the existence of various Labour parties: parliamentary and extra-parliamentary, professional and voluntary, and central and local. So, for example, the likelihood of a Labour-controlled local authority or a constituency Labour party doing or saying something at variance with the London-based party leadership was once considerable. This made the task of leading the party difficult, because not all elements necessarily sang from the same song sheet. Now, however, by a combination of authoritarianism and organizational discipline the leadership has established a more direct line of command downwards to all party units that had previously maintained a distinctiveness of their own.[42] New Labour is a more singular party than Old Labour.

Second, during previous Labour governments the potential for membership participation and voice was extensive. Earlier periods and practices should not be romanticized as some "golden age" since the party's democratic ethos and procedures were often more symbolic than real, because of oligarchic manipulation. Furthermore, the party's collective, delegatory procedures limited the possibilities of individual participation and influence. Nevertheless, accountability of the leadership to the party during earlier Labour governments was greater than today, and there were more opportunities for well-publicized initiatives and pressures from below. By contrast, the constant stress in contemporary times on the need for party unity, and the replacement of collective, delegatory structures with individual, representative structures, make it more difficult for the membership to hold the leadership to account. Immediately after the re-election of the Blair government, further reform of the party is already on the agenda. Proposals to reform local constituency parties, contained in a party report, *Twenty-First Century Party*,[43] could lead to their substantial modification and their becoming fundamentally different organizations. If implemented, the party will then have been completely transformed from top to bottom. Without doubt local parties require reinvigoration to stimulate both membership and activism, which, as we pointed out earlier, are declining. However, a successful membership-recruitment programme also requires institutions and procedures that facilitate varied forms of participation and accountability. The danger for Labour as a party is that, just as the reforms in the period of the first Blair government weakened leadership accountability, those now proposed for the second Blair term will continue this trend.

NOTES

1. See Tony Benn, *Conflicts of Interest: Diaries, 1977–80* (London: Arrow Books, 1991), 485–8.
2. See Peter Mandelson and Roger Liddle, *The Blair Revolution* (London: Faber, 1996).
3. For example: "Ill-discipline,... factionalism, navel-gazing or feuding of the Seventies and Eighties allowed us to be painted as extremist, out of touch and divided. It helped keep us out of power for 18 years. The 'culture of opposition' had to be eradicated and 'a modern, disciplined party with a strong centre' established." Blair, *Independent,* November 20, 1998.
4. Party general secretaries play an important bridgehead role between the party leadership, the party professional staff and the extra-parliamentary party. Tom Sawyer's career closely mirrors the transformation of the Labour Party. Initially, he was a close supporter of Tony Benn in the 1970s, but then became a key figure on the party's NEC in supporting Neil Kinnock's reform programme in the 1980s. When Blair became party leader in 1994, he was appointed general secretary and was the instigator of the major structural reforms to the party's policy-making procedures introduced in 1997. His successor in 1998 was Margaret McDonagh, a full-time party official for eleven years, who had played a key role in the organization of the party's 1997 general election victory.
5. A Labour prime minister's political staff maintains the links between the incumbent at Number 10 and the party in Parliament and beyond. Sally Morgan had been a full-time official at party headquarters before becoming Blair's political secretary in 1997.
6. For example, Stephen Byers suggested such a transformation of the relationship at an "off-the-record" dinner conversation at the Labour Party's 1996 annual conference.
7. These had first been initiated by Tom Sawyer's predecessor as the party's general secretary, Larry Whitty. See *Democracy and Policy Making for the 1990s* (London: Labour Party, 1990).
8. The four task forces examined the structure and role of the NEC, relationships between the NEC, the cabinet and the PLP, the party's policy-making structures and processes and, finally, the future role of the party member.
9. *Partnership in Power,* 8.
10. *Partnership in Power,* 10.
11. *Partnership in Power,* 11. The eight policy commissions covered foreign affairs; crime and justice; democracy and citizenship; economic affairs and social security; education and employment; environment, transport and regions; health; and industry, culture and agriculture.
12. *Partnership in Power,* 7.
13. *Labour into Power: A Framework for Partnership,* 13.
14. Brilliantly chronicled and analysed by Lewis Minkin, *The Labour Party Conference* (London: Allen Lane, 1978).
15. Ian McCartney, National Policy Forum, Durham, July 3, 2000.
16. The following observations are drawn from the author's attendance at meetings of the National Policy Forum and discussions with members of the policy commissions.
17. The initial discussions from which *Partnership in Power* eventually emerged took place at the Cranfield Management School. Tom Sawyer has close links with the academic staff at Cranfield. See Tom Sawyer, "Politics and Management: The Making of New Labour" (Inaugural lecture, University of Cranfield, 2000).
18. Sawyer, "Politics and Management", 8.
19. One such example would be the well-publicized debate at the party's conference in 2000 on pensions. Whether party members approved or disapproved of the demand from the conference floor for pensions to be linked to average earnings, they would have been made aware of the party's concern with the level of pensions and its commitment to an improvement in pensioners' standards of living.
20. Trade-union representatives attending the National Policy Forum meet as a bloc before the proceedings commence to discuss the overall agenda.
21. Further evidence of the trade unions' power is revealed in the sequel to this issue. At the following meeting of the National Policy Forum in July 2000, Alastair Darling, secretary of state for social security, was asked by trade unionists what enquiry had taken place. His unsatisfactory

replies prompted the NPF members to demand that the issue of pensions be discussed at the party's national conference in the autumn. At this conference a motion demanding that pensions be linked to average earnings was carried against the recommendations of the party leadership.

22. Jeremy Beecham, "Lessons from the Forum Process", *Tribune*, July 14, 2000.

23. For a powerful critique of the entire policy-making process from someone who was closely involved for two years between 1998 and 2000, see Liz Davies, *Through The Looking Glass: A Dissenter Inside New Labour* (London: Verso, 2001), 79–92 and 157–64.

24. *Partnership in Power*, 8. In addition to the leader, deputy leader and treasurer, representatives are now elected from the trade unions, constituency parties, socialist societies, youth, the government, Westminster and European parliamentary parties and local government.

25. The grassroots alliance was made up of Labour Reform, the Campaign for Labour Party Democracy, Labour Women's Action Committee, Labour Black Representation Committee, Campaign for Socialism (Scotland), Network of Socialist Campaign Groups, Chartist, Labour Left Briefing and Socialist Campaign Group News.

26. Four of the grassroots alliance candidates were elected in 1998, three in 1999, and two in 2000.

27. David Gardner, "The Selectors", *Tribune*, October 16, 1998.

28. Eric Shaw, "New Labour: New Pathways to Parliament", *Parliamentary Affairs* 54 (2001), 35–53.

29. Shaw, "New Labour", 42.

30. Two-thirds of members cast their votes for Morgan, yet Michael won the overall ballot by 53 to 47 per cent of the votes. The three trade unions which cast their votes for Michael without balloting their levy-paying members were the Transport and General Workers' Union, the General, Municipal, Boilermakers and Allied Trades Union, and the Amalgamated Engineering and Electrical Workers' Union.

31. Individual members cast their votes, as follows: 1st ballot — Livingstone 54.9 per cent, Dobson 35.3 per cent, Jackson 9.8 per cent; 2nd ballot — Livingstone 59.8 per cent, Dobson 40.2 per cent. Overall, however, Dobson defeated Livingstone by 51.5 to 48.5 per cent of the vote. Neither the AEEU nor the South London Cooperative Society balloted its members before casting their votes for Dobson. The MEP who cast her vote for Dobson even though she had resigned was Pauline Green. One constituency Labour party secretary publicly described the election result as "the biggest stitch up since the Bayeux Tapestry," and asked "Why should I continue giving up my spare time if party democracy is a sham?" (*Guardian*, February 22, 2000). Dobson received just 13.8 per cent of the total vote in the subsequent mayoral election.

32. What so annoyed many party members in Wales and London was that when Blair had been elected as leader in 1994 it was by ballot of members and affiliated organizations, and the votes of certain trade unions had been deemed out of order and therefore unacceptable because all their political levy-payers had not been balloted. However, in Wales and London it was the votes of such non-balloting organizations that were decisive in producing the outcomes desired by Blair. Since the debacles in Wales and London, the NEC has proposed a rule change for all future leadership elections in devolved institutions, and for choosing the party's nominees in city mayoral elections, stipulating that the choice will be based solely upon a ballot of individual members.

33. For example, in April 1999, in a letter sent to all individual party members, he stated: "Labour Party members are more important than ever. I am committed to a mass Labour Party, reaching into every community in the country... I want a mass party which turns outwards to the community — campaigning, consulting, communicating Labour's message... Labour members are essential to making Labour policy. The new policy forums mean that all can have their say in a process that is the most democratic of any party. It is Labour members who set the priorities for action because they are in tune with the people whom we seek to represent. Together, government and party combine to create a partnership in power, working together to produce policy and explain government's actions, as well as campaigning for Labour at every level... [L]et me say how highly I value the contribution of every single person who has made a commitment to our party by becoming a member, long-standing or new. In today's Labour Party, with our party in government, members matter more than ever before." Neither Wilson

nor Callaghan would have written in that vein during his time as prime minister. However, Liz Davies argues that in the relative privacy of NEC meetings Blair was constantly critical of the membership for its less than enthusiastic support for the government (See Davies, *Through The Looking Glass*).

34. Surveys of the party membership were conducted in 1989–90, 1997 and 1999. All the surveys used a two-stage systematic random sampling procedure to select the samples from lists of members held at national party headquarters. For the 1989–90 survey 480 constituencies were chosen at the first stage, stratified by Labour party regions, and a systematic random sample of one in thirty party members was selected at the second stage. The same procedure was used in 1997, except that a random sample of 200 constituencies stratified by region was selected at the first stage. The response rate in both 1989–90 and 1997 was 63 per cent. The 1999 survey was a panel; one-third of the 1997 respondents were selected at random and surveyed, producing a response rate of 69 per cent. For further details of the questionnaires, see Patrick Seyd and Paul Whiteley, *Labour's Grass Roots: The Politics of Party Membership* (Oxford: Clarendon Press, 1992) and Patrick Seyd and Paul Whiteley, *Labour's New Grassroots: The Transformation of the Party Membership* (London: Palgrave, forthcoming).

35. David Denver and Gordon Hands, *Modern Constituency Electioneering* (London: Cass, 1997).

36. I am grateful to Philip Cowley for providing me with up-to-date information upon which this section is based.

37. Hugh Berrington, *Backbench Opinion in the House of Commons, 1945–55* (Oxford: Pergamon, 1973).

38. Philip Gould, *The Unfinished Revolution* (London: Little, Brown, 1998), 353.

39. See Davies, *Through The Looking Glass*.

40. Samuel Beer, *Modern British Politics* (London: Faber, 1965).

41. Henry Drucker, *Doctrine and Ethos in the Labour Party* (London: Allen and Unwin, 1979).

42. This trend towards greater uniformity and singularity is likely to be temporary, however. The devolution of powers in Great Britain is beginning to produce policies in Labour-controlled Scotland and Wales that diverge from those of their London-based party headquarters.

43. *Twenty-First Century Party* (London: Labour Party, 2000).

CHAPTER 5

New Labour and the Media

Colin Seymour-Ure

NEW LABOUR HAD the editorial support of an even larger majority of the national daily and Sunday newspapers at the 2001 general election than in 1997. The only papers to come out plainly for the Conservatives (see Table 5.1 on p. 118) were the daily and Sunday *Telegraph* titles and the *Mail on Sunday*. The two former had an overwhelmingly Conservative readership and a historic reputation for determined loyalty to the party. The instincts of the *Mail on Sunday* were equally Conservative, but its support this time, though plain, was muted. Before 1997, Labour had never had the majority support of the national press at any general election. The most Labour could normally expect, certainly in the second half of the twentieth century, was the support of two each from about ten dailies and nine Sundays. In 1997, as Table 5.1 shows, six dailies and five Sundays gave the party largely unqualified endorsement. This shift of editorial attitude was as much a part of the New Labour landslide as a cause.

Greeted with such warmth in 1997, and buoyed by its Commons majority, the Blair government might have been expected to take a relaxed approach to media relations. Throughout its term, the performance of the economy was good; the divisive question of joining the euro was postponed; foreign policy brought no setbacks; the government as a whole (though not some individual ministers) proved fairly accident-free; the opposition was weak; the polls, with barely a swoop, flew high. Yet the government quickly acquired the reputation of being intensely, unprecedentedly and sometimes offensively preoccupied with presentation and media management.

At first, this preoccupation might have been just the appearance of a preoccupation, for the media soon put Downing Street news operations under the spotlight. They did so partly with the same curiosity they applied to the rest of the new government's arrangements, but more particularly because New Labour's renaissance during the previous ten years had seemed to owe much to skilful media management and marketing. Two of Blair's closest advisers, Peter Mandelson (an MP since 1992) and his press secretary, Alastair Campbell, were at

Table 5.1 National Daily and Sunday Press: Ownership, Circulation and Partisanship, 2001 compared with 1997

Newspaper	Owner		Circulation (000s)		Preferred Winner	
	2001	1997	May 2001	April 1997	2001	1997
Daily papers						
Daily Express	Desmond	MAI/United	956	1,220	Labour	Conservative
Daily Mail	Associated/Rothermere	(same as 2001)	2,415	2,151	(uncommitted)	Conservative
Daily Star	Desmond	MAI/United	694	648	Labour	Labour
Daily Telegraph	Hollinger/Black	(same as 2001)	1,020	1,134	Conservative	Conservative
Financial Times	Pearson	(same as 2001)	487	307	Labour	Labour
Guardian	Scott Trust	(same as 2001)	403	401	Labour	Labour
Independent	Independent/O'Reilly	Mirror Group	226	251	(not conservative)	Labour
Mirror	Trinity Mirror	Mirror Group	2,787	2,084	Labour	Labour
Sun	News Int'l./Murdoch	(same as 2001)	3,447	3,842	Labour	Labour
The Times	News Int'l./Murdoch	(same as 2001)	707	719	Labour	Eurosceptic
Pro-Conservative circulation			1,020 (8%)	4,504 (33%)		
Pro-Labour circulation			9,481 (72%)	8,533 (62%)		
Total circulation			13,142 (100%)	13,757 (100%)		
Sunday papers						
Independent on Sunday	Independent/O'Reilly	Mirror Group	253	276	(uncommitted)	(uncommitted)
Mail on Sunday	Associated/Rothermere	(same as 2001)	2,329	2,112	Conservative	Conservative
News of the World	News Int'l./Murdoch	(same as 2001)	3,899	4,365	Labour	Labour
Observer	Scott Trust	(same as 2001)	453	454	Labour	Labour
Sunday Express	Desmond	MAI/United	900	1,159	Labour	Conservative
Sunday Mirror	Trinity Mirror	Mirror Group	1,866	2,238	Labour	Labour
Sunday People	Trinity Mirror	Mirror Group	1,372	1,978	Labour	Labour
Sunday Telegraph	Hollinger/Black	(same as 2001)	795	909	Conservative	Conservative
Sunday Times	News Int'l./Murdoch	(same as 2001)	1,361	1,310	(uncommitted)	Conservative
Pro-Conservative circulation			3,124 (25%)	5,590 (37%)		
Pro-Labour circulation			8,490 (67%)	9,311 (63%)		
Total circulation			12,662 (100%)	14,801 (100%)		

Source: Circulation figures are from Audit Bureau of Circulations.

Notes: Figures are rounded. The *Mirror* figures include Scottish *Daily Record*.

least as well known to the interested public as most members of the shadow cabinet.

There was no room for doubt, however, as the government proceeded, that its media preoccupation was real. Symbolizing it, the imagery of "spinning" and the term "spin doctor", hardly part of the political vocabulary in the early 1990s, became commonplace. This intensity of preoccupation could explain why increasingly, too, the imagery was used cynically or disapprovingly. John Major, for example, referred in his Commons retirement speech to "the miserable political climate of spin and counter-spin that has grown up here in recent years", arguing that "the people who sent us here deserve more than to be spoonfed a cocktail of headline grabbing feelgood stories." John Major *would* say that; but his government did not have the same degree of preoccupation as New Labour, and more sympathetic commentators, such as the *Guardian,* grumbled too.[1]

If Labour's media preoccupation seemed, at first sight, both unnecessary and unpopular, why then did it exist? What forms did it take? What were its consequences? And what may we conclude about it?

WHY WAS NEW LABOUR SO PREOCCUPIED WITH MEDIA?

There was, first, a simple logic about the priority New Labour gave to communications. In the conduct of politics, broadly speaking, media are primary and political institutions secondary. The media can live without politics: indeed, surveys show that politics is one of the least appealing subjects to readers and audiences.[2] But politics cannot live without the media. The larger and more complex the media become, the more this is true. If politicians do not respond to changes in the media, by adapting their organization, their style, their language — or whatever else is appropriate — it is the politicians who suffer. The force of these claims can be seen in the way the parties' election campaigns changed with the growth of television from the 1960s onwards. But they are true for governments too. In particular, it is no use a prime minister adopting a policy if it cannot be sold to those responsible for effecting it (teachers, doctors) or for living with the consequences (parents, patients). Questions of substance (should we raise taxes?) are thus inextricable from questions of presentation (how can we raise taxes without losing voters?)[3]

Those arguments might appeal to any government, but there were several strong reasons why New Labour, in particular, could be expected to endorse them. During the nearly twenty years since the party was last in power, the media had become a much more intrusive presence in British politics. Some simple indicative measures are listed in Table 5.2 (p. 120). By 1997 people were reading thicker papers, more broadsheets and fewer tabloids. These papers, managed in London, still blanketed the nation (with the partial exceptions of Scotland and Wales); but increasingly people took at least their headline news from television, with virtually round-the-clock programming and an explosion of channels to choose from. National and local radio stations proliferated, too, even though their audiences

Table 5.2 Measures of Media Change during Labour's Years Out of Office

	1979	1997
National daily newspapers		
Broadsheets (4 titles 1979; 5 in 1997), circ. (000s)	2,300	2,900
Pages (approx. average)	30	66
Mid-market tabloids (2 titles), circ. (000s)	4,100	3,400
Pages (approx. average)	36	90
Down-market tabloids (3 titles), circ. (000s)	8,400	7,600
Pages (approx. average)	30	46
National Sunday newspapers		
Broadsheets (3 titles 1979; 4 in 1997) circ. (000s)	3,300	2,900
Mid-market tabloids (1 title 1979; 2 in 1997), circ. (000s)	3,000	3,300
Down-market tabloids (3 titles), circ. (000s)	12,000	8,600
Owners in 1979 still owning in 1997		
Daily papers	5	
Sunday papers	1	
Networked national TV channels		
BBC (no adverts.)	2	2
Independent TV (adverts.)	1	3
Satellite/Cable TV channels	–	many
audience share (%)	–	12
National radio stations		
BBC (no adverts.)	4	5
Independent (adverts.)	–	4
Local radio stations		
BBC (no adverts.)	20	38
Independent (adverts.)	19	207
Homes with more than one TV set (%)	24	75
Time spent on: TV (hrs.)	18	26
radio	9	16
Total BBC/ITV weekly programmes (hours)	256	562
News and current affairs	49	104
Sources of most news (%):		
TV	52	71
Newspapers	33	14
Radio	14	8
Perceptions of political bias on TV		
(% BBC/ITV believing party favoured)		
Conservative	16/4	16/4
Labour	3/6	7/9
Liberal Democrat	2/1	–/1
Number of lobby correspondents (approx.)	120	250

Sources: Various sources, including the Audit Bureau of Circulations, the BBC and ITC.

Notes: Some figures are rounded. Not all relate exactly to the calendar years 1979 and 1997.

were smaller. The number of political journalists at Westminster doubled. Political news operations had to be correspondingly sharper and quicker if New Labour were to manage the news agenda successfully. The spread of e-mail, pagers and mobile phones accelerated and complicated the would-be news manager's work.

Although cross-ownership between newspapers and television was still restricted by law, the main terrestrial ITV channel (Channel 3), funded by advertising, was moving in the direction of a single national market and away from its historic basis in fifteen networked but separately owned regional franchises. Overall, individual newspapers and broadcasting properties were typically located by 1997 in international multi-media conglomerates (often with non-media properties too), controlled by moguls such as Rupert Murdoch, Conrad Black and the Rothermere family. These groups had a greater and more comprehensive interest than they had had under previous Labour governments in a variety of government policies, some within the European Union framework, which could directly affect their businesses — such as competition policy, trade, industrial relations, sport and leisure, privacy and freedom of information. Moreover, no government could now escape the need to have specific media policies, to concert the development of the telecoms and information-technology industries.

At the level of day-to-day content, the diversification of broadcast outlets put under increasing strain the core "public service broadcasting" principles of political balance and non-partisanship. These go right back to the foundation of the BBC in 1926 and apply across all television and radio channels, regardless of their type of funding. The statutory ban on paid political advertising remains intact. But the other principles are more vulnerable. The larger the number of talk shows, interviews and phone-in programmes, the more difficult it becomes to monitor "balance". Similarly, the rule that broadcasters must not editorialize is weakened by the argument that selection and ranking of news items may amount to the same thing, by implicitly favouring one party more than another. For decades Labour could rely on these rules to ensure a broadcast "level playing field" for political coverage, which would offset in part the Conservative slant in the press. In an age of broadcast profusion, New Labour would have to work harder to be sure of getting its message across.

In the press, to quote an editor of the *Independent,* news often now "takes second place to analysis".[4] So much news comes electronically that papers see their distinctive role as contextualizing and evaluating it. During the eighteen years of Conservative dominance, the broadsheets in particular developed op-ed pages along American lines, diluting the single anonymous editorial voice. One consequence was that by 2001 papers made more of a virtue out of diversity of opinion. Named columnists were prized for their individuality. Two regular columnists on *The Times,* one on the *Guardian* and one on the *Daily Telegraph,* were former editors of their papers. The *Sun*'s political editor, Trevor Kavanagh, did not always follow the editorial line. At the *Daily Express* under the ownership of Labour supporter Lord Hollick (1996–2000), Peter Hitchens was kept on as "the voice of the old [i.e. Tory] *Express*".[5] During the uncertainty about postponement of the 2001 election date, to take two simple examples, *The Times*'s columnist Mary

Ann Sieghart and the *Guardian*'s Hugo Young both argued for June 7 while their editorialists preferred May 3.[6]

Those developments led to a chronic instability of editorial opinion, which must be the bane of spin doctors. Its marks were inconsistency, factionalism, chance enthusiasms, lack of proportion and a confusion of the newspaper and the news. The effects were accentuated by a simultaneous tendency for columnists and editors to jump from paper to paper. Paul Routledge, for instance, who had been political editor of the *Independent on Sunday*, after allegedly being offered the political editorship of the *Daily Express*, moved to the *Mirror*. Blair's press secretary, Alastair Campbell, was said to have brought pressure to bear on the *Express* against the appointment. "I'm off message!", Routledge boasted.[7]

By factionalism is meant here a consistent deviation from party orthodoxy on important issues. The best example was papers' attitudes to Europe. Conrad Black and Rupert Murdoch both supported Business for Sterling, an anti-euro group of industrialists. Both Mary Ann Sieghart and Anatole Kaletsky, respectively assistant and associate editor of *The Times,* not only endorsed but joined Lord Owen's New Europe Group. This group supported British membership of the European Union (EU) but not of the single European currency. Again, Simon Heffer and Christopher Booker, both columnists on the *Daily Mail,* belonged to the obscure British Weights and Measures Association, formed in 1995 to campaign for repeal of the compulsory metrication rules.

That last example arguably lies at the edge between lack of proportion and chance enthusiasm. The *Guardian*'s concentration on the venality of two disgraced former Conservative MPs, Neil Hamilton and Jonathan Aitken, similarly, seemed obsessive in relation to the political news agenda as a whole.[8] The Labour *Mirror*'s recommendation to its readers to vote Conservative in the election for the new London mayor in 2000 was clearly a chance enthusiasm. Again, the government was caught on the hop in 2000 by the scale of publicity mobilized by pensioners, indignant at a paltry 75 pence increase in the state pension. The chancellor later caved in and increased it by £5. The wretchedly unpopular Millennium Dome, enthusiasts believed, was killed by excessively negative media coverage.

Some of these enthusiasms, including the *Guardian*'s battle against sleaze, mixed up the story with the newspaper's involvement in it. Thus the *News of the World*'s emotive "name and shame" campaign late in 2000 against the anonymity of paedophiles may have been sincerely felt; but at the same time it was a provocative circulation booster by a new editor making her mark. Moreover, it distracted the attention of ministers. More harmlessly, the editor of the *Independent on Sunday* conducted a vigorous campaign for the legalization of cannabis, which ceased abruptly when she departed for the *Daily Express*.

The randomness of that set of examples is not inappropriate, for the conclusion to which the analysis leads is that the media clientele of Blair's Downing

Street was suited more naturally to the politics of interest groups than of parties. More than when Labour was last in power, newspapers were likely to take up single issues which were vigorously promoted by interest groups — and to do so unpredictably. Equally, many interest groups had themselves acquired more resources and media expertise during the Thatcher and Major era. Viewed from a party rather than an interest group perspective, there was no special reason why paedophile policy should have erupted in the media as and when it did, nor the moral panic about asylum seekers, nor the Dome disaster, nor the pensions row. Again, two of the political organizations that caught the government most unawares in their management of the news agenda were the People's Fuel Lobby and the Countryside Alliance. The former flashed like lightning in September 2000, via mobile phones and the internet, and it was all over in a week or so. The latter, in contrast, rumbled thunderously throughout the whole parliament. It used more traditional methods, such as mass marches converging on London, the last of which was cancelled because of the outbreak of foot and mouth disease. The government seemed unsure exactly how much weight to attach to it.

The modern politics of pluralism thus demands of governments a high priority for communications management because the media system, directly or indirectly, forms so much of the political arena. In the United States, this has been true far longer, and to some extent New Labour learnt from American experience. Philip Gould, one of the principal New Labour modernizers and latterly Blair's in-house pollster, observed the Clinton campaign at close quarters in 1992. Among modernizers, according to Mandelson's biographer, "Clintonization" became a kind of code word and a model; and Rawnsley, too, suggests that New Labour "certainly looted much of its rhetoric, many of its techniques and some of its policies" from Clinton. One specific example, much noticed at the time, was the party's purchase of the expensive Excalibur "rapid rebuttal" media software system in time for the 1997 campaign.[9]

If by any chance those arguments were insufficient, the Blair government could find ample support in history for the priority it gave communications. Old Labour generally governed with a hostile press. Must this not, Labour supporters could have been excused for thinking, have had at least something to do with its failure ever to have won two full consecutive terms? After the shambles following the Wilson–Callaghan era, furthermore, Labour had made itself electable again through a modernization in which effective communications were a key part. Both in 1987 and 1992 the party could consider itself unlucky to have lost. This time, post–1997, New Labour must govern in such a way as to ensure the second term. Unhampered by traditional ideological baggage, it should concentrate on effective marketing.

New Labour could find a more recent reminder of the hazards of poor news management — and of the suddenness with which they might strike — in the disastrous experience of the Major government. Major's victory in 1992 turned rapidly sour and was followed by five years of public-relations mismanagement and mishaps, accompanying party splits on European policy and uniquely low poll ratings for the prime minister personally. But Labour could not take it for granted, after the 1997 election, that the Conservatives would continue to self-destruct over Europe, nor, therefore, that the Conservative press would not at some stage come back on side.

Lastly, the lessons of the 1997 election themselves justified New Labour's high communications priority. The basic lesson was that Labour's unprecedented support in the press was due to a dealignment of newspaper partisanship, not a re-alignment. The shift started in 1992, when four out of eleven national daily papers were either highly qualified in their partisanship or else had none. With Britain's ignominious ejection from the European monetary system on "Black Wednes-day" — September 16, 1992 — editorial support for the Conservative government began to tumble. When John Major in July 1995 called for a leadership election within the Conservative Party in a bid to silence Conservative critics, only one paper, the *Daily Express,* favoured him staying on as prime minister.

Although Labour's support among the national dailies in 1997 was twice as high as ever before (six out of ten), there was only one straight conversion: the *Sun.* The *Daily Star* and the *Independent* had been uncommitted in 1992; the *Financial Times* had wanted a "non–Conservative majority" (and its support in 1997 for Labour was rather equivocal); and *The Times,* though anti-Conservative in 1997, was Eurosceptic, not pro-Labour. Furthermore, it was Blair whom papers backed, not New Labour the party. The headline with which the *Sun* made its pitch early in the 1997 campaign was simply "THE SUN BACKS BLAIR". Blair appealed by his personality and by his record as a modernizer rather than as an ideologue. In 2000 this was still his attraction to the *Sun*'s political editor: "Really, our trust is implicitly in Tony Blair".[10] In 1997, finally, papers were ready to take a chance on Blair because of the "time for a change" argument. Yet this hardly amounted to a firm basis for a long-term commitment. No more did the attraction of an unproven personality. Altogether, the press in 1997 had signalled the start of a conversation with New Labour, not a settled endorsement. Labour's communications managers knew that support during the years in office would have to be earned.

WHAT FORMS DID NEW LABOUR'S PREOCCUPATION WITH MEDIA TAKE?

However much weight those different arguments might carry, they provided plenty of incentives for the Blair government to take the media seriously. At root New Labour's preoccupation was a matter of priorities: a determination not to fail as a government through poor communication of good policies. It was summed up in the clumsy New Labour phrase, "on message". The government should decide the "message", and then everyone should ideally be "on" it.

Both the agenda of politics and its interpretation should follow the New Labour line. What government would not like to achieve such control? The novelty was that the Blair government sought it with unprecedented and sometimes brutish vigour.

One immediate sign was the new prime minister's readiness to confront, for certain Downing Street staff, the historic principle of civil service non-partisanship. Incoming administrations have often worried that the civil service has been contaminated by their predecessors: surely, they reason, the policies of a new government need implementing with a conviction that comes from explicit party loyalty? The argument has a particular appeal in the area of media relations. Some prime ministers, therefore, have brought in journalists as press secretaries, and these have nominally become civil servants. Others have employed career civil servants, often from the Foreign Office or the Treasury. Either way, the combination has involved contrivance. The journalist press secretaries have not always fitted in comfortably with civil service neutrality, while the extreme case of a career civil servant being accused of behaving like a partisan was Margaret Thatcher's press secretary, Bernard Ingham, who served for most of her eleven years in office.[11]

Blair put an end to this fudge. Like his chief of staff, Jonathan Powell, Alastair Campbell, as chief press secretary, was given a contract that not only acknowledged his partisanship but gave him executive authority over civil servants. Purists might grumble that Campbell behaved like a minister (indeed like a deputy prime minister) even though he was unelected, but there was no longer any need, or justification, to worry about distinguishing between what was, and was not, "partisan" behaviour. At the same time, Blair greatly increased the number of special advisers brought in by ministers across Whitehall as political appointees to their personal staff. By 2001 there were 27 in Downing Street alone, out of a total staff of 149 (John Major used to have six). The majority of these, too, did press relations or broader communications work: twelve in the Policy Unit, three in the Research and Information Unit and eight directly on media work.[12]

More broadly, the new government did not hesitate to bruise the professionalism of the Whitehall information officers: the Government Information Service. The head of the Treasury Information Division, Jill Rutter, was brusquely sidelined by Gordon Brown's press secretary, Charlie Whelan. Hers, by custom, was not an information officer grade post. But the government made equally clear that information services in the departments at large needed to be more pro-active, more alert to media needs and better at integrating policy and presentation. After an early efflux of senior staff, a Cabinet Office report steadied morale, clarified the ground rules and made various organizational changes. In a significant symbolic change, the service was renamed the Government Information *and Communication* Service to reflect its more contemporary vision. Within about three years, all the most senior press officers had been replaced.[13]

The government's determination had a grimmer side. What could not be fixed by organization and resources had to be done "up close". Alastair Campbell and Peter Mandelson acquired an unenviable reputation among the media for browbeating and bullying, well documented in the flow of books about New Labour.[14] Their minions, identified often in the recounting just as "spin doctors", followed their lead. Broadcast journalists and news executives — for example on BBC Radio 4's early morning *Today* programme and its follow-up programmes at lunchtime and in the evening — got used to being heavily leant on. A breaking story should be treated this way, shouldn't it? And that story yesterday certainly shouldn't have been treated that way, should it? "I'm fed up with the garbage you've been putting out. Where's your social responsibility?" Campbell typically complained to *Today*'s political correspondent, who became inured to such almost daily criticisms from one spin doctor or another.[15] Reporters were the ones most often abused. Where Ingham used the language of "bunkum and balderdash", Campbell talked of "bollocks" and "crap". Senior figures such as the *Newsnight* interviewer Jeremy Paxman and the veteran foreign correspondent John Simpson were rubbished. (Simpson was accused of presenting Serb propaganda at face value in his reporting from Belgrade.)[16] Managers received long letters of complaint. "If anyone needed further evidence of the dumbing down of TV news, they should look no further than your 6 o'clock bulletin earlier this evening," wrote Campbell to Tony Hall, the chief executive of BBC News. "The objective", one spin doctor was reported as saying, "is to grind the BBC down, to shake journalists' confidence, implanting a self-censor in every BBC brain."[17] But leaked to the press, these episodes appeared to strengthen media resolve and criticism, and they may well have sounded crass to readers and viewers.

Compared with the broadcast media, the press was more courted than bludgeoned. The *Sun,* as chief convert to New Labour in 1997, got special treatment, even being given advance notice of Blair's decision to delay the general election. Irredeemable opponents — notably the *Telegraph* papers — received no favours. The *Guardian,* which thought itself a "critical friend", was regarded with irritation in Downing Street. (Campbell had once been provoked to take a swing at its political editor, Michael White.)[18] The loyalist Labour *Mirror* resented the "prodigal son" favouritism shown to the *Sun;* and this may have been one reason for its startling recommendation to vote Conservative in the London mayoral election.

The government's preoccupation with the media was, second, a matter of personality. Blair himself was more sensitive to the potential of Downing Street news operations as a tool of government than any prime minister since Wilson. John Major, not surprisingly, had seen news media as a threat, and he fulminated about them in his memoirs.[19] Blair saw them, in the cant contrast, as an "opportunity". Mandelson and Campbell, the two closest relevant advisers, were both media people. Mandelson had worked in current affairs television, and Campbell, as political editor of the *Daily Mirror* from 1989 to 1993, knew the machinery of political journalism inside out. Campbell was also the only press secretary to have worked for a prime minister before they both first entered Downing Street. He joined Blair formally in September 1994 and had advised him informally earlier than that. Moreover, no one can have had a stronger awareness than Campbell of the way in which Thatcher cemented her relationship with the key newspaper proprietors, through honours, hospitality and the distribution of political favours, and of the dividends all this paid in sympathetic news coverage. He saw, too, how fatally John Major had lacked the same touch, so that the press "threw off the Tory agenda and set about creating one of its own. It turned on the Conservative Party with an unspeakable ferocity and tore it apart."[20]

Blair's communications team thus moved smoothly from opposition to government, with a clear and dedicated mission. Campbell's partner, Fiona Millar, became Cherie Blair's part-time press secretary; and next door at Number 11 Gordon Brown, too, had Charlie Whelan in tow. Throughout Downing Street, at lower levels, recruits among the political appointees came with media experience and a media mindset. Some had worked at Labour's Millbank headquarters in opposition (for example, Hillary Coffman of the Press Office). Others came from the BBC (such as Lance Price of the Press Office and Bill Bush of the new Research and Information Unit). Others again had newspaper backgrounds (Philip Bassett and David Bradshaw of the Strategic Communications Unit). As time went on, they departed in the same way. For instance, Tim Allan, one of the journalists in the Press Office, went on to be head of corporate public relations at Rupert Murdoch's BSkyB.

Such examples illustrate the fact that in the organization and running of Blair's Downing Street considerations of public communication were at the heart. They went far beyond day-to-day relations with news media, for they included matters such as polling, media monitoring and presentational strategy. Rather as Ronald Reagan's White House was permeated by communication priorities, so there was a seamless-web quality about links between communication and other functions in the Blair machine. The Policy Unit, for example, a group of about a dozen people specializing in different fields, was principally concerned with policy development — yet policy development almost inevitably involved them in speechwriting and issues of presentation, prioritization and public opinion.[21]

Communication priorities — and Campbell's personal importance — were reflected in Campbell's regular attendance at the weekly meeting of the cabinet: even Ingham very rarely did that. The cabinet had a new agenda item, "Current Events", under which the relevant minister (Mo Mowlam at the time of the 2001 general election) took people through the policy announcements for the coming week. Every day, too, a cabinet "presentation" committee met to consider and coordinate presentation and policy. This had been a Heseltine innovation under John Major. Under Labour its membership brought together officials and advisers from the Press Office, the Policy Unit, the Cabinet Office, the whips, the Labour Party and the main Whitehall departments. Mandelson chaired it, until he became a departmental cabinet minister in July 1998, after which its chairmanship varied. On Monday mornings Blair, like his predecessors, had a routine office meeting with his political staff and advisers to review the week ahead. Campbell was there; so was Mandelson until he joined the cabinet. At 9.45 a follow-up meeting, concerned with "tone", was joined by the pollster Philip Gould and by Philip Bassett from the new Strategic Communications Unit. Campbell and Bassett took part also in the preparatory sessions before Prime Minister's Questions in the House of Commons on Wednesdays.

Blair's Press Office had a staff of fourteen. This was little larger than John Major's, but more of them (five) were political appointees. Campbell's deputy, Godric Smith, was a career civil servant. This arrangement provided a sensible balance. Smith was responsible for much of the office management. He also took on an increasing number of the routine twice-daily briefings of the lobby correspondents, after Campbell had become particularly exposed and controversial ("embattled", to use the vernacular) in the summer of 2000. (This was due partly to a television documentary about Campbell and partly to a general run of bad publicity.)[22] For party political matters, Smith was assisted at the briefings by two of the political appointees.

Three new units (the name denotes their modest scale) were associated with communications work at Number 10. Two were relatively trivial: the Media Monitoring Unit, which operated inside the Press Office, and the Research and Information Unit. The latter, established a couple of years before the 2001 election, produced the kind of data that fed into the preparations for Prime Minister's Questions. The third body, the Strategic Communications Unit, was not as grand as its name might suggest. It was set up in 1998, with a staff of about ten, at the suggestion of the Cabinet Office review of the Government Information Service. Its tasks included running a Whitehall electronic diary and briefing service, coordinating departmental news agendas with Downing Street (it distributed several hundred pages of copy each day), drafting ministerial speeches and articles, and despatching every evening to one hundred ministers an electronic fax intended to keep them on message about the next day's news agenda. The unit also produced that characteristic Blair innovation, the government's "Annual Report", setting out achievements and promises met during the previous year.[23]

Another of the SCU's products was an impressive weekly grid. This detailed a spate of forthcoming events, statistics, parliamentary and political news ("Fur Farming Bill: 2nd Reading"), EU goings-on and general events, such as the Cup Final and high profile rape trials, that might eclipse the latest statistics on hospital waiting lists.[24] The grid was pored over at lunchtime on Wednesdays in a meeting of senior staff chaired by Jonathan Powell. Six months before the 2001 election, it was supplemented by a Euro grid, distributed by the Foreign Office.

This gave notice of forthcoming decisions by the European Commission or European Parliament that might have damaging implications for Britain and/or for the government's popularity.[25]

The only one of these bodies to attract much notice was the Press Office itself. Ever since the office took its modern form after 1945, its routines have always been fixed to a great extent by the needs of its news media clientele. The chief press secretary, which is the title in use since Bernard Ingham (1979–90), deals privily and individually, in person and by phone, with most kinds of journalists and news executives, domestic and foreign. But the rhythm of the press secretary's day is set by the two mid-morning and afternoon meetings with the lobby correspondents. This group takes its name from the lobby outside the House of Commons, which it became the group's unique privilege to frequent after the public were banned in 1885.

The lobby correspondents' quest is for news, not think-pieces, so much so that until 1960 full membership was granted only to daily, not Sunday, papers and to a couple of broadcasters. Lobby journalists got more news if the press secretary spoke privately, off the record or at least unattributably. For years the system was in equilibrium. Critics occasionally carped about pack journalism, but the press got their daily story and Downing Street got its line out. The growth of political broadcasting, fat newspapers and mean journalists, however, all put it under strain. Leaks became common. John Major's second press secretary, Chris Meyer, gave up thinking he could brief off the record, though he maintained the pretence. Meyer was a career diplomat without a public profile (he became ambassador in Washington under Blair), whereas Alastair Campbell was already a familiar figure by Blair's side and lacked even that protection.

Campbell agreed on a compromise. He put his twice-daily briefings on the record, in the interests, he claimed, of "transparency". But in order to allow himself a little scope for speaking frankly, he would not allow them to be recorded or filmed or to be sourced to himself by name. The Press Office kept its own tape recording, apparently for only a day or two. This arrangement was unsustainable. Campbell ended up being explicitly identified, and by 2000 an official record of the briefings was routinely put on the Downing Street website. (A nice paradoxical touch was that the names of the lobby correspondents asking questions were concealed.) The ultimate result of making the collective lobby briefings effectively public, on much the same footing as the White House press secretary's briefings, was of course not to make the sources of Downing Street news more open but to drive underground Campbell's serious dealings with political editors and lobby journalists.

Campbell's relationship with his prime minister was, for a press secretary, uniquely close. As Blair's principal adviser and most trusted political friend, he was often described, as Anthony King points out in Chapter 1, as the real deputy prime minister. In a government so consumed with communications, the press secretary's remit involved him anyway in many aspects of strategy. Also, Blair's initial resolution of the blur between partisans and civil servants in Downing Street enabled Campbell to avoid being hounded for behaving "politically". Indeed, given Campbell's clout in the administration, Blair had no need of a minister to oversee communications. The obvious person to do such a job would have been Peter Mandelson, a key strategist in opposition. But at first he could not do it officially, since he was only a junior minister; and when he achieved cabinet rank in 1998 his job as trade and industry secretary left him no time for detailed communications work. Nor could he do the job during his period out of office or as Northern Ireland secretary later. The only ministerial job, therefore, was the rather feeble coordination role played by the minister for the Cabinet Office, latterly Mo Mowlam.

Overall, then, the Blair communications machine was rather more rugged and well oiled than John Major's, but it was still basically of the same construction. The prime minister's own involvement, given the factors discussed in the previous section and his personal alertness to the media's potential, was considerable. His participation in some of the regular meetings has already been indicated. He was also a willing and assiduous public performer for the benefit of the media. His speeches were written according to the logic of the Downing Street organization. That is, contributions came from the Press Office, the Policy Unit, the Private Office (acting as liaison with government departments) and the Strategic Communications Unit. Details varied according to how far a speech was about one or another policy field or was for a party audience. Campbell, being so busy, mainly had an "editorial" role. Blair himself evidently quite enjoyed speechwriting.[26]

Far more than any of his predecessors, Blair also "wrote" articles for the papers. The articles were a simple way of rewarding — and perhaps making — friends. The effort could be justified, too, as enabling the prime minister to bypass editorialists and the lobby. Particular attention was paid to the *Sun* and *Mirror,* because of their mass readerships among both Labour loyalists and target voters. But the currency became devalued (certainly among journalists) as it became obvious that the articles must have been largely ghosted. For example, at one press awards ceremony Blair was ironically declared "Freelance of the Year" for having published more than 250 articles over his name in 47 publications during 1999. In 1998 Campbell allegedly managed to palm an identical "exclusive" article by Blair onto more than a hundred regional papers, each distinguished by a sole paragraph appropriate to the local readership.[27] Fellow cabinet ministers wrote press articles equally freely, often to rebut a criticism.

As a broadcaster, Blair avoided the gaffes and rows with broadcasters that had punctuated the Thatcher and Major years. But this may partly have been due to his avoidance of set-piece studio encounters, tough interviewers and the more intensely political programmes such as the BBC's *Newsnight* and *Panorama.*

One innovation, possibly to help counter accusations of getting out of touch, was an hour-long *Ask the Prime Minister* programme run by David Dimbleby in December 2000, in which Blair answered questions from a studio audience and telephone callers. Also, he took further the trend towards prime ministers giving press conferences. He gave a wide-ranging one in July 2000, to launch expenditure initiatives, and three on successive days — a record for a British prime minister — during the petrol crisis of the following September. He often used the roadway outside Number 10 to make shorter announcements, including about the build-up to the bombing of Iraq in November 1998, the progress of the outbreak of foot and mouth and the consequent postponement of the local elections (and implicitly the general election) fixed for May 3, 2001.

Blair was diligent, too, at schmoozing with media barons and editors. He kept up the courtship of Rupert Murdoch that had arguably helped bring into the Labour fold in 1997 Murdoch's working-class *Sun,* a perverse supporter of the Conservatives, in view of its working-class readership, throughout the Thatcher era. Not only was he in regular contact with Murdoch personally and by phone; but he reportedly intervened with Italian Prime Minister Romano Prodi about the possible purchase of an interest in Italian television by Murdoch's BSkyB satellite television company.[28] At the memorial service in 1998 for Lord Rothermere, owner of the *Daily Mail,* which appealed across all classes and was a bastion of Conservative support, Blair read one of the lessons. When the *Express* titles, shaky in both circulation and political inclination, were sold late in 2000 to an unexpected purchaser, the soft-porn merchant Richard Desmond, the Blairs promptly gave him and his wife a friendly welcome to tea in Downing Street. It was too much to expect that the *Mail* might endorse him editorially in 2001 (though it came closer than ever before), but such gestures could do no harm. Under Desmond, who became a very "hands on" proprietor, the *Express* did indeed firm up its inclinations and came out categorically for Labour on polling day.

More generally, Blair personified New Labour's streak of populism in his approach to public communication. A dramatic early illustration in September 1997 was the prominent role he took by reading a lesson at the funeral of Princess Diana. There was no reason of protocol for him to do that at all, unless he wanted to, but what an opportunity only a few months into his premiership! — and linking him emotionally with one of the great popular icons of the age. Campbell coined the phrase, "the people's princess", which Blair used, with contrived spontaneity and to great effect, in his encomium before the television cameras on the morning after she died.[29] "The people's . . . " became a quintessential New Labour sobriquet, attached (by others, often ironically) to anything with populist connotations, such as the Millennium Dome and even the new brand of man/woman-in-the-street peers.

Blair's personal style was populist — and classless, in the sense of being adjustable to circumstances. The British ear for accent meant that his changeable vowels were quickly noticed. To working-class audiences he spoke "estuarine English" or "mockney" — some way distant from the accents of his public school and the bar. At the Lord Mayor's annual Guildhall banquet, the gorblimey touch was missing.[30] Much was made of his enthusiasm — and that of Downing Street staff at large — for football, of his shirtsleeve working habits, initially on the sofa rather than at a table or desk, of his liking for pop music and of his undergraduate group, the Ugly Rumours. His children stayed within the state education system but were ferried to high-quality schools. Cherie and the family featured in staged photo opportunities. But when a former *au pair* girl prepared to publish an insider memoir, the Blairs invoked the law to squelch it. When baby Leo was born, Blair took time out to do some parenting.

Blair modulated the attachment of his name to particular issues and policies, in a manner familiar to American presidents. He kept well clear of the fiasco of the Millennium Dome (except the very special fiasco of its opening party on the Millennium Eve). Later, when the government had to decide whether to veto Rupert Murdoch's bid to buy the football champions Manchester United, Blair made clear that the decision was up to the trade secretary, Stephen Byers: not for Blair the responsibility for irking Murdoch.[31] More substantially, Blair intervened at crucial moments, for instance in Northern Ireland, in the fuel crisis of September 2000 and in the foot and mouth crisis that eventually delayed the election.

Not surprisingly, Blair's approach to public communications contributed to the claim that he was running a "presidential" government. Announcements that might by convention have been made first in Parliament were made straight to the media, a practice that, while not unprecedented, drew protests from the Speaker. Blair himself virtually shunned the House of Commons as an arena for the public prime minister. He took part in proceedings less than any of his predecessors and he allowed MPs to quiz him at Question Time only once a week instead of the normal twice (though he did answer for half an hour instead of fifteen minutes).[32] He sought to maintain his personal popularity by diligent attention to focus groups and pollsters, and he concentrated control of communications in Downing Street. By such means he hoped to increase his authority over ministers.

WHAT WERE THE CONSEQUENCES OF NEW LABOUR'S PREOCCUPATION?

The new government's communications activity naturally caught the interest of those at whom it was directed. Media are always self-obsessed. Right from the start, Mandelson and Campbell, whose reputations were well established in opposition, came under scrutiny, first in press articles, later in books and television documentaries. *The Times* even ran a weekly strip, called "Alisdair", about a spin doctor. The government soon discovered, too, that the proliferation of ministerial press secretaries might help keep people on message but that it also increased the scope for crossed wires and amplified the noise of internecine rows. The best example was Gordon Brown's press secretary, Charlie Whelan. Real or alleged differences between Blair and Brown could easily be pumped up when journalists had both Campbell and Whelan to talk to. Moreover, Whelan did not get on with Mandelson and he was an irritant to Campbell, since he was seen as having a separate media power base in the Treasury (figuratively, since he operated frequently and convivially from pubs). Not surprisingly, Whelan left after eighteen months, caught in the wash from the resignations of Peter Mandelson and Geoffrey Robinson.[33] Equally, the government's very success in maintaining its popularity, measured by a clear lead in the opinion polls, built up a certain resentment. Whether they thought this popularity was because of the government's efforts to control its image or despite them, editors could not be expected to enjoy the implication that their papers and programmes were being manipulated. The result, one observer argued, was that they "made a fetish of criticising the concept and the practice of so-called 'spin' and... turned Campbell, if not into a household name, into a Machiavellian bogey figure". The government's response was yet more spin.[34]

The first consequence of the government's media fixation, then, was that its news operations and the personalities involved frequently became part of the story they sought to tell. Campbell's desire to be quoted as an "official spokesman", not by name, showed a sound instinct to avoid this, even though his importance in the prime minister's entourage obviously meant that it was wishful thinking. Similarly, Whelan was right when he observed, upon his own departure, that "the job of press secretary becomes extremely difficult if the press secretary and not the department he serves, becomes the story and the subject of excessive attention".[35]

A second consequence had to do with the fragility of reputation. Much of Blair's original appeal was due to a media image emphasizing his qualities of personality and promise rather than ideological convictions or a record of achievement. To the extent that he was a creature of the media, however, he was vulnerable in principle to quite rapid changes in how the media treated him. The polls showed that he got away with it; but in the summer of 2000 they showed, too, the nature of this vulnerability. The first shock came on June 7, when Blair misjudged the mood of delegates at the Women's Institute conference at Wembley. A few days later, the first of a number of stories broke about four leaked memos, sent to and from Blair and Philip Gould between April 29 and June 4. The first one reported Gould telling Blair that focus groups found him uncaring, out of touch, lacking in conviction and failing to deliver on promises.[36] Then on July 2 a prominent early Blairite, the popular novelist Ken Follett, let off a blast of disappointment with Blair's record (Campbell spun a quick riposte for the *Mirror*). Four days later, Blair's teenage son Euan was picked up by the police late at night drunk and incapable, after celebrating the end of his exams. Next, a heavily trailed BBC television documentary about Campbell and the Press Office, shown on July 15, drew strongly critical publicity. This was followed shortly by the second leak in the sequence of Blair/Gould memos, this one reporting that the prime minister was perceived as arrogant and that the New Labour brand, in the words of a Policy Unit member, was "badly contaminated". "All the recent leaks have one central theme," the official said: "that Tony Blair is all spin and no substance".[37]

The bad news continued with the petrol crisis in September. On three successive days, September 12, 13 and 14, Blair gave early evening televised press conferences — a first for any British prime minister. But his initial claims about solving the dispute proved wrong. By late September, polls showed the government's standing had plummeted. MORI registered a record fall for a single month, and ICM in the *Guardian* showed the Conservatives actually ahead, by 38 per cent to 34 per cent, with most people blaming the government for the fuel crisis and only a handful blaming the hauliers. Blair's personal rating dived from +2 in July to −34 in late September.[38] New Labour's friends in the press, such as the *Mirror*, the *Sun* and the *News of the World,* joined the Conservative press in criticizing Blair for arrogance, not listening and sidelining Parliament. This proved a blip. The government recovered. Nonetheless, if Blair's reputation ever were to collapse, that is how quickly it might happen.

A third consequence of active communications management was the larger-than-usual possibility of government crises having a media sub-plot: the media would not only become part of the story but be blamed for creating or heightening the crisis. The Bernie Ecclestone Formula One affair was one example. The relationship between the Hinduja brothers and Peter Mandelson and Keith Vaz were another. Ministerial changes were a third — and the most important. Table 5.3 lists cabinet reshuffles during comparable periods in the Thatcher, Major and Blair administrations. Thatcher and Major each made four reshuffles. None of Thatcher's had a media sub-plot and only one of Major's.[39] Blair, in contrast, made seven reshuffles, no fewer than five of which were provoked to a greater or lesser extent by media speculation and exposure. These included the rubbishing of social security minister Harriet Harman, a media frenzy about the bizarre late-night escapade of Welsh secretary Ron Davies on Clapham Common, the resignation of trade secretary Peter Mandelson only five months after entering the cabinet, the denigration (allegedly by Alastair Campbell) of the Northern Ireland secretary, Mo Mowlam, and the second resignation of Peter Mandelson, who had been brought back as Mowlam's replacement.

As to substantive policy, two possible consequences of a preoccupation with the media may be mentioned. First, Blair's populism, epitomized in this context by the claims made for Gould's focus groups, showed itself occasionally in

Table 5.3 Cabinet Reshuffles and Media "Sub-Plots": Thatcher, Major, Blair

	Margaret Thatcher May 1979–June 1983	John Major April 1992–May 1997	Tony Blair May 1997–June 2001
Total reshuffles	4	4	7
Total with media "sub-plot"	0	1	5
Cabinet ministers at start	21	23	22
Cabinet ministers replaced	7	10	9

Note: Margaret Thatcher's full period in office was from May 1979 to November 1990. John Major's full period was from November 1990 to May 1997.

impetuous policy changes and commitments. The most derided was an off-the-cuff proposal (unlikely to have been cleared by the Home Office) to frogmarch drunken louts to cash machines for payment of on-the-spot fines. Less impractical but just as startling, because unheralded, was Blair's undertaking to a television interviewer that he would definitely proceed to allow Parliament to ban foxhunting, made at a time when the government seemed to be equivocating on an issue that aroused conflicting passions.

More significantly, the government was repeatedly chided for unnecessary and excessive caution ("prudence", when applied to economic policy) in a wide range of domestic policy — and all because it did not wish to antagonize the press. New Labour had celebrated victory in 1997 to the sound of "Things can only get better", a pop song of the time. Four years later, supporters who felt things were not getting better fast enough, by no means all in the Old Labour camp, were ready to push the prime minister towards a more radical agenda after the 2001 election. "We cannot spend another four years watching Tony Blair respond to the agenda of the *Daily Mail*," one of them told the *Guardian*.[40] However, Ben Pimlott, a sympathizer who evidently thought the government had been quite radical, could suggest there was "a neat paradox at the heart of New Labour practice: a left-wing government playing down its achievements because of its fear of alienating Middle England".[41] Either way — whether one thought the government had or had not been too cautious — it could be argued that too much attention had been paid by Blair to the presumed influence of the press over the voters.

In a few areas, this nervousness about media reactions seemed to produce policies that could have come straight from the Thatcher era. The best examples were crime and the treatment of asylum seekers and illegal immigrants. In economic and social policy, the criticism was less about the absolute levels of planned public expenditure than about a reluctance to redistribute wealth, though Gordon Brown's budgets contained more redistribution than met the eye. The policy area in which Blair was most open to the charge of procrastinating for fear of the media was the European Union and specifically the issue of a common currency. It was soon clear that he wished to be safely into his second term before

Table 5.4 Editorial Attitudes to the European Union, 2001 compared with 1997

Paper	2001	1997
Daily Express	Sympathetic	Eurosceptic
Daily Mail	Eurosceptic	Eurosceptic
Daily Star	Sympathetic	Eurosceptic
Daily Telegraph	Eurosceptic	Eurosceptic
Financial Times	Sympathetic	Sympathetic
Guardian	Sympathetic	Sympathetic
Independent	Sympathetic	Sympathetic
Mirror	Sympathetic	Sympathetic
Sun	Eurosceptic	Eurosceptic
The Times	Eurosceptic	Eurosceptic
Circulation ('000s):		
Eurosceptic	7,589 (58%)	9,714 (71%)
Sympathetic	5,553 (42%)	4,043 (29%)

Source: Audit Bureau of Circulations for circulation figures.

confronting it. This position was certainly understandable. As Table 5.4 shows, a majority of the daily press (nearly three-quarters, measured by circulation) had been Eurosceptic in 1997, including traditional Labour enemies (notably the *Daily Mail* and *Daily Telegraph*) but also its most widely read new-found friends (notably the *Sun*). Before long, after the 1997 election, the *Sun* was asking about Blair, in a headline filling the front page, "IS THIS THE MOST DANGEROUS MAN IN BRITAIN?"[42] The reason was Blair's dangerous leanings towards the single European currency. Precipitately handled, the euro was thus *the* issue that could make the press round on Blair and threaten his prospects of winning a second term. In the 2001 campaign the Eurosceptic dominance in the press was less, but only because the *Daily Express* and *Daily Star* had been bought by a sympathetic proprietor.

The same caution permeated the government's media policy itself. Having won a majority of press support in 1997, why upset the moguls needlessly? The veto of Murdoch's Manchester United takeover was a rare exception. The government made no move to limit concentration of newspaper ownership, or cross-ownership with broadcast interests, or ownership by foreign nationals. In 1998 it used the whips to defeat Commons amendments to competition law that would have banned the kind of predatory price subsidies with which Rupert Murdoch sought to weaken the competitors of *The Times*.[43] The government also backed away from the idea of a privacy law, to protect people against media intrusion. It rejected the proposal by a working party chaired by a New Labour economist, Gavyn Davies, for a "digital TV tax". The BBC's income is derived largely from a fixed annual licence fee, payable by everyone with a television set. The Davies proposal would have made digital television users pay more. But Murdoch's BSkyB group sets its own subscription levels and was strongly opposed to any new levy—with Campbell's former deputy in the Press Office, Tim Allan, making the case.

Was New Labour Right to be Preoccupied with the Media?

President Eisenhower is said to have believed in "letting the facts speak for themselves". But that is one thing facts never do (and fortunately Eisenhower had a good press secretary). All governments manage the news. The question is whether Blair needed to be so preoccupied and was right to use his particular methods.

The government's top priority with the broadcast media, banned from editorializing, was to control the news agenda. This meant both the topics in the news and the interpretation put upon them. Failure to try and impose its own agenda, however unpopular this might turn out to be, would have been unthinkable. It would have meant surrendering the initiative to the opposition or to a random set of political influences. The same priority applied to its treatment of the press, but with the important extra objective of securing editorial support. Here the crucial factor for New Labour, mentioned earlier, was that its historic majority of editorial supporters in 1997 reflected more a partisan dealignment of the press than a permanent realignment. It was thus the start, not the end, of an argument.

The fact that newspapers did not renege on their 1997 commitments does not mean that the government need not have bothered with them. On domestic policy in general, traditional supporters like the *Mirror* and the *Guardian* were not going to abandon the government when it mimicked "Tory policies", nor were converts such as the *Express* titles: none of them had anywhere else to go. But that did not prevent them sniping. Issues such as crime, immigration, health care and poor schools are notoriously difficult to protect from bad news, and the Blair government therefore received its fair share. On one issue above all — relations with Europe, as we have seen — both its remaining enemies and its most widely read new friends were deeply suspicious of its intentions. Across the board, the government could not afford to let up in its media operations.

The full difference between dealignment and realignment was encapsulated in the newspaper editorials as the 2001 campaign reached its climax. Papers' general sympathies were in every case clear: superficially, Table 5.1 is accurate. But almost none could look its readers in the eye: Table 5.1 does not tell the whole story. Long-term Labour papers (the *Mirror* titles, *Guardian, Observer, Sunday People*) had reservations on public expenditure issues, such as health and pensions. The Murdoch papers, 1997 converts, gave dire warnings about the euro: the *Sun* promised "unprecedentedly ferocious opposition", "deeply, even mortally damaging", if the government sought to join it.[44] *The Times* was more restrained, as it did not think the government would be able to obtain a majority in a referendum anyway. In contrast, the *Financial Times* approved of the government's approach to Europe (and its economic management) but disliked its illiberalism and arrogance.

Arrogance was a common complaint, in addition to specific policy criticisms and anxieties about Europe. Since the remaining Conservative papers voiced the same types of complaint, these same papers' reluctance to shout themselves hoarse was all the stranger. "It's a great thing to be a Conservative", cried the *Daily Telegraph,* looking the reader in the eye; and then, shifting its gaze, "If that's what you are, capitalise on it, and vote Conservative." The *Daily Mail* confessed, straight to the reader, its "deeply felt Conservative instincts"; then it looked away and pronounced delphically, "If the Tories haven't done enough to win, surely Labour, with this track record, doesn't merit an overwhelming victory."[45] So newspaper partisanship both for Labour and, residually, for the Conservatives was allusive and hedged with reservations. As the likely scale of Labour's victory became clear towards polling day, several papers voiced concern about the harmful implications of a second landslide. This was another sign of partisan dealignment rather than realignment: true loyalists like to win big. The anxiety was that a landslide might buttress illiberalism and arrogance and make a policy of further European involvement easier.

There is a useful distinction to be made between "strong opinions, weakly held" and "weak opinions, strongly held". On the evidence of the 2001 campaign, New Labour was in receipt more of the latter. It had won its argument with the press over its four years in office, but not on all counts. The government could certainly argue, therefore, that it had not taken such pains with the media unnecessarily. The possibility remains, however, that its sustained success in the opinion polls, and eventually in the 2001 election, did not happen because of its news operations but despite them — or at least regardless of them. For this view, the main argument is the parlous state of the opposition. William Hague was regularly judged to have got the better of Blair in the House of Commons, especially in Prime Minister's Questions. But he may be the first party leader to have suffered personally from televised parliamentary proceedings (introduced in the Commons at the end of the Thatcher era), since his rhetorical success did not overcome the disadvantages, apparently, of his appearance and voice (let alone the party's wider problems), and it never translated into popular success. A stronger opposition performance, in and out of the Commons, would probably have increased the government's difficulties in keeping the media initiative. But it is not possible to claim more than that.[46]

A final measure of the Blair government's preoccupation with media can be made by comparison with its predecessors. There are two positions. One is the "control freakery" view: that Blair's government was more spin than substance, that its priorities were set by what it could sell and that no previous minister had presided over media management to such an extent. The other view sees the Blair government driven by traditional political and (once in power) administrative dynamics, which were simply "modernized" to fit the conditions of its time. The two views go back to the propositions about media and politics put forward at the start of this chapter. To oversimplify, the control freakery view assumes that the institutions of party and government are autonomous and that prime ministers can choose whether or not to apply the potential of the media to their purposes (winning elections, implementing policies). On this argument, Blair could have governed just as well — and at no greater risk — if he had chosen not to use the instruments of control freakery but to work instead to gentler harmonies than those of the mobile phone. The "modernizing" view, in contrast, sees political institutions — party organizations, parliaments, cabinets, bureaucracies, interest groups — as working in an environment that is both permeated by the media and increasingly conditioned by the media. On this argument, a prime minister can no more ignore the technology that keeps MPs on message and that underpins, say, the Strategic Communications Unit than Balfour could hold out against the newspaper technology that forced him, in 1902, to change Commons Question Time in order to meet the deadlines of the provincial evening papers.[47] Blair was simply adapting Downing Street to the latest media technology, and any failure to do so would assuredly have brought avoidable risks. In the same circumstances, can one really envisage Margaret Thatcher failing to do the same? Going back further, the prime ministers who saw the potential of television — Harold Macmillan, Harold Wilson — sought innovatory ways of exploiting it. Even Edward Heath staged televised press conferences in the grand surroundings of Lancaster House, an aristocratic mansion turned conference centre not far from Westminster. Heath's initiative failed because it affronted the print media, and he felt obliged to back down.

Downing Street news operations work in that most sensitive area where the overlapping but ultimately conflicting goals of governments and media institutions touch. These are rarely in equilibrium. Sometimes government seems on top, as Heath was not — but as New Labour was during its first term. At other times the media rough up the government, as when they made John Major's life miserable. Part of the fascination of the second New Labour term will be to see whether, when and why the current balance shifts: for sooner or later it surely will. When the opposition is weak, as in 1997–2001, the media take over part of its role. But they are uncomfortable doing so in a vacuum: they want a parliamentary opposition with gumption, to provide them with a point of reference. That is why the government's second landslide was anticipated — and then greeted — with a certain editorial concern among both supporters and opponents. This concern was joined in more than one paper with calls for an end to "spin-doctor politics". This in turn was linked to the issue of low turnout. "Spin doctor politics have been shown to be a huge turn-off", reflected the *Sunday Times,* "and millions of people, especially younger ones, have become disengaged from the political process."[48] If an end to spin-doctor politics does happen, therefore, it is likely to be the result not only of changed attitudes in the Blair government but also of changed attitudes in the media and, not least, of a changed and revived Conservative Party.

NOTES

1. John Major, 365 House of Commons Debates, col. 657, March 12, 2001. Cf. Alan Rusbridger, editor of the *Guardian*, "The word 'spin' is to this Government what 'sleaze' was to the last", *Guardian*, July 15, 2000.

2. See, e.g., Jeremy Tunstall, *Newspaper Power* (Oxford: Clarendon Press, 1996; Colin Seymour-Ure, *The British Press and Broadcasting since 1945*, 2nd edn (Oxford: Blackwell, 1996).

3. Mrs Thatcher, if the judgement of her press secretary Bernard Ingham is good, would not accept the argument of this paragraph (Ingham, *Kill the Messenger* (London: HarperCollins, 1991), 169–70). But her fatal experience with the reviled "poll tax", which she completely failed to sell to the public and which indirectly brought her down, seems to bear it out. See David Butler, Andrew Adonis and Tony Travers, *Failure in British Government* (Oxford: Oxford University Press, 1994).

4. Andrew Marr (later political editor of the BBC), quoted in Jean Seaton, ed., *Politics and the Media* (Oxford: Blackwell, 1998), 46.

5. Interview with the then editor, Rosie Boycott, *Guardian*, April 19, 1999.

6. *The Times*, March 30, 2001; *Guardian*, March 30, 2001.

7. *Guardian*, June 1, 1998. The editor of the *Daily Express* denied she had been pressured not to appoint Routledge. Other examples included Polly Toynbee, who went from the *Independent* to the *Guardian* in 1998; Andrew Marr, who went from editing the *Independent* to writing for the *Express* and then to the political editorship of the BBC, plus a column in *The Times;* and Tony Bevins, who left the *Observer* for the *Daily Express*, from which he resigned when it was bought by Richard Desmond. After he joined the *Mirror,* Routledge continued to trade as being "off message". His columns during the election campaign were headed as such.

8. Hamilton lost his seat in 1997, after being exposed as having accepted payment for parliamentary services ("cash for questions"). Aitken resigned as a minister following accusations of having had free hospitality at the Paris Ritz. He lost his seat in 1997 and was later imprisoned for perjury committed during a libel trial against the *Guardian*.

9. Peter Oborne, *Alastair Campbell: New Labour and the Rise of the Media Class* (London: Aurum Press, 1999), 111; Paul Routledge, *Mandy: The Unauthorised Biography of Peter Mandelson* (London: Simon and Schuster, 1999), 143; Andrew Rawnsley, *Servants of the People* (London: Hamish Hamilton, 2000), 5–6; David Butler and Dennis Kavanagh, *The British General Election of 1997* (London: Macmillan, 1997), 58–9.

10. Trevor Kavanagh, interviewed by Roy Greenslade, the *Guardian,* January 2, 2000.

11. See Robert Harris, *Good and Faithful Servant* (London: Faber and Faber, 1990), e.g. 114–20.

12. Public Administration Committee, *Fourth Report, Special Advisers: Boon or Bane?* HC 293 (2001), paras 6, 14.

13. *Report of the Working Group on the Government Information Service,* Cabinet Office, November 1997. The figures on press officers are from Dennis Kavanagh and Anthony Seldon, *The Powers Behind the Prime Minister* (London: HarperCollins, 2000), 254. This book has a very useful detailed chapter about Blair's Downing Street.

14. Those of the BBC reporter Nicholas Jones repay particular attention, as he was one of the journalists regularly abused (Nicholas Jones, *Soundbites and Spin Doctors* (London: Cassell, 1995); Nicholas Jones, *Campaign 1997* (London: Indigo, 1997); Nicholas Jones, *The Control Freaks* (London: Politico's, 2001). See also Oborne, *Alastair Campbell;* Routledge, *Mandy;* Rawnsley, *Servants of the People;* Philip Gould, *The Unfinished Revolution: How the Modernisers Saved the Labour Party* (London: Abacus, 1999); Donald Macintyre, *Mandelson and the Making of New Labour* (London: HarperCollins, 2000); Tom Bower, *The Paymaster: Geoffrey Robinson, Maxwell and New Labour* (London: Simon & Schuster, 2001)).

15. *Guardian,* January 6, 2000.

16. *Independent on Sunday,* July 5, 1998; *Guardian*, April 17, 1999; April 19, 1999.

17. *Guardian,* March 24, 2000, February 9, 1998.

18. Oborne, *Alastair Campbell*, 90–4. Later the Commons Public Administration Committee recommended that Campbell's authority to issue orders to civil servants should be removed (*Guardian*, 13 March 2001).

19. John Major, *John Major: The Autobiography* (London: HarperCollins, 2000). See, e.g., the introduction.

20. Oborne, *Alastair Campbell*, 119. As an instance of Major's lack of touch, Oborne describes his reluctance to elevate the chairman of the *Daily Mail* group, already a knight, to the peerage. Major resented the *Mail's* attacks on his government. Tony Blair had no such hesitation, though David English died a few days before the peerage was announced (Oborne, *Alastair Campbell*, 178).

21. Kavanagh and Seldon, *The Powers Behind the Prime Minister*, 266. The Policy Unit was first established by Harold Wilson. It has become a Downing Street fixture.

22. Rawnsley, *Servants of the People*, 377–82. For Godric Smith's briefing role, see the *Guardian*, June 14, 2000.

23. For the Research and Information Unit and the Strategic Communications Unit, see Kavanagh and Seldon, *The Powers Behind the Prime Minister*, 289; and for the latter only, see the Cabinet Office *Report of the Working Group*.

24. For an example of the grid, see Kavanagh and Seldon, *The Powers Behind the Prime Minister*, 255–6.

25. *Guardian*, November 21, 2000.

26. Kavanagh and Seldon, *The Powers Behind the Prime Minister*, 283.

27. Oborne, *Alastair Campbell*, 143, 199.

28. *Financial Times*, March 24, 1998; Oborne, *Alastair Campbell*, 192–3.

29. Rawnsley, *Servants of the People*, 60–3.

30. The English accent known in the last twenty years as "estuarine" is spoken in the areas adjoining the Thames Estuary east of London and some sixty miles to the sea. "Mockney" is a more recent term, meaning "mock cockney" and referring to a middle-class person's conscious adoption of a working-class central and east London accent, for the purpose (say) of concealing their class position. "Gorblimey" is a historic corruption of an old oath ("God blind me!"), associated again with traditional working-class speech patterns.

31. Rawnsley, *Servants of the People*, 293–4.

32. J. Burnham and G. Jones, "Accounting to Parliament by British Prime Ministers" (paper presented to the Political Studies Association 50th Annual Conference, April, 2000).

33. Peter Mandelson resigned in December 1998, after disclosure of the fact that he had received a large undeclared loan from his ministerial colleague Geoffrey Robinson for the purpose of buying a house.

34. Roy Greenslade, *Guardian*, May 8, 2000.

35. *Daily Telegraph*, January 5, 1999; quoted, Oborne, *Alastair Campbell*, 162.

36. *Sunday Times*, June 11, 2000.

37. *The Times, Guardian, Sun*, July 19, 2000.

38. *The Times*, September 28, 2000, *Guardian*, September 19, 2000.

39. Major's media-provoked reshuffle involved the humiliation of the philandering heritage secretary, David Mellor. Major also had to replace a number of junior ministers as a result of 'sleaze' incidents in which media played a part.

40. *Guardian*, June 5, 2001.

41. *Guardian*, March 10, 2001.

42. *Sun*, June 24, 1998.

43. Murdoch sold *The Times* for 10p on Mondays, instead of the normal 35p. The losses were made up from profits elsewhere in his empire. The aim was to eat into the circulation of competitors, especially the *Daily Telegraph*.

44. *Sun*, May 28, 2001.

45. *Daily Telegraph*, June 6, 2001; *Daily Mail*, June 6, 2001.

46. For two articles in *The Economist*, typical of many concerning implications of a weak

opposition, see Bagehot, "Over, before it's begun", *The Economist,* January 13, 2001, and "Teflon Tony", *The Economist,* March 24, 2001.

47. As part of wider procedural reforms in 1902, Question Time was brought forward earlier in the day by Arthur Balfour, then Leader of the Commons, for the convenience of the press (Colin Seymour-Ure, "Parliament and Mass Communications in the Twentieth Century", in S.A. Walkland, ed., *The House of Commons in the Twentieth Century* (Oxford: Clarendon Press, 1979), 533).

48. *Sunday Times,* June 10, 2001. Cf. *Guardian,* June 9, 2001: "The public is — rightly — cynical about spin, over-promising, double-accounting and phoney initiatives".

CHAPTER 6

The Liberal Democrats in "Constructive Opposition"

David Denver

FROM THE TIME they were founded in 1988, as the result of a merger between the Social Democratic Party (SDP) and the old Liberal Party, the Liberal Democrats have faced a fundamental strategic problem. How should they position themselves in relation to the two major parties and what kind of relationships could be established with them without compromising their own independence and integrity? The problem is complicated by the need to fight on two electoral fronts. In most places where they are strong, the Liberal Democrats are in competition with the Conservatives, with Labour being largely out of the running. In some areas, however — mainly in the north of England and including cities such as Liverpool and Sheffield — the Liberal Democrats are in contention with Labour and relations between the two parties are characterized by mutual hostility.

Initially the solution was to maintain a stance of "equidistance" between the other two parties — refusing to indicate a preference for one or the other or to rule out cooperating with either. Between 1992 and 1997, however, the Liberal Democrats significantly redefined their position. Almost immediately after the 1992 general election the then party leader, Paddy Ashdown, announced that the party should "work with others to assemble the idea around which a non-socialist alternative to the Conservatives can be constructed".[1] This caused some consternation among Liberal Democrats in areas where Labour was perceived to be the principal enemy, but Ashdown continued to press his case. This was made easier by the policies and performance of the Conservative government, but a spur to concrete action was provided by the emergence of Tony Blair as Labour leader in July 1994 and the subsequent transformation of the party into New Labour. Blair was receptive to the idea of cooperation and appeared in tune with many Liberal Democrat values. Within a relatively short time he had virtually turned the Labour Party into just the sort of "non-socialist alternative" to the Conservatives to which Ashdown aspired. In addition, New Labour's clear moves towards the centre-ground of politics and the popularity of Blair and his party among voters threatened the electoral prospects of the Liberal Democrats. The claim that they had no preference between the other parties began to look increasingly threadbare, and in September 1995 the Liberal Democrat conference adopted a statement prescribing a new approach. Their primary aim was now to defeat the Conservatives, and it was asserted that Liberal Democrat MPs would not sustain a Conservative government in office. At the same time, the party would keep its distance from Labour. Equidistance had been abandoned. This was hailed as a historic development in some quarters since it opened up the possibility, in the long term, of a major realignment of the left in British politics.[2] Indeed, achieving such a realignment became known to New Labour and Liberal Democrat insiders as "the project" and was, initially at least, central to the thinking of both Blair and Ashdown. Both believed that the division between the two parties on the left, dating from the early years of the twentieth century, had allowed the Conservatives to dominate British politics. If the division could be healed in some way, then the prize would be great — the future for their kind of progressive politics would be secured.

In the months that followed the ditching of equidistance, relations between the two parties became closer in public and this process culminated in the autumn of 1996 when they agreed to hold joint talks with a view to potential collaboration on constitutional reform, in particular devolution, reform of the House of Lords and reform of the electoral system, the latter being the holy grail of Liberal Democrat politics. These "Cook–Maclennan" talks (the Labour side being led by Robin Cook and the Liberal Democrats by Robert Maclennan) paved the way for subsequent legislation. It emerged later, however, with the publication of Paddy Ashdown's diaries, that relations between the two party leaders had been much closer than anyone suspected at the time.[3] According to Ashdown, he and Blair began to have informal meetings shortly after the latter became Labour leader. Only a small circle of leading politicians in each party were aware of these meetings, in which possible forms of future cooperation were discussed. It appears that the discussions went as far as to include the possibility of a coalition government, with Ashdown and one other Liberal Democrat having seats in the cabinet. The price of Liberal Democrat support would be a commitment to electoral reform on Blair's part.

Whatever the truth about the details of what was and was not discussed — and there were some suggestions that Ashdown's account may have exaggerated Blair's enthusiasm for joint action — there is no doubt that these meetings took place and that the two parties, at least at the top, were now closer together than they had ever been. This was not lost on the electorate. In the past, British Election Study (BES) surveys have regularly found that voters were more likely to believe that the Liberal Democrats and their predecessors were closer to the Conservatives than they were to Labour. In 1992 the respective figures were 39 per cent

Table 6.1 Liberal Democrat Performance in the 1992 and 1997 General Elections

	1992	1997
Percentage share of votes	18.3	17.2
Seats won	20	46
Second place	153	104
(to Conservatives)	(144)	(73)
(to Labour)	(8)	(31)
(to other)	(1)	–
Third place or lower	461	490

and 33 per cent. In the 1997 BES survey, however, 57 per cent considered the Liberal Democrats closer to Labour and only 18 per cent closer to the Conservatives. Other evidence points to the same conclusion. Whereas in 1992 42 per cent of Liberal Democrat voters opted for the Conservatives as their second-choice party and 36 per cent for Labour, in 1997 the Conservatives were chosen by only 22 per cent and Labour by 64 per cent. Between 1992 and 1997 the proportion of Conservatives choosing the Liberal Democrats as their second choice fell from 69 per cent to 53 per cent while the proportion of Labour voters doing the same rose from 53 per cent to 65 per cent.

THE 1997 ELECTION

Table 6.1 gives details of the performance of the Liberal Democrats in the 1992 and 1997 general elections. In 1997 the share of the vote that they gained fell by just over one point but the number of seats they won more than doubled, from 20 to 46. This apparently paradoxical outcome resulted from two developments. The first was an increase in tactical voting. In constituencies that they held or where they were in second place behind the Conservatives and less than 30 percentage points behind, the Liberal Democrat vote actually increased.[4] Second, the Liberal Democrats successfully targeted their constituency campaign effort on a relatively small number of seats.[5] It is noticeable that, as well as winning more seats in 1997, there was also an increase in the number of seats where the Liberal Democrats did very badly, coming third or worse. This demonstrates the limitations inherent in a strategy of targeting constituencies. It may win some seats, but in order to be a major national force the party needs to be seriously challenging in many more constituencies.

The data in the table also illustrate the electoral logic underlying the Liberal Democrats' 1995 change of tack in that in the 1992 election they were second to the Conservatives in 144 constituencies but to Labour in only eight. Moreover, of the twenty seats that they won in 1992, the Conservatives were second in sixteen. However, the Liberal Democrats were now second to Labour in 31 seats. Seven of these were in Wales and seventeen in the North of England (including five in Liverpool and four each in Sheffield and Greater Manchester). In these areas the task was to remove Labour MPs, and this would not be helped by ever-closer links between the two parties.

It would seem, nonetheless, that the abandonment of equidistance paid dividends for the Liberal Democrats in the 1997 election. In the words of Curtice and Steed, "Voters exhibited a striking tendency to opt for whichever of the two opposition parties appeared best placed to defeat the Conservatives locally," and the party won more seats than the old Liberals had at any election since the 1920s.[6] In the 1950s it used to be said, with only slight exaggeration, that all the Liberal MPs could ride to the House of Commons in a single taxi; after 1997 the Liberal Democrats would have required a decent-sized coach.

Yet the achievement of the Liberal Democrats was overshadowed by that of New Labour. If the two major parties had been more evenly balanced in the House of Commons, the Liberal Democrats would have been in a strong position to influence the incoming government. As it was, however, the strongest Liberal Democrat showing in many years coincided with a Labour landslide. With an overall majority of 179, Labour had little need of support from Paddy Ashdown and his sizeable band of MPs.

"CONSTRUCTIVE OPPOSITION"

In this situation talk of coalition was redundant, and even hopes that the Liberal Democrats would exert a strong influence over the government receded. Nonetheless, on the day after the election Ashdown announced that his party would be a voice of "constructive opposition" in the new parliament, saying that "Mr Blair and the Labour Party have entered into an agreement with the Liberal Democrats. I expect that to be delivered. I do not believe that that agreement was entered into in bad faith nor indeed that Mr Blair is a dishonourable man."[7] The agreement he had in mind, presumably, was the decision to collaborate on constitutional reform that resulted from the Cook–Maclennan talks.

Shortly afterwards, in the debate on the Queen's Speech in the House of Commons, Ashdown gave a more elaborate account of what he meant by "constructive opposition":

> If a generation of progressive change, founded on constitutional and electoral reform, is what the Government intend, the Prime Minister can count on the Liberal Democrats to be critical but firm supporters of every step that he takes along the way. Of course we shall criticise the Government when we believe that they are wrong, and especially when their actions fall short of the programme of reform that the country needs. I have to say that there are some rather worrying examples of that in the programme with which they have presented us today. Our aim, however, will be to provide a constructive opposition, and if that breaks the outmoded convention that Oppositions must always oppose, whatever the merits of the case, we make no apologies for it.[8]

The centrality in Ashdown's thinking of the need for constitutional reform is clear.

The rewards for Ashdown and the Liberal Democrats were not long in coming. The government almost immediately began the process that would lead to (successful) referendums on devolution in Scotland and Wales in September 1997. It also promised to establish a commission on electoral reform. More surprisingly, in July Tony Blair, in an unprecedented and unexpected move, announced the creation of a Joint Cabinet Committee (JCC) comprising himself and senior members of the government together with Ashdown and four leading Liberal Democrats (Alan Beith, Menzies Campbell, Robert Maclennan and Lord Holme). When it first met in September the committee was described by the *Guardian* (September 18) as 'the biggest experiment in cross-party co-operation since the Lib–Lab pact in the 1970s'. In fact it was bigger than that since, unlike the previous example of cooperation, the committee had formal cabinet status and allowed the Liberal Democrats to be at the heart of government. Initially the JCC was to discuss constitutional reform, but it was to meet every two months and was expected to go on to other matters.

Repaying his part of the bargain, Blair also established in December 1997 an independent commission on the electoral system headed by Lord Jenkins who, as Roy Jenkins, had been one of the original "Gang of Four" which split off from the Labour Party to form the Social Democratic Party in 1981. Labour's 1997 election manifesto had promised that there would be a referendum on the system used to elect the House of Commons, and the commission's brief was to recommend a system that could be put to the electorate as an alternative to the established first-past-the-post system. Evidence was taken from interested parties (including academics in the field), and a good deal of analysis of the effects of various systems was undertaken. The commission produced its report in October 1998 and recommended a mixed system that involved electing constituency MPs by the Alternative Vote method but also the creation of additional regional members. These extra regional members would "top up" the constituency representatives in a way that made overall representation more proportional to the votes cast. The recommendation was carefully crafted to make it more palatable than a straightforwardly proportional system to sceptical MPs. In the event, however, the report was quietly shelved by the government, which claimed that pressure of time made it difficult to organize a referendum but was also wary of a distinct lack of enthusiasm for change among its own backbenchers. Little more was heard of the commission and its recommendations before the 2001 election.

Shortly after the first meeting of the JCC the Liberal Democrats held their annual conference at Eastbourne and all the talk was of relations with Labour. Critics of recent developments, among them Charles Kennedy, were highly suspicious, warning that the party should not be seduced by Blair and fearing that too cosy a link with Labour would erode the party's distinctive identity. Some detected a secret leadership agenda for a formal coalition, or even merger, in the longer term. In response to these fears, leadership loyalists roundly attacked the government's timidity and its performance on the economy, the National Health Service and the single European currency. Nonetheless, Ashdown in his leader's speech once again spelled out his conception of constructive opposition and, according to Michael White in the *Guardian* (September 25) "the underlying thrust of his message to party activists was that they must adjust to the prospect of coalition politics within a decade".

Constructive opposition, then, defined relations between the Liberal Democrats and the new government after 1997. Discussion of how far inter-party cooperation should go continued to dominate the party conference in September 1998 when, with the Jenkins commission about to report, delegates insistently demanded that Blair had to deliver on electoral reform before there could be moves to a closer relationship. In November, however, matters took an unexpected turn. To the general astonishment of their parties, Blair and Ashdown issued a joint statement announcing that the role of the JCC would be extended to allow cooperation on health, education, modernization of the welfare state and pushing for European integration. In their statement they said that "This will be an important step in challenging the destructive tribalism that can afflict British politics even where parties find themselves in agreement". The long-term aim was "to ensure the ascendancy of progressive politics in Britain". In order to reassure their own party members and activists, however, the party leaders also said "[We] are two sovereign and independent parties working together where we agree and opposing each other where we do not. Our parties will continue to offer different choices to the British people in the ballot box."[9] This development outraged those in the Labour Party who opposed Blair's strategy of pursuing cooperation with the Liberal Democrats — including heavyweights such as John Prescott (deputy prime minister), Gordon Brown (chancellor of the exchequer) and Jack Straw (home secretary). "The project" was very much a product of New Labour thinking, and more traditional Old Labour people saw no need for it now that Labour on its own had won a landslide election victory. Among Liberal Democrat MPs the new development was generally accepted as a logical consequence of the party's espousal of proportional representation and pluralist politics. Among activists jealous of the party's independence, however, it increased suspicion of Ashdown's long-term plans.

What did constructive opposition mean in practice on the floor of the House of Commons? Table 6.2 shows the pattern of voting by Liberal Democrat MPs on whipped votes in the House of Commons in the first three sessions of the parliament. Votes on the second and third reading of bills are concerned with the broad principles of the legislation and the bill as finally constituted, and it can be seen that on these divisions, despite sitting on the opposition benches, Liberal Democrat MPs were much more likely to support the government than to side with

Table 6.2 Votes of Liberal Democrat MPs in the House of Commons

	May '97– November '98 %	November '98– November '99 %	November '99– November '00 %
(a) Votes on Second and Third Readings			
With Labour vs. Conservatives	63	52	66
With Conservatives vs. Labour	17	36	21
With both	13	0	5
Against both	8	12	8
(N)	(48)	(42)	(38)
(b) Votes on Details			
With Labour vs. Conservatives	58	44	35
With Conservatives vs. Labour	23	43	43
With both	1	0	0
Against both	19	13	22
(N)	(199)	(130)	(145)

Source: Philip Cowley, Darren Darcy, Colin Mellors, Jon Neal and Mark Stuart, "Mr. Blair's Loyal Opposition? The Liberal Democrats in Parliament", *British Elections & Parties Review* 10 (1998), 100–16. Data for the third session were kindly made available to the author by Philip Cowley and Mark Stuart.

Note: "Votes on Details" refers to those on the Report Stage, Committee Stage (when taken on the floor of the House) and during consideration of Lords' amendments.

the official opposition, especially during the first parliamentary session. This is in line with the strategy of constructive opposition. It might be argued, however, that the strategy should also involve trying to improve legislation by proposing and supporting amendments when bills are considered in detail. Examination of these sorts of votes in the second part of Table 6.2 shows a rather different picture. Initially the Liberal Democrats were a little less likely to vote with Labour than they were on broad principles. At this stage, therefore, inter-party cooperation was not confined to discussions in the JCC but was manifested in the votes of MPs in the House. In the second and third sessions, however, Liberal Democrats appear to have become more critical of the government. By the third session they were more likely to vote with the Conservatives on matters of detail than they were with Labour, supporting the government on just over one-third of votes. Cowley and Stuart suggest that the figures show that Liberal Democrat MPs began increasingly to stress the "opposition" part of the strategy while retaining the "constructive" part.[10]

ASHDOWN'S RESIGNATION AND THE ELECTION OF KENNEDY

In July 1998 Paddy Ashdown celebrated ten years as leader of the Liberal Democrats. Ten years before, he had taken over a party that had a low membership, was in a precarious financial position and was unsure of what to call itself. Throughout 1989 more of the public thought that he was not proving a good leader of the party than thought he was, and the party languished at below 10 per cent of voting intentions in opinion polls. In June 1989 the party was humiliated at the European elections, gaining less than half the share of votes won by the Greens.[11] Now he presided over a healthy party which, with 46 MPs and almost as many local councillors as the Tories, was the strongest third force in British politics since before the war. Addressing speculation about his possible retirement, Ashdown commented, "You must be joking. This is where the fun begins. Let me make my intention absolutely clear — I intend to lead this party through this parliament, through the next election and into the next government."[12]

In January 1999, however, Ashdown announced that he intended to retire in the following summer. This was undoubtedly the most significant event of the 1997–2001 parliament for the Liberal Democrats. Ashdown claimed that his decision to retire around this time had been made a long time before and that his previous denials had been politically necessary for the good of the party. He said that he had achieved what he had set out to do and wanted to go out on a high while he was still young enough to try his hand at something else.[13] Others suggested less worthy motives — that Ashdown hoped to be given a high-level job with the European Union, for example. It was also suggested that the real reason for his resignation was that his core political strategy — continued and developing cooperation with New Labour — was running into difficulties. On the Labour side, the report of the Jenkins commission on electoral reform, as noted above, had been very coolly received, and no early referendum on its recommended alternative to first-past-the-post was in sight. In addition, the resignation of Peter Mandelson from the cabinet in December 1998 removed a strong and influential supporter of "the project" from the front rank. There was also growing resistance to Ashdown's strategy within his own party. A grass-roots Campaign for Liberal Democracy had been formed to organize resistance and there were growing grumblings about Ashdown's autocratic style.

Divisions among party members on the question of relations with Labour are revealed by the results of a survey of party members carried out during 1999. When asked whether the Liberal Democrats should have maintained the policy of equidistance between Labour and the Conservatives, 38 per cent of members agreed that they should have as compared with 44 per cent disagreeing. In response to a further question, 33 per cent agreed that Labour politicians could not be trusted and that the Liberal Democrats should keep their distance; 44 per cent disagreed (in both cases the remainder had no opinion either way).[14] Similar evidence of a dissatisfaction among party activists emerged from data derived from a survey of candidates for the Scottish Parliament and Welsh Assembly — and also local council candidates in both countries — undertaken in May–June 1999. Respondents were presented with a ten-point scale relating to the stance that should be taken towards the Labour government, with "constructive opposition" at one end and "keep your distance" at the other. They were

Table 6.3 Liberal Democrat Activists' Attitudes towards Relations with Labour

	Scottish Parliament/ Welsh Assembly candidates		Scottish/Welsh council candidates	
	Ashdown %	Self %	Ashdown %	Self %
Favours "constructive opposition"	90	43	81	53
In between	8	24	13	25
Favours "keeping distance"	2	33	6	22
(N)	(102)	(102)	(287)	(290)

Source: Surveys of candidates undertaken by the author and colleagues in May–June 1999.

asked to indicate both where they would place themselves on this issue and also where they would place Paddy Ashdown. Table 6.3 summarizes the results.

Unsurprisingly, Ashdown's position was very widely recognized: 90 per cent of Parliament/Assembly candidates and 81 per cent of council candidates placed him towards the "constructive opposition" end of the scale. Indeed, the real puzzle is why these figures were not even larger. However, fewer than half (43 per cent) of Parliament/Assembly candidates and a bare majority (53 per cent) of council candidates took the same position, while significant minorities clearly leaned towards the view that the party should "keep its distance" from Labour.

Reading behind the lines of Ashdown's "political testament" (an article written by him in the *Guardian* when his resignation took effect was headlined PADDY ASHDOWN BEQUEATHS HIS POLITICAL TESTAMENT) one gets the impression that he resigned because he was simply tired and fed up trying to lead a cantankerous and difficult party in the direction that he wanted it to go.[15] Although written in an ostensibly affectionate way, one detects a sense of frustration, and perhaps relief, when he writes that the Liberal Democrats are:

> inveterately sceptical of authority, often exasperating to the point of dementia, as difficult to lead where they don't want to go as a mule and as curmudgeonly about success as one of those football supporters who regards his team's promotion to the premier league as insufficient because they haven't also won the FA cup!

Whatever the real reasons for Ashdown's retirement, his January 1997 announcement left potential successors plenty of time to consider their options and to begin their campaigns for the leadership (although formal campaigning did not begin until after his resignation took effect in June). The absence of an obvious heir-apparent made for a crowded field — within days thirteen possible contenders had been named in the press (in other words almost 30 per cent of the parliamentary party) — and this threatened to turn the election into something of a farce.

However, two leading contenders (and supporters of Ashdown), Alan Beith,

Table 6.4 Liberal Democrat Leadership Election Result, August 1997

	Round 1	Round 2	Round 3	Round 4	Final (%)
Kennedy	22,724	23,619	25,164	28,425	56.6
		(+895)	(+1,545)	(+3,261)	
Hughes	16,233	17,378	19,360	21,833	43.4
		(+1,145)	(+1,982)	(+2,473)	
Bruce	4,643	5,241	6,068		
		(+598)	(+827)		
Ballard	3,978	4,605			
		(+627)			
Rendel	3,428				

Source: Keith Alderman and Neil Carter, "The Lib-Dem Leadership Election", *Parliamentary Affairs* 53 (2000), 311–27.

the deputy leader, and Menzies Campbell, the party's foreign affairs spokesman, quickly decided not to run. Campbell in particular was a heavyweight and impressive figure, whom many believed to be the obvious successor to Ashdown, but he may have thought that his age (57) would count against him, given the youthfulness of the other major party leaders. Eventually five people contested the election: one woman, Jackie Ballard; and four men — Malcolm Bruce, Simon Hughes, Charles Kennedy and David Rendel. Kennedy, a genial and gregarious figure, and Hughes, a rather more austere and earnest character, had something of a national profile (the former mainly because of his appearances on television chat shows and quizzes), but the rather colourless Bruce was not well known and Ballard (who had only been elected as an MP in 1997) and Rendel were virtually unknown outside Liberal Democrat circles — and not that well-known inside them.

The central issue of the leadership campaign was future relations with Labour and, curiously, none of the candidates was a great enthusiast for Ashdown's strategy. Nevertheless, in his campaign literature Kennedy, despite previous misgivings, did repeat the Ashdown formula: "we are right to co-operate with the Government where — as on constitutional reform — we agree. But we are equally right to oppose them when we disagree".[16] Bruce largely ignored the issue while the other three sent thinly veiled messages of scepticism. A Hughes leaflet, for example, was headed "Your vote for Simon — the only guarantee of an independent and successful future for the Liberal Democrats".

The leadership election result was announced on August 9 (voting being by the single transferable vote method) and is reported in Table 6.4. As it turned out, the election was a two-horse race between Kennedy and Hughes, but the former led comfortably on first preferences (by 44.6 per cent to 31.8 per cent). Hughes picked up slightly more second preferences from Rendel and Ballard supporters than did Kennedy, but Kennedy maintained his lead and emerged as a comfortable, if not overwhelming, winner. Nonetheless, the extent of support for Hughes hinted at the depth of opposition to the Blair–Ashdown project.

KENNEDY AS LEADER

The new leader, at 39 the youngest of the serious contenders, had once been witheringly dismissed by Paddy Ashdown as "that ambitious young man",[17] and after the 1997 election he had been consigned to the relative obscurity of being the party's agriculture and rural affairs spokesman. He had been regarded as something of a political lightweight, more interested in appearing on television and radio (rivals described him as 'Chatshow Charlie') than in the grind of day-to-day politics at Westminster. Nonetheless, Kennedy emerged as the candidate of the party establishment — he had the support of 25 of the party's 46 MPs — and was the one least sceptical of cooperation with Labour. In addition, according to Alderman and Carter, during the campaign "Kennedy alone made a real effort to present a broader view of the future", setting out a wide-ranging policy programme in his manifesto.[18]

It was reported that Tony Blair welcomed Kennedy's success, and in a carefully crafted victory speech the latter trod a fine line, promising to maintain the legacy of cooperation while at the same time preserving the distinctiveness and independence of the Liberal Democrats. In his first conference speech as party leader, at Harrogate in September, under strong pressure from both sides in the debate, he maintained this position, ruling out any extension of the remit of the JCC on the one hand but extolling the benefits of cooperation on the other.

During 2000, however, relations between the government and the Liberal Democrats became distinctly cooler. The main reason was the apparent unwillingness of the government to do anything about electoral reform or the Jenkins report. A referendum before the next election was now clearly off the agenda, and the issue became whether or not Labour would commit itself to a referendum in the next parliament. On the eve of the Liberal Democrats' spring conference in March, Kennedy declared that without a firm Labour manifesto commitment to holding a referendum on reforming the Westminster electoral system he could not see "much basis for further meaningful co-operation" between the two parties.[19] At the conference itself, his speech focused almost entirely on environmental issues, trying to define a more strongly distinctive identity for the party and himself (and with half an eye on the electoral threat that the Green Party might pose to the Liberal Democrats). The *Guardian* dismissed Kennedy's implied threat to Tony Blair as a "macho gesture", reminding readers that "he is … no Paddy Ashdown" and that continued cooperation was more vital to Kennedy's prospects than to Blair's.[20] At an upbeat party conference (delegates being encouraged by a sudden upsurge in support for the party in opinion polls) in September, however, Kennedy resisted calls to abandon the JCC. He concentrated on courting disaffected moderate Tories put off by what he claimed was the reactionary course being followed by William Hague and attacking Labour for its timidity over a range of issues. Signs of Labour impatience were obvious, however, in a speech given on the conference fringe by Charles Clarke, a Home Office minister who, in the face of considerable heckling, told his audience that the Liberal Democrats should choose "constructive engagement rather than oppositionism and cheap sound-bites".[21] The two parties continued to drift apart at national level. The JCC met for the last time in July 2000, and in January 2001 Kennedy declared that "the project" was in a coma. He saw little point in maintaining the JCC if Labour would not shift its stance on proportional representation, and so it was mothballed until after the general election. Future cooperation would depend on the contents of the Labour election manifesto.

As the general election approached, the wisdom of Kennedy's strategy — wooing moderate Conservatives by attacking William Hague and at the same time sniping at Labour from the left — was being questioned in some quarters. Labour campaign strategists were reported as believing that he was becoming a liability. One commented, "It's very difficult to work out what Charles Kennedy thinks his strategy is, if he has a strategy."[22] The point being made was that those who had deserted the Tories for the Liberal Democrats in 1997 would not be retained by promises of higher taxation, greater public spending and radical environmental and civil liberties policies. In addition, the gradual distancing of the Liberal Democrats from Labour at national level sat oddly with more local developments. In the Scottish Parliament and the Welsh Assembly the two were in coalition (see below), and the same was true in numerous local councils up and down the country. After all that had happened after 1997, including a change of leader, the Liberal Democrats were actually little nearer a solution to the conundrum of how to position themselves in relation to the two larger parties while still maintaining their distinctiveness and at the same time achieving enough electoral support to allow them to influence government policy.

The reaction of the electorate to Kennedy's leadership was generally favourable. Throughout his period in office more people were satisfied rather than dissatisfied with the way that he is doing his job as leader of the Liberal Democrats. Table 6.5 shows the monthly figures in summary form. The first thing to notice is that, unsurprisingly, Ashdown had a much higher profile among the electorate than Kennedy. In the last seven months of his leadership around 28 per cent of survey respondents had no opinion on Ashdown's performance whereas 50 per cent or more had no opinion on Kennedy in the first thirteen months of his leadership. The proportion declined after that but, even so, in the run up to the general election Kennedy appears to have had a lower profile than Ashdown in the run up to the 1997 election. Whereas an average of 30 per cent had no opinion on Ashdown's leadership from January to April 1997, the figure for Kennedy

Table 6.5 Satisfaction Ratings for Ashdown and Kennedy as Lib Dem Leaders

	1999	2000	2001
Ashdown			
	Jan +39 (27)	Jan +14 (58)	Jan +14 (48)
	Feb +37 (29)	Feb +11 (59)	Feb +16 (36)
	Mar +35 (29)	Mar +14 (54)	Mar +18 (38)
	Apr +37 (27)	Apr +18 (50)	Apr +15 (45)
	May +32 (28)	May +17 (53)	
	June +33 (27)	June +14 (52)	
	July +39 (29)	July +13 (50)	
Kennedy		Aug +14 (50)	
	Aug +11 (69)	Sept +25 (41)	
	Sept +13 (65)	Oct +15 (47)	
	Oct +10 (64)	Nov +18 (50)	
	Nov +17 (61)	Dec +17 (47)	
	Dec +14 (56)		

Source: MORI Ltd.

Note: The satisfaction rating figures represent the percentage satisfied with how Ashdown/ Kennedy was doing his job as leader of the Liberal Democrats minus the percentage dissatisfied. The figures in brackets indicate the percentages having no opinion.

was 45 per cent in April 2001. Given that the electoral appeal of the leader has been an important element in Liberal Democrat support, this must have been worrying for campaign strategists. Their hope was that the campaign itself would enable Kennedy to make a greater impact on voters. Second, Kennedy's ratings among those having an opinion were consistently positive. This was in marked contrast to Ashdown's early experience as leader; Ashdown did not achieve a positive rating until just over two years after his elevation to the position. Once again, however, the most relevant comparison is with the period preceding the 1997 election, and from January to April in that year Ashdown's ratings were, respectively, +19, +20, +38 and +41. His standing with the electorate clearly improved as the election approached, and Liberal Democrats hoped that the same would happen in 2001, though Kennedy had rather more to do.

The relative standing of the major party leaders among voters is indicated by their responses to a standard poll question asking who would make the best prime minister and the proportions nominating Paddy Ashdown or Charles Kennedy from 1999 onwards are shown in Table 6.6. Apart from a temporary blip around the time of public demonstrations against petrol prices in the autumn of 2000, Kennedy's support in this respect hovered around 12–13 per cent. This was significantly lower than Ashdown achieved in the months before his retirement but very similar to the latter's scores in early 1997 (14 per cent in January, 13 per cent in February and 12 per cent in March). Overall, then, the polls gave no indication that the replacement of Ashdown by Kennedy would prove electorally disastrous.

Table 6.6 Percentage Nominating Ashdown and Kennedy as Best Prime Minister

	1999		2000		2001	
Ashdown		%		%		%
	Jan	17	Jan	12	Jan	13
	Feb	18	Feb	13	Feb	13
	Mar	20	Mar	12	Mar	13
	Apr	19	Apr	12	Apr	13
	May	19	May	12		
	June	21	June	12		
	July	19	July	13		
Kennedy			Aug	14		
	Sept	14	Sept	19		
	Oct	11	Oct	17		
	Nov	12	Nov	15		
	Dec	11	Dec	13		

Source: Gallup Political and Economic Index.

Kennedy had a positive image, was no less likely to be thought the best prime minister and, it could be argued, had every chance of raising his profile during the general election campaign.

ELECTORAL UPS AND DOWNS, 1997–2001

In a perceptive newspaper article written at the time of Kennedy's election as leader of the Liberal Democrats, Steve Richards argued that "Blair will remain interested in the Liberal Democrats as long as they are a potent electoral force".[23] Blair, he suggested, had wooed Ashdown because the Liberal Democrats were a useful electoral ally and the challenge for Kennedy was "to build on Ashdown's electoral success rather than get bogged down in endless internal strategic debates". If the popularity of the party slumped, then closer cooperation would be off Blair's agenda.

This was sound advice to the Liberal Democrat leader. Between 1992 and 1997 the Liberal Democrats had shown their potential value to Labour by taking four seats from the Conservatives in parliamentary by-elections (three of which Labour could never win in normal circumstances) and increasing their representation in local government across the country from 3,728 councillors in 1992 to 5,078 in 1996. In the same period the number of councils they controlled rose from 27 to 55.[24] As already noted, they then went on to more than double the number of seats won in the general election. After 1997, however, the situation was different. In the past, the Liberals had tended to prosper under Conservative governments but to make little headway when Labour was in power. Now, for the first time since the Liberal Democrats were formed, there was a Labour government in power and the Liberal Democrats themselves were fairly closely associated with it. In these new circumstances the electoral performance of the Liberal Democrats proved to be patchy.

Parliamentary By-elections

There were sixteen parliamentary by-elections (excluding Northern Ireland) between 1997 and 2001. One of these was the very unusual re-run of the general election contest in Winchester ordered by the courts. Winchester had been narrowly won by the Liberal Democrats, but allegations of flaws in the counting process were upheld. The Liberal Democrat candidate won the re-run handsomely. Excluding Winchester (and also the seat vacated by the Speaker), the average change in the Liberal Democrats' share of the votes between the general election and the by-elections was +3.5 points (compared with +5.3 points between 1992 and 1997). In part this weaker performance was a result of sheer bad luck in that only one seat fell vacant in which the Liberal Democrats were the clear challengers to the Conservatives — precisely the type of seat in which the party would hope to make significant advances. This was Romsey. At the general election the Conservatives held the seat with 46.0 per cent of the vote; the Liberal Democrats were in second place with 29.4 per cent and Labour third with 18.6 per cent. In the by-election held in May 2000 the Liberal Democrats took the seat with 50.6 per cent of votes, with the Conservatives second on 42.0 per cent and Labour trailing (and losing their deposit) on a paltry 3.7 per cent. The result suggested massive tactical voting by former Labour voters and perfectly illustrated the electoral pay-off from enhanced cooperation between Labour and the Liberal Democrats, since Romsey was a typical Conservative-held seat in the south of England that Labour could not hope to win. This was the only seat to change hands in any by-election between 1992 and 1997 and the reaction of the Liberal Democrats to their victory was, not unnaturally, euphoric. Kennedy suggested that it was now reasonable to expect that in the next general election the party could hold on to all of its current seats and could set its sights on winning at least an additional 50 from the Tories.[25] Curiously, however, the by-election victory produced no "afterglow" effect in the polls (see below).

Local Elections and European Parliament Elections

Local elections in Britain are held annually in different parts of the country, and their results are widely interpreted as indicators of the national standing of the parties. Moreover, success at local level can provide a springboard for advances in general elections. Unlike in the 1992–97 period, however, the Liberal Democrats did not make spectacular gains in local elections after 1997. Indeed, in each round (1998, 1999, 2000) they suffered a net loss of council seats (doing better, however, in Labour areas in the north of England than in the Conservative-dominated south). By 2000 the total number of Liberal Democrat councillors had fallen to 4,450 and the number of councils controlled was back down to 27. However, the

Liberal Democrats made stronger showings in these elections than they did in contemporary opinion polls. In both 1998 and 1999 their "national equivalent" share of the vote was 25 per cent, and in 2000 it was 27 per cent.[26] There is clear evidence, however, that the Liberal Democrats tend to do better in local than in general elections so that these relatively strong performances were unlikely to be repeated in the general election.[27]

The elections for the new position of London mayor and the new London-wide Assembly in May 2000 provided another potential opportunity for commentators (and the parties themselves) to assess the current standings of the parties among the voters. With around 5 million electors in the capital these elections were significant contests. In fact, however, the mayoral election was dominated by Ken Livingstone, the maverick Labour MP standing as an independent, and little can be read into the fact that the Liberal Democrat, Susan Kramer, widely agreed to be an attractive and effective candidate, obtained only 11.9 per cent of first-preference votes.[28] This compared with the 14.6 per cent of votes that the party had won in London in the 1997 general election. In the Assembly elections voters were asked to vote separately for a constituency representative (the fourteen constituencies being formed by combinations of the 74 parliamentary constituencies) and for a party list. In the constituency voting, the Liberal Democrats won 18.9 per cent of the votes (but no seats) while in the list voting they had 14.8 per cent. The difference between the two may reflect tactical voting at constituency level or the performance of particularly popular individual candidates. While not disastrous, the Liberal Democrats' performance was far from outstanding, although they could draw satisfaction from the fact that the electoral system used (a version of the additional member system (AMS)) awarded them four seats in the 25–member assembly. Party headquarters probably had similarly mixed feelings in the wake of the elections to the European Parliament held in June 1999. On this occasion the Liberal Democrats won only 12.7 per cent of votes. Yet a proportional representation system was used for this election and ten Liberal Democrats were elected, eight more than they had ever had in the European Parliament.

Scotland and Wales

The first elections for the devolved Scottish Parliament and Welsh Assembly took place in May 1999, again using AMS, with voters choosing a constituency representative and also voting for a regional party list. Besides indicating the levels of support for the Liberal Democrats in the areas concerned, these elections had important consequences in terms of relations with Labour. In both countries the constituency voting showed a small increase in support for the party as compared with the general election — from 13.0 per cent to 14.2 per cent in Scotland and from 12.3 per cent to 13.5 per cent in Wales. All constituencies won in the general election were held and one more was added in each case.[29] Support in the voting for party lists was slightly lower (12.4 per cent and 12.5 per cent respectively) but enabled the party to add five additional representatives in Scotland and three in Wales.

The Liberal Democrats thus emerged from the Scottish elections with seventeen seats in a Parliament of 129 members (MSPs). Labour had 56 seats, the SNP 35, the Conservatives eighteen and the others three so that the Liberal Democrats were in a position to hold the balance of power. It had been anticipated that no party would have an overall majority in the Parliament and, given developments in party relations at U.K. level (as well as marked hostility between Labour on the one hand and the SNP and Conservatives on the other), a Labour–Liberal Democrat arrangement was the obvious solution to the problem of providing a government for Scotland. Negotiations between the two parties began almost immediately, and shortly afterwards the two Scottish party leaders, Donald Dewar and Jim Wallace, issued a joint statement ("Partnership for Scotland") stating that they were "determined to serve the people of Scotland by working together in partnership in the Parliament and in Government". In short, a coalition government was formed in which the Liberal Democrats had two cabinet positions — Jim Wallace as deputy first minister and minister for justice and Ross Finnie as minister for rural development — as well as two junior posts. The biggest stumbling block to coalition was the issue of student tuition fees. These had been introduced by the Labour government in London, but the Liberal Democrats had campaigned strongly for their abolition in Scotland. In the event, the issue was fudged and the joint programme agreed between the parties announced that a committee of inquiry would be set up to make recommendations on the issue. The joint programme also included a commitment to make progress on introducing proportional representation in Scottish local government elections. With their inclusion in the Scottish executive, the Liberal Democrats had their first-ever taste of government above local level. During the next two years they could claim some successes in influencing policy in Scotland. Perhaps most notably, tuition fees for Scottish students were indeed abolished.

The Welsh Assembly elections also resulted in no party having an overall majority. Somewhat surprisingly, Labour fell three seats short of the 31 required for a majority while the Liberal Democrats won six seats. In this case Labour initially decided to go it alone as a minority administration, but the first year of the Assembly was not a happy one, largely because the original first secretary, Alun Michael, appeared to have been foisted on Welsh Labour by the London leadership and was unable to shrug off the impression that he was Blair's man in Cardiff. In February 2000, however, Michael resigned and was replaced by his previous rival for the leadership, Rhodri Morgan. In the following October there was an almost exact re-run of earlier events in Scotland. Morgan and the leader of the Welsh Liberal Democrats, Michael German, issued a joint statement ("Putting Wales First") outlining an agreed programme and setting up a "partnership government". German became deputy first secretary and minister

Table 6.7 Trends in Liberal Democrat Support, 1997–2001

	1997 %	1998 %	1999 %	2000 %	2001 %
Jan		14	14	15	14
Feb		15	14	16	15
Mar		15	13	14	14
Apr		15	14	14	13
May	17	14	15	15	13
June	14	15	16	15	
July	14	16	14	14	
Aug	13	14	15	15	
Sept	14	16	15	18	
Oct	12	16	14	18	
Nov	14	14	14	15	
Dec	15	14	15	15	

Source: MORI website.

Note: The figures shown are means of all published polls in the month concerned; that for May 1997 is the general election result, and that for May 2001 is derived from four polls conducted before the date of the election was announced.

for economic development while another Liberal Democrat, Jenny Randerson, joined the Welsh cabinet as minister for culture, sport and the Welsh language. In the partnership document it was even intimated that an independent committee would be set up to investigate "options for tackling problems inherent in the current system of student maintenance and support".

By the end of 2000, therefore, the Liberal Democrats were playing a significant part in the government of Scotland and Wales — a major development for a party that, in previous incarnations, had not played a significant role in government since 1922. Both countries exhibited the "new politics" of cooperation in action and to some extent were acting as testing grounds for what might be possible at national level. There were costs to be borne, however. By firmly allying themselves with Labour, the Scottish and Welsh Liberal Democrats appeared to be virtually ruling themselves out as an alternative for disenchanted Conservatives. Moreover, if the Scottish and Welsh governments became unpopular, it was likely that the Liberal Democrats as well as Labour would suffer. Finally, it is likely that being widely perceived as being in bed with Labour in Scotland and Wales would make it more difficult for the Liberal Democrats to campaign credibly against Labour, at least within those two countries.

Opinion Polls

There are difficulties in using by-elections, local elections and devolved elections to estimate the likely support for parties in general elections. They are episodic, take place in specific parts of the country and are increasingly likely to be affected by idiosyncratic local influences. Monthly opinion polls provide more reliable

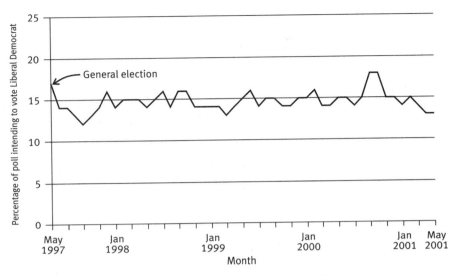

Figure 6.1 Liberal Democrat Share of Monthly Voting Intentions

Source: MORI website.

evidence of trends in party support over the country as a whole. Table 6.7 shows the mean monthly share of voting intentions obtained by the Liberal Democrats between 1997 and 2001 and the data are presented in graphical form in Figure 6.1. After the general election, as is customary, Liberal Democrat support declined somewhat, reaching a low of 12 per cent in October 1997. Thereafter, as the graph illustrates, it is difficult to imagine a clearer case of a party's support "flatlining". As suggested above, the party's share of vote intentions was not affected when Kennedy replaced Ashdown in late 1999 and, indeed, only twice strayed outside a very narrow band of 13 per cent to 16 per cent. In the autumn of 2000, at the time of the fuel tax protests, the government became unpopular and the Liberal Democrats benefited, scoring 18 per cent in successive months. Eight individual polls in late September put them at 20 per cent or more. This surge created a sense of euphoria at the party conference, leading Lord Razzall, campaigns chairman, to declare, "Order the champagne for the day after the election. We will be celebrating winning more seats and more votes than in 1997."[30] As a hostage to fortune, this ranks with David Steel's famous call to delegates at the 1981 Liberal Assembly to "go back to your constituencies and prepare for government" (the party won seventeen seats in the next election).[31] Wiser heads were more cautious, including that of Lord (Chris) Rennard, the party's campaign guru, who restricted himself to pointing out that their poll ratings were stronger than they had been before the 1997 election, that they usually made progress during the campaign and that they might expect to benefit from an "incumbency effect" in the seats that were won for the first time in 1997. In any event, the autumn 2000 surge in support for the Liberal Democrats proved temporary and from November to early May support returned to around the level that had been sustained from late 1997.

CONCLUSION

The Liberal Democrats could enter the 2001 general election campaign in reasonable heart. Relations with Labour remained difficult and controversial within both parties, but, despite the loss of a popular leader, the Liberal Democrats appeared to have a solid core of support among the electorate which had been maintained at about 15 per cent for most of the previous four years. Their position in the last three months before the election was called was similar to what it had been in 1997, though the slight downward trend was unsettling. In addition they remained a significant force in local government, had more members of the European Parliament than ever and were partners in ruling coalitions in Scotland and Wales. With a Labour government in power, support for the Liberal Democrats had not evaporated, as some had feared it might. However, advances in Europe and the devolved institutions were achieved under a more proportional electoral system and reform of the Westminster system — the key to the creation of a new kind of politics and, in particular, to the long-term role of the Liberal Democrats — remained an only slightly less distant prospect than ever. In its election manifesto, Labour promised only to "review" the operation of the electoral systems introduced for Scotland and Wales, and also the Jenkins report, in order "to assess whether changes might be made" to the Westminster system. As on previous occasions, the best hope for movement in this direction was for the Liberal Democrats to win enough seats in the general election either (optimistically) to hold the balance of power in the House of Commons or (more realistically) to convince Labour doubters that they were a formidable electoral ally. It remained to be seen, however, whether previous experience would be repeated and the Liberal Democrats would gather momentum during the campaign and convert generalized support into seats. It was also unclear whether the party would benefit from tactical voting as it had done in 1997. In that election Labour supporters had a strong incentive to vote tactically in seats where the Liberal Democrats were in second place: it was a means of removing the Conservatives from office. In 2001, however, Labour were in government and were expected to win the election comfortably, so that the need to vote tactically against the Conservatives was less pressing. Overall, much rested on the genial shoulders of Charles Kennedy. As yet untested as party leader in a general election, only time would tell whether he could emulate Paddy Ashdown's successful *bravura* campaigning style and lead the party into a renewed dialogue on the left of British politics.

NOTES

1. Quoted in David Butler and Dennis Kavanagh, *The British General Election of 1997* (Basingstoke: Macmillan, 1997), 68.
2. See Alan Leaman, "Ending Equidistance", *Political Quarterly* 69 (1998): 160–9.
3. Paddy Ashdown, *The Ashdown Diaries Vol. 1 1988–97* (London: Allen Lane The Penguin Press, 2000).
4. See John Curtice and Michael Steed, "The Results Analysed", in Butler and Kavanagh, *The British General Election of 1997*, 309–10.
5. David Denver, Gordon Hands and Simon Henig, "Triumph of Targeting? Constituency Campaigning in the 1997 Election", *British Elections & Parties Review* 8 (1998), 171–90.
6. Curtice and Steed, "The Results Analysed", 309.
7. *Daily Telegraph*, May 3, 1997.
8. *Hansard*, May 14, 1997: col. 71.
9. The full text of the Blair/Ashdown statement can be found in the *Guardian*, November 12, 1998.
10. Philip Cowley and Mark Stuart, "The poodle gives a nip", *Guardian*, November 27, 2000.
11. See David Denver, "The Centre", in Anthony King, ed., *Britain at the Polls 1992* (Chatham, N.J.: Chatham House, 1992), 101–28.
12. *Guardian*, July 23, 1998.
13. A full account of Ashdown's resignation and the subsequent leadership contest can be found in Keith Alderman and Neil Carter, "The Lib-Dem Leadership Election", *Parliamentary Affairs* 53 (2000): 311–27.
14. The Liberal Democrat members' survey, which had 2,866 respondents, was conducted by Patrick Seyd and Paul Whiteley, who kindly supplied these data.
15. *Guardian*, June 11, 1999.
16. Liberal Democrats, *Manifesto Booklet*, Leadership Election 1999.
17. Reported in the *Guardian*, September 21, 1998.
18. Alderman and Carter, "The Lib-Dem Leadership Election", 321.
19. *Guardian*, March 20, 2000.
20. *Guardian*, March 21, 2000.
21. *Guardian*, September 19, 2000.
22. *Daily Telegraph*, April 10, 2001.
23. Steve Richards, "The best way to get Tony's attention is stay successful", *Guardian*, August 10, 1999.
24. Local government statistics are taken from Colin Rallings and Michael Thrasher, *British Electoral Facts 1832–1999* (Aldershot: Ashgate, 2000), 245–6.
25. *Guardian*, April 11, 2000.
26. Local elections take place in different parts of the country each year and never encompass the whole of Britain. Nationwide levels of support for the parties can, therefore, only be estimated. The estimates quoted here are from Rallings and Thrasher (*British Electoral Facts*, 247).
27. See Colin Rallings and Michael Thrasher, "Split-Ticket Voting at the 1997 British General and Local Elections: An Aggregate Analysis", *British Elections & Parties Review* 8 (1998), 111–34.
28. The supplementary vote system was used to elect the London mayor with voters casting both a first and second preference vote.
29. In addition, the fact that the Orkney and Shetland constituency was split into two enabled the Liberal Democrats in Scotland to pick up an extra seat in the Scottish Parliament.
30. *Guardian*, September 20, 2000.
31. Quoted in Ivor Crewe and Anthony King, *SDP: The Birth, Life and Death of the Social Democratic Party* (Oxford: Oxford University Press, 1995), 140.

CHAPTER 7

Why Labour Won — Again

John Bartle

NEW LABOUR HAD triumphed in 1997. The party was swept to power by the largest swing to any party since 1945, won more seats than ever before and obtained the largest majority that a Labour government had ever had.[1] In some ways, however, Labour's second victory in June 2001 represented an even greater triumph. As Table 7.1 shows, the party was returned to office with a slightly reduced share of the vote, down from 44.4 to 42.0 per cent. Yet the swing to the Conservatives, at a mere 1.8 per cent, was one of the smallest swings since 1945. Labour's haul of 412 seats in the House of Commons, represented a net loss of just six seats compared with 1997. The party's landslide majority was therefore barely touched. After the dust had settled, Labour had a majority of 167 seats over all other parties in the new House of Commons.

Labour's triumph was all the greater on this occasion because it could not rely on an intensely unpopular Conservative government or the easy promises of opposition to win support; it had to govern and be held accountable for actions that affected the lives of every man, woman and child in the country. If it failed, there was every reason to believe that it would be punished and its term in office would be short. Moreover, if the past record was any guide, there was every reason to expect that Labour would fail. Every previous Labour government had been

Table 7.1 Results of the 2001 General Election

	Share of vote (Great Britain)			Seats in Parliament (United Kingdom)		
	Vote 1997	Vote 2001	Change 97–01	Seats 1997	Seats 2001	Change 97–01
Labour	44.4	42.0	-2.4	418	412	-6
Conservative	31.5	32.7	+1.2	165	166	+1
Liberal Democrat	17.2	18.8	+1.6	46	52	+6
Others	6.9	6.5	-0.4	30	29	-1

Source: House of Commons Library Research Paper 01/54, Table 1e, 15.

associated with one economic crisis or another, a devaluation of the currency, runaway inflation or bitter industrial disputes. Every Labour government since 1964 had similarly failed to deliver on their promise of a more caring society in which there would be opportunity for all and high quality public services. Viewed from this side of the June 2001 election, it is all too easy to forget that Labour leaders like Tony Blair and Gordon Brown were haunted by the knowledge that Labour had so often failed in the past.

When judged in historical terms — or more specifically in terms of its own history — Labour's second victory was undoubtedly impressive. Tony Blair, Gordon Brown, John Prescott *et al.* had achieved what Clement Attlee, Hugh Gaitskell, Harold Wilson, James Callaghan and all those other towering figures in Labour's past had failed to do: they had won a second full term in office. Yet, impressive as Labour's victory was, it was rather less impressive than had looked likely for virtually the whole of its first term. This is shown by Figure 1.3 (p. 41), which displays trends in party support from 1997 to 2001. On the basis of the findings illustrated in the figure, Labour was better placed to win an election than any other government since the war. Even the short-lived petrol crisis in September 2000 did little to hinder Labour's almost stately progress. In the whole of the first five months of 2001 the polls suggested an average share of 49 per cent for Labour, 31 per cent for the Conservatives and 14 per cent for the Liberal Democrats. This represented an astonishing additional 2 per cent swing from the Conservatives to Labour since the 1997 general election and, if projected into an election, would have produced a Labour majority of 224 in the House of Commons. By the time that Tony Blair on May 8 finally made his short journey to Buckingham Palace to request a general election, virtually every commentator in the land expected Labour to win.[2] For most people the only real question was the size of the majority.

However, when judged by the benchmark of the mid-term polls Labour's actual 42.0 per cent share of the vote in June 2001 begins to look disappointing. The Liberal Democrats' performance, in contrast, looks like a minor triumph. They increased their vote share by 1.6 points compared with 1997 and made a net gain of six seats. Charles Kennedy had every reason to be pleased with his party's performance: centre party representation in the new House of Commons would be at its highest since 1929, when David Lloyd George led the old Liberal Party.

Whatever benchmark is chosen, the Conservatives' performance appears uniformly disastrous. They barely improved on their disastrous performance four years earlier. Their share of the vote nudged up only 1.2 points, from 31.5 to 32.7 per cent, and they made a net gain of just one seat (and then only because they recovered Tatton, the seat that the "anti-sleaze" candidate Martin Bell had won in 1997). The 2001 general election represented the Conservatives' second worst performance in terms of share of the vote since 1832 and second worst performance in terms of seats in the House of Commons since the Liberal landslide of

1906. Worse still, though they gained a solitary seat in Scotland, they became the fourth party in terms of vote share north of the border and once again failed to win a single seat in Wales. The Conservative Party's claim to be the party of the union looks increasingly tenuous.

Viewed from another perspective, Labour's landslide share of the vote also looks somewhat less impressive. Its share of the vote among the eligible electorate fell to just 25 per cent, compared with 31 per cent in 1997. According to this measure, Labour's victory represented a less than emphatic endorsement of either the party's programme or its record in office. While voters may have indicated their general satisfaction with Labour in the polls, fewer than ever before were prepared to pay the small cost of a short walk or a missed television programme to ensure a second Labour term. The result hardly appeared the mandate or "instruction" to deliver that Tony Blair had asked voters to give him before the election.

The outcome of the 2001 general election sets a series of puzzles. Why did Labour enjoy such unprecedented leads in the polls for four years? Why did Labour win more votes than the Conservatives? Did the polls overestimate Labour support as they did in 1992 and 1997, or was the discrepancy between the polls and the final vote a result of differential turnout? Why did a 4-point reduction in Labour's lead result in roughly the same outcome in terms of seats? Finally, why did so few voters participate in the June 2001 general election? The answers to all these puzzles will require a deal of research, but in the meantime the evidence from the national opinion polls and the constituency results should make it possible to make a start towards explaining these puzzles. The answers provided in this chapter must be regarded as provisional; but there is little reason to suspect that deeper analysis will produce markedly different answers.

THREE APPROACHES TO THE 2001 GENERAL ELECTION

Any account of "why Labour won" logically involves three inter-related questions. First, why did any given individual vote for one party rather than another? What social, psychological or political characteristics appear to differentiate a Conservative from a Labour voter or a Conservative from a Liberal Democrat? Second, why did Labour receive so many more votes than either the Conservatives or the Liberal Democrats? What factors contributed most to Labour's victory? Third, how did the first-past-the-post electoral system translate votes into seats?

The next three sections examine three different approaches to explaining individual vote decisions. Each approach adopts a very different perspective on the election. The "sociological approach" assumes that political preferences are determined by voters' socio-economic characteristics and that there is overwhelming continuity of political preferences. The "campaign approach" assumes that voters make their decisions during the campaign itself after listening to the arguments of the parties and acquiring enough information to arrive at a reasonable decision. The "political approach" steers a middle course between the sociological and campaign approaches. It maintains that election outcomes are neither set in sociological stone nor greatly influenced by the formal campaign; instead they are determined both by the performance of the government and the decisions of the opposition parties.[3] Since this represents by far the most plausible approach to the study of general elections, this chapter will explore this approach in depth. However, before proceeding any further it is necessary to assess what the sociological and campaign approaches have to say about the 2001 general election.

A Sociological Approach

The sociological approach suggests that both political behaviour and political opinion have their origins in voters' socio-economic characteristics. It assumes that the interests of one group (employees, taxpayers or homeowners) inevitably conflict with those of another (employers, welfare beneficiaries or council tenants). Voters support a particular party to express both their agreement with its values and disagreement with others. According to other accounts, however, group behaviour results from a more tribal sense of "belonging" that does not presume any negative feelings towards other groups.[4] In either case, however, it is assumed that people with common identities, interests and experiences tend to speak together and that political conversation sustains shared values. Group loyalties are also reinforced by the activities of the parties themselves, who tailor their programmes to appeal to such groups and then provide an organization capable of mobilizing them on election day itself.

Analyses of general elections often begin by examining how politically relevant social groups divide their support between parties. It has long been assumed, for example, that younger voters, the working class, council tenants, trade-union members, those who are employed in the public sector or are dependent on state benefits, northerners, the Scots and Welsh represent what might be thought of as Labour's core vote. These groups are commonly referred to as "Labour's heartlands". It has equally long been assumed that the middle class, owner-occupiers, those who work in the private sector and southerners constitute the Conservatives' core vote.[5] These groups are commonly referred to as "middle England".

The terms "Labour's heartlands" and "middle England" convey valuable information about voting behaviour. However, many voters possess some social characteristics that incline them to one party and others that incline them to another. The behaviour of such "cross-pressured" voters is not predictable on the basis of social characteristics alone. Moreover, the sociological approach tends to assume that it is natural or even inevitable for certain groups to support one party rather than another. Yet both New Labour and the old Tory Party chose to portray themselves as parties that transcended sectional interests and served all groups. But the most important limitation to the sociological approach is empirical. It is simply that it is increasingly difficult to predict the political preferences

Table 7.2 Socioeconomic Characteristics and the Vote

	1992			1997			2001			Swing '97–'01	Swing '92–'01
	Con	Lab	Lib	Con	Lab	Lib-Dem	Con	Lab	Lib-Dem		
Gender											
Male	40	37	20	30	49	14	34	46	14	+3.5	-7.5
Female	46	34	17	30	49	16	33	46	16	+3.0	-12.5
Age											
18–34	43	36	18	25	54	19	37	48	12	+9.0	-9.0
35–54	47	32	19	28	51	19	32	45	16	+5.0	-14.0
55+	48	36	15	35	47	15	33	46	16	-1.0	-12.5
Social Class											
Professional & managerial (AB)	59	16	21	36	36	21	43	33	19	+5.0	-16.5
Routine white-collar (C1)	50	27	20	31	46	18	35	40	14	+5.0	-14.0
Skilled manual (C2)	38	41	18	28	58	9	31	57	10	+2.0	-11.5
Unskilled manual (DE)	30	50	15	24	58	12	25	56	16	+1.5	-5.5

Source: King, *New Labour Triumphs,* 11; ICM and the British Election Study.

Note: The table shows the percentage of each socioeconomic group voting Conservative, Labour or Liberal Democrat.

of any individual on the basis of social characteristics (and in particular social class) alone.[6] Indeed, support for the Liberals and Liberal Democrats — which increased sharply in the 1970s and has not returned to previous levels — has defied characterization in purely sociological terms. They draw their support from all age groups, all social classes, just about all regions and both the private and public sector.[7] Whether the rise of the Liberal Democrats was the cause or consequence of this social dealignment is much debated; but the essential truth, that British politics is far less tribal than in the past, is not.[8]

Table 7.2 makes a first pass at assessing how social groups divided their support between the parties on June 7, 2001. Unfortunately, the polling companies have not made detailed information on the behaviour of certain groups such as homeowners, trade-union members and those who work in the private or public sectors available.[9] The data for 1997 are based on figures previously reported in *New Labour Triumphs,* while the data for 2001 are based on responses to the ICM survey carried out between May 31 and June 1.[10] This poll suggested a very slight half a per cent swing to the Conservatives since 1997, compared to the 1.8 per cent swing that actually occurred in the general election.[11] Together with virtually every other survey in the campaign, this poll overstated Labour support prior to the election. However, the ICM survey has the virtue of overstating Labour's lead by one of the lowest amounts (just four points) of any survey conducted during the 2001 campaign. The overestimate of the Labour vote should not therefore greatly distort the findings.

The first thing to note about Table 7.2 is that it shows that support for Labour in 2001 was remarkably consistent across all the age groups.[12] The young, the middle aged and older voters all gave Labour 46 per cent of the vote, plus or minus two points. However, between 1997 and 2001, those aged between 18 and 34 swung from Labour to the Conservatives by 9 per cent while those aged 35 to 54 swung by 5 per cent and the oldest age group swung hardly at all. This finding is exactly what one would expect from a theory of party identification. This suggests that the more political experience voters accrue, the more likely they are to form an attachment to a party and the less likely they are to be influenced by "short-term" factors. Recent research has found a great deal of support for this argument. Around 44 per cent of voters aged 18 to 34 do not identify with a party at all, compared with just 15 per cent among those aged 55 or over.[13] It is unclear what short-term factors may have been responsible for this swing among the young. Labour's introduction of student loans (an unpopular decision among the very young, who make up a large portion of this group) may be part of the explanation, but it may also simply reflect the tendency of younger voters to swing whichever way the country is swinging — but more so.[14]

Table 7.2 demonstrates that men and women divided their support in exactly the same way in 2001. Both gave Labour around 46 per cent of the vote and both swung by about 3 points since 1997 to the Conservatives. Although there was talk, before the election, that Labour might become the "natural party of women" — like the Democrats in the United States — this did not materialize.[15] However, it is worth noting that between 1992 and 1997, the swing among women from Conservative to Labour was 13 per cent, compared with just 8 per cent among men. Although New Labour eliminated the old gender gap which meant that women favoured the Conservatives in 1997, it has not subsequently established a new gap in its favour.

Table 7.2 also examines the voting behaviour of various occupational groups. It demonstrates that, as usual, Labour performed best among its traditional supporters: skilled and unskilled manual workers, obtaining leads of 26 points among the C2s and 31 points among the DEs. However, Labour also performed well among routine non-manual voters, obtaining a 5-point lead among the C1s, a group that had tended to favour the Conservatives before 1997. The only group that gave the Conservatives a lead in 2001 was the professional, managerial and executive class, the ABs, who divided 43 to 33 in their favour. Between 1997 and 2001 the traditional middle class, the ABs and C1s, swung to the Conservatives by 5 per cent, while the traditional working class, the C2s and DEs swung more modestly by about 2 per cent. This swing between 1997 and 2001, therefore, served to increase the differences between the classes, despite earlier reports that the class differences in voting behaviour might have vanished altogether.[16] However, the consequences of this apparent polarization must not be overstated. The more instructive comparison is the voting behaviour of these groups in 1992

Table 7.3 Three Nations

	1997					2001						
	Turn-out	Con	Lab	Lib Dem	Nat	Turn-out	Con	Lab	Lib Dem	Nat	Change in turnout	Swing '97–'01
Regions of England												
South East	73.7	41.4	31.9	21.4		61.3	42.6	31.7	21.6		-12.4	-0.7
South West	74.9	36.7	26.4	31.3		64.9	38.5	26.2	31.2		-10.1	-1.0
London	67.6	31.2	49.5	14.6		55.2	30.5	47.3	17.5		-12.4	-0.8
East Midlands	73.2	34.9	47.8	13.6		60.9	37.3	45.1	15.4		-12.3	-2.5
West Midlands	70.8	33.7	47.8	13.8		58.5	35.0	44.8	14.7		-12.4	-2.1
East Anglia	74.4	38.7	38.3	17.9		63.7	41.7	35.8	19.0		-10.7	-2.8
North West	69.9	27.1	54.2	14.3		55.3	28.3	51.8	16.5		-14.6	-1.8
Yorkshire	68.3	28.0	51.9	16.0		56.7	30.2	48.6	17.1		-11.6	-2.7
Northern	69.4	22.2	60.9	13.3		57.6	24.6	55.7	17.1		-11.8	-3.8
Nation												
Scotland	71.3	17.5	45.6	13.0	22.1	58.1	15.6	43.9	16.4	20.1	-13.2	+0.1
Wales	73.4	19.6	54.7	12.4	9.9	61.6	21.0	48.6	13.8	14.3	-11.8	-3.8
England	71.4	33.7	43.6	17.9		59.2	35.2	41.4	19.4		-12.0	-1.4

Source: Butler and Kavanagh, *The British General Election of 1997;* BBC Online.

and 2001. Between 1992 and 1997 the middle class swung much more heavily to Labour than the working class. The relatively small difference in swing back to the Conservatives among the middle classes between 1997 and 2001 therefore did little to increase the distinctiveness of the classes. Over the period between 1992 and 2001, the ABs swung by 16.5 per cent and the C1s by 14.0 per cent in Labour's favour, compared with a mere 5.5 per cent swing among DEs. The 2001 general election witnessed a very slight reversion to pre-1997 levels of class voting, but it would still be thoroughly misleading to suggest that British society is deeply class-ridden or that social class is in any way the fundamental basis of party politics. The middle class remains disproportionately Conservative, but it is no longer a Labour-free zone, as it was during much of the 1980s.

While there was a very mild reversion in the class basis of the vote, there was a continued decline in its regional basis.[17] This decline is illustrated by Table 7.3, which examines voting behaviour by the eleven "standard regions". As in 1997 Labour's support was greatest in its geographical heartlands (the North, North West and Yorkshire) and weakest in much of the South (the South East, South West and East Anglia). However, between 1997 and 2001 the swing to the Conservatives in Labour's heartlands exceeded that in the South, further reducing regional polarization. The Liberal Democrats again performed well in their own heartland of the South West, despite polling evidence that the party had lost a great deal of support to Labour between 1997 and 2000.[18]

The outcome of the general election in Scotland merits particular attention. Support for the Scottish National Party (SNP) fell back by 2 points compared with 1997 and the party suffered a net loss of one seat. The SNP also performed considerably less well than it had in the 1999 elections to the Scottish Parliament, when it received 29 per cent of the constituency vote. The 2001 election therefore appears to confirm the evidence of recent polls that, while people are prepared to vote for the SNP in elections to Holyrood, they are less willing to vote for it in elections to Westminster. For the moment at least, devolution appears to have stopped the tide of nationalism in its tracks. The Liberal Democrats, who feared that their coalition with Labour would lead to their being punished for the Scottish executive's failings, must have been pleasantly surprised by the results. Their share of the vote increased by three points compared with 1997. The reasons for this progress are not clear, but it may be that their trenchant advocacy of increased spending on public services appealed to the Scots, who are thought to be more collectively minded than voters elsewhere in Britain.

However, it is the fate of the Conservative Party in Scotland that deserves most attention.[19] Throughout the 1950s the Conservatives were a strong — if not the strongest — force in Scottish politics. In 1979 the party had 22 MPs north of the border. As late as 1992 it still had ten MPs. Yet from 1997 to 2001 not a single Conservative sat for a constituency north of the border. The parlous state of the Conservatives in Scotland was emphasized by the relief that was expressed when the party won a single seat, Galloway and Upper Nithsdale, in 2001. However, this news was immediately soured by the realization that by the end of the night the Conservatives were the fourth party in Scottish politics — not just in terms of seats — but in terms of share of the vote, receiving just 15.6 per cent. The Conservatives are not just in fourth place because of the electoral system but because they genuinely are the fourth choice among Scottish voters. The Tories appear to be in a state of terminal decline in Scotland.

There are other geographical features of the 2001 general election worth emphasizing. For the second election in a row, the Conservatives failed to win seats in the following inner cities: Leeds, Sheffield, Birmingham, Leicester, Sunderland, Newcastle, Coventry, Glasgow, Cardiff and Liverpool. In 2001 the Conservative Party remained a predominantly rural and suburban party. The appearance of foot and mouth disease in the countryside appears to have had little effect on the outcome. The swing to the Conservatives in rural seats does not appear to have been much higher than in urban seats, though they did well in some badly affected constituencies such as Penrith and the Border.[20]

As Table 7.4 (p. 172) shows, Northern Ireland once again proved to be another country altogether. While the rest of the United Kingdom was drearily choosing political moderation, Northern Ireland made what appeared to be a positive choice for conflict. It was the only part of the United Kingdom where turnout actually rose, from 67.1 to 68.0 per cent. It was also almost the only part of the country where support for extremism rose. On the nationalist side of the divide Sinn Féin gained two additional seats to take their tally up to four. Sinn

Table 7.4 Northern Ireland

	Share of vote (Northern Ireland)			Seats in Parliament (United Kingdom)		
	Vote 1997	Vote 2001	Change 97–01	Seats 1997	Seats 2001	Change 97–01
Ulster Unionist	32.7	26.8	-5.9	10	6	-4
Democratic Unionist	13.6	22.5	+8.9	2	5	+3
Sinn Féin	16.0	21.7	+5.7	2	4	+2
SDLP	24.2	21.0	-3.2	3	3	0
Alliance	8.0	3.6	-4.4	0	0	0
Others	5.5	4.4	-1.1	1	0	-1

Source: House of Commons Library Research Paper 01/54, Table 1f, 16.

Féin also, for the first time ever, polled slightly more votes than the moderate Social Democratic and Labour Party. On the Unionist side, Ian Paisley's Democratic Unionists gained an additional three seats, taking their tally up to five, while the more moderate Ulster Unionists under David Trimble lost four seats. The non-sectarian Alliance Party of Northern Ireland could not match the performance of its British sister party, the Liberal Democrats. Its share of the vote fell by 4.4 points and it won no seats.

A Campaign-based Approach

A brief analysis of the sociology of the vote provides some clues about those factors that caused individuals to support one party or another at the 2001 general election but leaves many questions unanswered, simply because social characteristics alone account for little of the variation in political preferences. In theory the formal campaign is thought to be important, since it provides voters with sufficient information, argument and debate to arrive at a reasonable vote decision. The following section, therefore, adopts a rather different temporal perspective and enquires what effect the four-week campaign appears to have had on voters' decisions.

The first task is to assess what actually changed during the four-week campaign. The average results from the four major polling organizations taken before May 8, suggested that Labour had the support of 49 per cent of voters, the Conservatives 33 per cent and the Liberal Democrats 13 per cent.[21] Table 7.5, which displays the average share of the polls during each week of the campaign, suggests that there was hardly any change at all until the final week, when Labour slipped three points and the Liberal Democrats moved up four points. On June 7 Labour actually received 42 per cent of the vote, the Conservatives 33 per cent and the Liberal Democrats 19 per cent. If the original baseline of the polls is to be believed, Labour lost 7 points during the campaign, while the Liberal Democrats gained 6 and the Conservatives made no progress at all. A straightforward

Table 7.5 The Campaign Polls, May 8 to June 7, 2001

	Labour	Conservative	Liberal Democrat
Week 1	49	32	14
Week 2	49	30	14
Week 3	49	30	15
Week 4	46	31	18

Note: The table shows the percentage share of each party averaged from all published opinion polls in those weeks.

interpretation of this evidence is that the Liberal Democrats recruited an extra 1.5 million voters during the four weeks of the campaign.[22]

If the evidence of the polls is taken at face value, then it appears that the only party able to claim that it "won" the campaign was the Liberal Democrats, the party that had least to spend on complex market research and communications. By contrast, the well-equipped Labour party machine at Millbank appears to have "lost" the campaign, while the equally well-equipped Conservatives at Central Office had no effect at all. It appears that voters were won over by some combination of Charles Kennedy's charm, the Liberal Democrats' "honest" approach to taxation and public spending, their ability to stick to their preferred agenda of public services, and focusing on the last-minute tactical voting decisions.

This simple analysis, however, probably overstates the amount of campaign change that took place. There is evidence, for example, that pre-election polls overstate support for Labour and understate support for the Liberal Democrats. To some extent this is a result of the hypothetical nature of the question, which asks, "If there were a general election tomorrow, which party would you vote for?" When asked outside an election campaign, some voters quite simply forget about the Liberal Democrats, since they receive far less coverage in the media than the two major parties. When the question is asked, moreover, voters are not made to think about the tactical situation in their constituency. This may inflate Labour's support while deflating support for the Liberal Democrats, because these two parties may be seen as effective substitutes for anti-Conservative voters. Some evidence that Labour and the Liberal Democrats were so seen is provided by MORI. In the run up to the general election MORI asked, "How do you intend to vote in the General Election on June 7?" When nominations closed, however, MORI presented voters with a ballot paper showing the names and affiliations of the candidates in their constituency. This change in methodology coincided with an increase in support for the Liberal Democrats of about 3 or 4 points and a decrease in support for Labour of a similar amount. This suggests that a great deal of the campaign change occurred as voters worked out which party was best placed to defeat the Conservatives, but it hardly suggests that voters were persuaded by the arguments of the parties.

There is another possible explanation of the difference between Labour's lead in the polls and its actual lead on election day itself that should be examined. Towards the end of the campaign, when it appeared that Labour was on course for another landslide victory, the Conservatives urged voters to act to reduce Labour's majority and "wipe the smile off Tony Blair's face". While there is little evidence that many voters did switch to the Conservatives, there is some indication that the polls may have somewhat reduced the Labour vote. Late in the campaign ICM asked, "Does the prospect of another Labour landslide make you more or less likely to vote Labour or does it make no difference?"[23] While there was some evidence of a "bandwagon" effect, with some 5 per cent replying "more likely", far more, 14 per cent, said the prospect would make them "less likely" to vote Labour. It is not possible to determine the exact effect that anticipation of another Labour landslide had on voters. It may have had some impact on sophisticated voters, but its main effect may have been to persuade a small number of Labour voters that they could stay at home on June 7.

It would, therefore, appear unwise to think that all of the apparent 7-point decline in support for Labour and the 6-point rise in Liberal Democrat support are "real" or the result of voters responding to arguments raised or information acquired during the campaign. Some of this change was the entirely predictable effect of variations in the election context. Some of this apparent change may also be simply the result of a tendency for the national polls to overstate support for Labour for other reasons.[24] It is quite possible that the polls have overstated Labour support for a considerable time and this is a possibility that the polling industry will clearly wish to investigate.

In the meantime it is very clear that the campaign itself does not provide an explanation of why Labour received so many more votes than the Conservatives. The factors that contributed to Labour's victory were in place long before the campaign was announced, long before a campaign poster was launched and long before a party election broadcast was aired. Any examination of political factors must therefore adopt a somewhat longer temporal perspective and examine the actions of the parties between 1997 and 2001.

A Political Approach

In the wake of the 1997 general election, one commentator observed that, "There is an old saying in British politics: 'Oppositions don't win elections. Governments lose them'". He went on to add, "Like so many old sayings, this one needs to be rephrased. It should read: 'Governments are capable of losing elections — but only if there is an Opposition party available that people are willing to vote for.'".[25] It is the contention of this chapter that the 2001 general election provides further support for this general proposition. The outcome of this election was not set in sociological stone nor was it greatly influenced by the four-week campaign. Instead the election was both won and lost in the long haul between May 2, 1997 and June 7, 2001. The outcome of the election represented a *political* evaluation of the parties.[26]

WAS NEW LABOUR CAPABLE OF LOSING THE ELECTION?
The Economy: Restoring a Tarnished Reputation?

Throughout its long history Labour has been regarded as a caring party, one that wished to do many noble things such as reduce poverty, create full employment and provide high-quality public services. Yet, equally throughout its history, Labour has been regarded as an incompetent party, one that messed things up, that produced industrial chaos, soaraway inflation and a devalued currency. While Labour governments have often been thought to be desirable in the abstract, they have been thought to involve a great deal of risk. In a competition between a caring but incompetent Labour Party and a less caring but undoubtedly competent Conservative Party, the latter had almost invariably triumphed at the polls. The emergence of what political scientists have referred to as "the Conservative century" therefore undoubtedly owed much to the perception that they were more competent than Labour.

So Labour's path to power in 1997 required it to reassure voters, many of whom had never voted Labour in the past, that the party could be trusted to manage the economy. In opposition Tony Blair and Gordon Brown had sought to achieve this by re-writing Clause 4, the basic statement of the Labour Party's aims and objectives. They further sought to reassure former Conservative voters by promising that "key elements of the 1980s trade union reforms" would be preserved and that they would "take no risks with inflation".[27] They also promised that there would be no "return to penal taxes" and therefore pledged not to increase the basic or top rates of income tax.[28] Their faith in Conservative economic competence having been shattered by the events of Black Wednesday, many voters decided that the risk of a Labour government was worth taking. However, even as Gordon Brown occupied his desk in the Treasury, many voters still expressed residual doubts as to whether Labour would increase taxes and let inflation rip. In a Gallup survey in late April 1997, 67 per cent of voters indicated that they were concerned that inflation "might rise sharply" under a Labour government and 64 per cent thought that "taxes might go up so much that people would be squeezed financially".[29]

Once settled in the Treasury Gordon Brown further reassured voters and financial markets alike by giving the Bank of England control over interest rates and announcing that Labour would stick to planned public spending limits for its first two years in office. These announcements served to further reassure former Conservatives that Labour did not represent a threat to their standards of living. This is illustrated in Table 7.6, which displays voters' responses to the following

Table 7.6 One Nation

"Some people say that all political parties look after certain groups and are not so concerned about others. How closely do you think that the Conservative/Labour Party looks after the interests of ..."

Percentage saying very closely or fairly closely

	Conservative			Labour		
	1987	1997	2000	1987	1997	2000
The middle class	84.9	79.3	84.8	57.6	80.9	73.0
The working class	38.0	28.6	33.1	88.8	90.8	69.6
The trade unions	22.2	17.6	16.5	93.0	83.8	59.7

Source: The British Election Studies 1987, 1997, and British Election Panel Study, 2000.

question, "How closely do you think that the Conservative/Labour Party looks after the interests of the _____ class/trade unions?" In 1987, 89 per cent of voters thought that Labour looked after the interests of the working class either "very closely" or "fairly closely", while only 58 per cent thought that it looked after the middle class "very" or "fairly" closely, a difference of some 31 points. By 1997 91 per cent thought that Labour looked after the working class, but fully 81 per cent thought that it looked after the middle class; the gap thus closed to just 10 points. By 1997, therefore, voters' perceptions of Labour's basic socio-economic stance had been transformed and its claim to be a "one nation" party that transcended sectional interests looked plausible.[30] By mid-2000 the proportion thinking Labour looked after the middle class had fallen to 73 per cent, but this was still far higher than in 1987.

One consequence of committing Labour not to raise the basic or top rates of income tax was that Brown was forced to find funds for the public services from other forms of taxation. He achieved this by a number of expedients: increasing duties on alcohol and cigarettes, abolishing some tax concessions for pension funds and advance corporation tax. As Table 7.7 shows, each of Brown's individual budgets was popular with the electorate and certainly more popular than any budget introduced by the Conservatives between 1992 and 1997. The first budget in 1997 was enormously popular. Fully 82 per cent thought it was "fair", even though a small majority thought that they would be worse off; large majorities approved of the decisions to reduce VAT on domestic fuel to 5 per cent and to increase spending on the NHS by £1.2 billion. The only budget measure of which people emphatically disapproved was the decision to increase petrol by 4p per litre. The data displayed in Table 7.7 suggest that the 1998 and 1999 budgets were similarly popular. However, by 2000 the public had grown less enthusiastic. While 26 per cent thought that the budget would be good for themselves personally, some 49 per cent thought that it would be bad, yielding a net score of −21. Moreover, while 42 per cent agreed that the budget would improve the state of the economy in the long term, 39 per cent disagreed, yielding a net score of

Table 7.7 Assessments of Labour's Budgets

(a) "Do you think the Budget is a fair one or not?"

	Fair	Not fair	Don't know	Net approval
1997	82	12	5	+70
1998	65	31	3	+34
1999	–	–	–	–
2000	55	38	7	+17
2001	71	23	6	+48

Source: Gallup Political and Economic Index, various dates.

(b) "From what you know, or have heard of, do you think the Budget proposals are a good thing… for you personally…for the country as a whole?"

	Self				Country as a whole			
	Good	Bad	DK	Net	Good	Bad	DK	Net
1997	29	37	34	-8	56	20	24	+36
1998	33	39	28	-6	57	22	26	+25
1999	36	42	22	-6	46	33	21	+13
2000	26	49	25	-21	48	27	25	+21
2001	42	30	28	+12	52	25	23	+27

Source: MORI website, various dates.
Budget 1997: www.mori.com/polls/trends/budgeteffect.shtml.
Budget 1998: www.mori.com/polls/1998/t980323.shtml.
Budget 1999: www.mori.com/polls/1999/t990322.shtml.
Budget 2000: www.mori.com/polls2000/t000328.shtml.
Budget 2001: www.mori.com/polls/2001/t010327.shtml.

(c) "On balance, do you agree or disagree with the statement that in the long term, the government's budget will improve the state of Britain's economy?"

	Agree	Disagree	Don't know	Net
1997	–	–	–	–
1998	54	29	17	+25
1999	49	32	19	+17
2000	42	39	19	+3
2001	48	36	16	+12

Source: See Table 7.7b.

(d) "Are you satisfied or dissatisfied with the way Gordon Brown is doing his job as Chancellor of the Exchequer?"

	Satisfied	Dissatisfied	Don't know	Net
1997	–	–	–	–
1998	56	24	20	+32
1999	50	33	17	+17
2000	48	37	15	+11
2001	55	32	13	+23

Source: See Table 7.7b.

+3, the lowest evaluation. Pensioners in particular felt aggrieved by the decision to increase pensions by only 75p in the year 2000/1 and there were growing signs that voters resented the relentless increase in petrol tax. Labour's lead in the polls accordingly slid in 2000, as did satisfaction with Gordon Brown as chancellor.

Perhaps the most important consequence, however, of the Blair/Brown strategy of reassurance was that it brought a measure of economic success. Inflation, which had threatened to get out of control, fell within the government's target band and averaged 2.3 per cent in the first five months of 2001. Interest rates, which had increased from 6 per cent in May 1997 to 7.5 per cent in June 1998 were progressively cut from October 1998 onwards.[31] By April 2001 they stood at 5.5 per cent. Since many people have variable-rate mortgages or sizeable loans, these cuts led to an increased sense of economic optimism. The "feel-good factor", the difference between those thinking that their personal financial situation would get better and those thinking that it would get worse, averaged +11 points in the first five months of 2001; these were exactly the sorts of conditions that had allowed Conservative governments to feel confident of victory in 1983 and 1987. Moreover, unemployment continued to fall throughout Labour's first four years in office. By spring 2001 the "misery index", the simple sum of inflation and unemployment, was at its lowest level for 30 years.[32] On the eve of the general election campaign the *Daily Telegraph* admitted that, "things can't get any better for Blair".[33]

Not only the Conservative press took note of the state of the economy: so did the electorate. In late April 1997, shortly before the 1997 election Labour led the Conservatives as the best party to handle the issue of unemployment by fully 30 points; by 2001 this had increased to 48 points.[34] Indeed, 34 per cent of Conservative voters thought Labour best on this issue by 2001. In 1997 Labour actually trailed the Conservatives as the best party to handle the problem of inflation by 3 points.[35] However, by 2001 Labour had moved into a 30-point lead. Again, even one in five Conservative voters thought Labour best on the issue of inflation.[36] Labour had demonstrated to former Conservative voters that they would not allow inflation to erode the value of their savings. Labour had a little less success on the issue of taxation. In 1997 Labour also enjoyed a narrow 7-point lead on taxation. This had grown by 2001, to 16 points.[37] Nevertheless, Labour received high marks for delivering on its economic promises. This is illustrated in Table 1.3 (p. 24), which displays responses to the following question, "There is a lot of talk at the moment about whether the present Government is or is not 'delivering'. From what you know, do you think that it is or is not delivering on each of the following?" In August 2000 Labour was widely thought to have delivered on its economic promises. Some 62 per cent said that Labour had delivered on its promises of "getting people back to work", while 47 per cent agreed that Labour had put an end to the "boom and bust economic cycle".

Delivery on the economy fed through into more general perceptions of

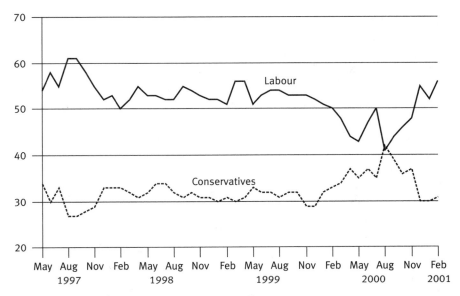

Figure 7.1 Evaluations of Economic Competence, 1997–2001

Source: Anthony King and Robert J. Wybrow, *British Public Opinion, 1937–2000: The Gallup Polls* (London: Politico's, 2001), 118–19; *Gallup Political and Economic Index,* April 2001, Issue no. 489.

Labour's economic competence. When voters in 1997 were asked "With Britain in economic difficulties, which party do you think could handle the problem best — the Conservatives under _____ or Labour under _____?" In April 1997 Labour enjoyed a lead of 6 points (44 to 38 per cent).[38] However, in contrast with all other Labour governments, this lead was consolidated in office. Figure 7.1, sets out responses to this question for every month between May 1997 and May 2001. With the sole exception of the petrol crisis in September 2000 Labour continued to enjoy sizeable leads on this measure. Its lead averaged 28 points from May to December 1997, 21 points in 1998, 22 points in 1999 and 12 points in 2000 (still higher than in 1997). After the short-lived petrol crisis, it rallied again and averaged 23 points in the first five months of 2001. No wonder that Tony Blair paid the following tribute to his chancellor: "The Labour Party could not have won a bigger political prize than, in a single Parliament, to be so firmly established as the party of economic competence."[39]

In recent years it has become fashionable to think that votes are primarily influenced by the state of the economy. Indeed the phrase, "It's the economy, stupid" has been elevated into a sort of eleventh commandment for political scientists, journalists and campaigners alike. However, this assumption has been questioned by recent British experience. To be sure, the argument fits the British case in 1987 when a buoyant economy helped secure Thatcher's third victory, but the Conservatives won in spite of a recession in 1992 and lost in 1997 despite a booming economy.[40] Labour undoubtedly received some reward for its economic record in 2001. Yet previous studies have suggested that many of those voters who felt that their standard of living had risen wisely attributed this to their own hard work — or the success of previous Conservative chancellors — rather than Gordon Brown's skilful management of the economy.[41] If such perceptions existed, they almost certainly reduced Labour's electoral reward. Moreover, as economic problems such as unemployment were solved, they were replaced by renewed concerns about the state of the National Health Service, education and transport. Paradoxically, Labour's new-found reputation for fiscal prudence and in particular its decision to stick within Conservative expenditure plans prevented it from delivering on the public services. In Britain, therefore, another old saying needs to be rephrased to read, "It's the economy *and public services,* stupid".[42]

The Public Services: Making Things Better?

When MORI asked voters in their twentieth-century poll "Which two or three achievements by government would you say have contributed most to British life?" their answers left little doubt that most Britons were attached to the public services. Fully 46 per cent (and 49 per cent of Conservative voters) named "the introduction of the NHS" and 18 per cent (including 18 per cent of Conservative voters) named "establishing the welfare state" as the most important achievements of government.[43] Other public services such as "expanding higher education" and the introduction of state pensions also figured high on the list. Yet, as proud as many people were of the public services, the state of services was a matter of growing concern in Britain by the mid 1990s. It was widely felt that the Conservatives had allowed them to be run down. As economic problems such as unemployment were solved, voters indicated that "health care" and "education" were the "most important issues facing Britain today".

The 1997 Labour manifesto had promised to save the NHS and Tony Blair had maintained that his three priorities for government were "education, education, education". Unsurprisingly, therefore, when Gallup asked Labour voters in May 1997 to select from a list of things that might happen under a Labour government, 90 per cent selected the option "Labour will improve public services like the NHS and education".[44] However, it was here that Labour's desire to establish its economic competence became a double handicap. It forced Gordon Brown to increase "stealth taxes" on petrol, cigarettes, alcohol and pension funds to raise revenue. Voters noticed and often resented these taxes, particularly those relating to petrol.[45] By the time of the 2001 election around 62 per cent of voters agreed with the proposition that Labour had introduced a lot of "hidden taxes".[46] Brown's fiscal prudence also meant that increases in spending on the NHS and education were limited and simply not sufficient to improve these services noticeably. Waiting lists in the NHS remained stubbornly long and the media continued to be awash with horror stories of lengthy waits to see doctors, bed shortages and patients waiting on trolleys in corridors. Unsurprisingly, many voters doubted that Labour was saving the NHS. In February 2000, only 28 per cent thought that Labour was delivering on improving the NHS while 71 per cent thought that it was not.[47] Labour was failing to live up to the expectations of its supporters: core Labour voters and former Conservatives alike.

Voters were undoubtedly disappointed in Labour's performance in relation to the public services. However, the party largely escaped punishment for its failures. Many voters thought that the problems of the public services were not necessarily Labour's fault. When voters were asked in January 2000, "Which one of the following do you think is most to blame for the current crisis in the NHS?", 17 per cent blamed Tony Blair and 13 per cent blamed Frank Dobson, the former secretary of state for health, while only 3 per cent blamed Alan Milburn, the new minister in charge. However, fully 42 per cent blamed Thatcher, someone who had had no responsibility for the NHS since she left office in November 1990![48] Gordon Brown's long-awaited comprehensive spending review, which finally announced substantial increases in spending, also appears to have reassured voters that Labour was beginning to tackle the problem of underfunding in the NHS. In February 2000 Labour had scored −43 on this "net delivery" index, but as Table 1.3 (p. 24) shows, this had risen dramatically to −18 by August 2000. Labour was still a disappointment but not as large a disappointment. Moreover, no matter how disappointed voters were in the Labour government few thought the Conservatives would be any better. When voters were asked which party was best to handle the issue of the NHS in May 2001 Labour enjoyed a lead of 28 points over the Conservatives. This was way down on the 54-point lead that it had enjoyed four years earlier but still impressive. The apparent lack of an alternative cushioned Labour from the full impact of the public's wrath.[49] However, continuing public concern about the state of the health service resulted in one nasty surprise for Labour on election night. In the constituency of Wyre Forest in the West Midlands, Richard Taylor — a former hospital consultant — stood as an Independent candidate opposing the downgrading of Kidderminster hospital's facilities. In a stunning result, he received 58.1 per cent of the vote, became only the second Independent MP elected in the last twenty years and sent a clear message about the importance that voters attach to local services.

The slippage between expectation and delivery undoubtedly contributed to the erosion of Labour's approval ratings. Figure 1.2 (p. 19) displays Labour's approval ratings. The average net approval ratings gradually deteriorated from 1997 through to 1999. Had assessments of Labour's performance on the economy not been so good, then the large poll lead that it enjoyed throughout 1999 and 2000 might have eroded more rapidly, particularly as Labour lost its reputation for honesty and trustworthiness. By 2000, the critics outnumbered the cheerleaders and its net approval ratings fell to an average of –8. Labour maintained its impressive lead in the polls not as a result of great faith in the government but for want of a credible opposition. Had Labour faced a more credible opposition, its position would have been jeopardized.

The Tax-and-spend Conundrum

The 2001 campaign focused on the issues of tax and spending — at times almost to the exclusion of any other issue. Therefore, it seems appropriate to discuss whether the balance that New Labour struck was the most appropriate in the circumstances. When Gordon Brown announced the results of the spending review in the House of Commons on July 18, 2000 he claimed:

> We have made our choice: improved investment in health, education, transport and social services, and in our communities. It is now for those who oppose our spending plans to state clearly where their cuts would fall. This government has been prudent for a purpose. Our choice is stability, employment and sustained long-term investment into the next Parliament, to create a Britain of security and opportunity for all.[50]

This strategy laid the foundation for economic growth and a remarkable transformation in voters' assessment of Labour's competence. It also posed the Conservatives with a real problem: to explain just how they could cut taxes without harming the services. Yet by sticking to the Conservatives' spending plans Brown delayed a much-needed injection of funds into the NHS and education. A great deal of survey evidence suggested that many Britons were prepared to pay higher taxes in order to improve public services. In both June 1997 and March 1998 ICM asked voters, "Which of the two would you most prefer the Labour government to do: (a) honour their election pledge to stick to the Conservatives' tax and spending plans even if it means limiting spending on public services, or (b) spend more on public services even if it means breaking the pledge on tax and spending?"[51] In June 1997 38 per cent chose honouring the pledge and 55 per cent breaking it. In March 1998 the figures remained broadly similar, with 36 per cent choosing honouring the pledge and 56 per cent breaking it. This appears good evidence that voters were prepared to contemplate higher taxes in the early part of Labour's first term. Moreover, it is supported by additional evidence from Gallup in Table 7.8, which suggests that voters were prepared to pay higher taxes to fund public spending. Indeed, if Table 7.8 is to believed, in 2001, a majority — 55 per cent — of Conservative voters were prepared to pay higher taxes to fund public services.

Table 7.8 also suggests that public enthusiasm for increased spending and taxes had *decreased* after four years of Labour government (as indicated by the decline in the net score from +65 to +55).[52] In part this decline may have been the

Table 7.8 Taxation versus Government Spending

Question: "People have different views about whether it is more important to reduce taxes or to keep up government spending. How about you? Which of these statements comes closest to your own view?"

	1997	May 14–15, 2001			
	All	All	Con	Lab	Lib Dem
Taxes should be cut, even if it means some reduction in government services, such as health, education and welfare.	7	11	20	8	6
Things should be left as they are.	18	20	21	22	11
Government services such as health, education, and welfare should be extended, even if it means some increases in taxes.	72	66	55	68	82
Don't Know.	3	3	4	2	1
Net support for increases in spending and taxes	+65	+55	+35	+60	+76

Source: Gallup website at
http://www.gallup.com/Poll/Surveys/2001/Topline010515/index. asp.

result of the "stealth taxes" experienced by voters, but it also may have stemmed from the realization that increased spending did not necessarily produce improvements. In August 2000, just after Gordon Brown had outlined the results of his spending review, Gallup asked, "From what you know, do you think the extra money will or will not actually bring about real improvements in the quality of the NHS, the education service, the roads and public transport over the next few years?" While 60 per cent thought that the new spending would bring about improvements in the public services, fully 35 per cent thought that it would not.[53] It may be that voters are far too sophisticated to measure the quality of the public services only by what is spent on them. Moreover, alternative ways of measuring attitudes revealed far less support for increased spending. Rasmussen, for example, used a computer to read out questions to respondents who were asked to type in a number on their telephone to indicate their response. This method, designed to reduce the tendency to give socially desirable responses, appears to have done just that. At the same time that the majority of voters were telling Gallup that they were prepared to pay higher taxes, 42 per cent were telling Rasmussen that they wanted taxes and spending kept as they were and only 21 per cent wished to increase taxes and spending. In this survey fully 34 per cent wished taxes and spending to be reduced.[54] This evidence provides a very different impression of the electorate's appetite for extra taxes from that contained in Table 7.8, even though these polls were both conducted at approximately the same time during the 2001 campaign. Moreover, if Labour had broken its pledge not to raise the top and basic rate of taxes, public trust might have snapped. The pledge on income tax was probably unnecessary in 1997, but sticking to it between 1997 and 2001 may well have been vital, particularly if Labour had been faced with a stronger challenge from the Conservatives.

In the face of less than overwhelming evidence that voters are prepared to pay higher taxes, Gordon Brown may have been wise in 2001 to repeat his pledge not to raise the basic and top rates of income tax. The problem for Blair government — indeed all governments — is that voters have conflicting considerations when it comes to tax and spending. It is therefore difficult to take any simple yardstick as a perfect measure of those attitudes. Some indication of this ambivalence is provided by voters' responses to slightly different questions about tax and spending.[55] In May 1997, for example, Gallup found that 85 per cent of voters approved of a policy of "a penny on income tax to be spent on education", but at the same time 59 per cent said that they wanted "no increase in any rates of income tax".[56] In Britain it is certainly the case that "it is economy *and the public services* stupid", but this revelation is not news — and does little to assist chancellors as they make their budget judgements and struggle to reconcile the public's appetite for both higher spending and lower taxation.

A New Style of Politics: Whiter than White?

Labour replaced a Conservative government that had gained a reputation for sleaze and scandal at a time when public levels of trust in politicians appeared to have reached an all-time low; but, as Anthony King has shown in Chapter 1, Labour quickly ran into its own problems with sleaze. In a MORI poll for the *Mail on Sunday* in July 2000, 34 per cent "strongly agreed" and 26 per cent "tended to agree" with the statement "Tony Blair is more concerned with image than with dealing with the real issues."[57] The issue of delivery became increasingly linked to Labour's reputation for spinning and media manipulation. Slow progress coupled with superb spinning combined to produce a growing sense that, in the words of William Hague, New Labour was "all spin and no delivery".

Further evidence of Labour's fall from grace comes from responses to the following question, "Do you think the Government has, on balance, been honest and trustworthy?" During the final phases of the last Conservative government in March 1997 only 29 per cent — most of them were Conservative voters — thought that the government was "basically honest", while 67 per cent thought that it had been basically dishonest, a net score of −38. This question was asked regularly from mid-1998 and the responses are displayed in Figure 1.2 (p. 19). Initially voters thought that Labour had, on balance, been basically honest. The average net-scores for 1998 and 1999 were +14 and +6 points respectively. By 2000 however, the net score fell to −12 as the drip-drip of scandals took their toll and as the media increasingly examined the claims of Labour achievement. In the first four months of 2001 Labour's net score averaged –9, indicating that long-term damage had been done.

Yet again, had Labour faced more credible opposition, this deterioration in Labour's reputation would probably have reduced support for Labour in the national opinion polls and at the subsequent general election. In January 2001 voters were asked, "Do you think the current Labour government is more or less sleazy than the previous Conservative government or is there no difference between the two?" Only 12 per cent thought Labour was "more sleazy" than the Conservatives, while 30 per cent thought it "less sleazy" and fully 54 per cent thought that there was no difference.[58] The Conservatives were unable to take advantage of examples of Labour sleaze simply because many voters thought the Conservatives would be even worse.

Broadly speaking, voters thought that both major parties were as bad as the other so that this contributed little to Labour's lead compared with 1997. The increased concern with the style of politics may have contributed a little to the rise in support for the Liberal Democrats who gained a reputation for honesty throughout the campaign (see below). Revealingly, in a post-election survey 91 per cent of all voters agreed with the suggestion that, in the next term, Labour "place more emphasis on practical achievements and less on presentation".[59] The main effect of these developments may have been to increase cynicism and further depress turnout.

Unity and Strong Leadership?

If voters were asked which party, the Conservatives or Labour, was the most united before 1992, it was a good bet that most would opt for the Conservatives. Just as the Labour Party had a reputation for economic incompetence, so too it had a reputation for being a divided party, whose members were permanently at each others' throats. By contrast it was often said that the Conservative Party's secret weapon was loyalty. Conservative leaders stuck together in order to keep the socialists out. After 1992, however, something odd happened. For these purposes, the Labour Party became the Conservative Party and vice versa. Tony Blair and New Labour gained an enviable reputation for discipline and staying on message, while John Major's Conservatives gained a well-earned reputation for being permanently at each others' throats, particularly over the issue of Europe.[60] Since, other things being equal, it is better to be united rather than divided, the perception that Labour was more united was thought to have contributed to Labour's victory in 1997.

These perceptions are reflected in Figure 7.2, which displays responses to the question, "Do you think that the _____ Party is united or divided at the present time?" The graph displays the "net unity" score, which is calculated by subtracting the proportion thinking a party is "divided" from the proportion

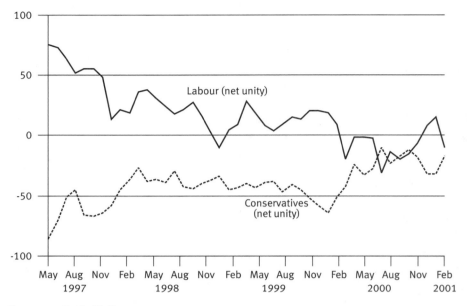

Figure 7.2 Party Unity, 1997–2001

Source: King and Wybrow, *British Public Opinion, 1937–2000: The Gallup Polls,* 37–51; *Gallup Political and Economic Index,* April 2001, Issue no. 489.

thinking it is "united". It can quickly be seen that the trend lines for the two parties slowly converged. Not only does the Labour line trend toward zero, so does the Conservative line. The relentless stories of cabinet splits and disputes about the selection of candidates for the mayor of London and the leader of the Welsh Assembly eroded Labour's reputation for unity and being on message. Conversely the fact that the Conservatives no longer had to make decisions about Europe helped to improve public perceptions of that party. By early 2001 Labour was perceived to be only slightly more united than the Conservatives, but they still went on to win the election. Figure 7.2 therefore appears to contain an important lesson for the Conservatives. Simply being on message does not appear to be enough to win elections. The party must also have a message that voters like.

In 1997 many observers believed that favourable evaluations of Tony Blair had contributed to Labour's victory. However, subsequent research suggested that Tony Blair as an individual, net of all other factors, resulted in a modest advantage of around six seats.[61] During the early years of the Labour government, Blair's "net approval ratings" (those approving of his performance as prime minister less those disapproving) far exceeded the net approval ratings for his government as a whole. The extent to which Blair represented an asset is illustrated in Figure 7.3,

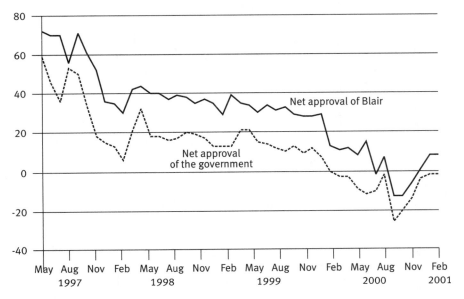

Figure 7.3 The Declining Pull of Blair, 1997–2001

Source: King and Wybrow, *British Political Opinion, 1937–2000: The Gallup Polls,* 177–8, 197–8; *Gallup Political and Economic Index,* April 2001, Issue no. 489.

which shows that his approval ratings ran constantly ahead of the government's until their third year in power. However, as time wore on the difference between approval ratings for both government and leader diminished.[62] It appears that, even if Blair was a modest asset to the party in the early stages of the government, the magnitude of this advantage diminished over time.

So Was the Government Capable of Losing?

The evidence examined so far presents a mixed picture. By early 2001 many voters thought that Labour had done well in managing the economy. Gordon Brown had gone a long way to restoring Labour's reputation as a party of economic competence and reassuring former Conservatives. However, Labour had disappointed voters by failing to produce substantial changes in the NHS, education and public transport. The fact that many voters were willing to blame the previous Conservative government for the problems of the public services suggests that they thought Labour needed more time to put things right. However, it is clear that more voters agreed with Labour's campaign slogan "a lot to do" than with the words that appeared immediately before it in the slogan "a lot done". Moreover, after four years in office Labour was thought to be little more honest and little less sleazy than the previous Conservative government. Labour's reputation for honesty, trustworthiness and unity having been eroded and Tony Blair's personal appeal having diminished, it appears only fair to conclude that Labour was capable of losing the election. But was there an opposition party that voters thought worth voting for?

WAS THERE AN OPPOSITION WORTH VOTING FOR?

"Governments are capable of losing elections, but only if there is an opposition party worth voting for." In 2001 the first condition may well have been satisfied; the second most certainly was not. Even though many voters were critical of the Labour government, they were less than convinced by the Conservative opposition. Some rather direct confirmation of this proposition was found in responses to a question posed by Gallup in May 2001, "[Do you agree or disagree that] the Labour government isn't up to much but the Tories don't offer a real alternative?"[63] Fully 61 per cent of all voters (including 59 per cent of Labour voters) agreed with this statement. However, a rather more detailed exploration of the Conservative Party's image is required in order to understand fully why so many agreed.

THE CONSERVATIVES
The Conservatives and the Economy: Losing Credibility

The Conservatives dominated British politics throughout the twentieth century at least in part because they were thought to be the party of economic competence: the party that understood money. This long-term advantage vanished in September 1992 when Britain was forced to leave the ERM. From September 1992 through to the general election in 1997 the party trailed behind Labour. The long shadow of Black Wednesday hung like a pall over the Conservative Party as evidenced by this (unprompted) explanation offered by a self-employed bricklayer and former Conservative voter.

> Then we had the ERM debacle, interest rates went doolally, the building industry couldn't operate, I had to take a 50 per cent pay cut overnight and my mortgage went up £150 a month. I went to Germany looking for work but that didn't pan out very well so, for a time, we had to rent out the home and move in with [his wife's] parents just to hang on to [the home]. She took a job as a cleaner to help make ends meet. So that's why I finished with the Tories, and it's never again so far as I'm concerned.[64]

During the 1997 campaign Labour posters sought to remind voters of Black Wednesday. Many Conservative politicians contented themselves with the knowledge that Labour would fail in office. Yet New Labour did not fail on the economy and Gordon Brown had become the most well-respected chancellor since polling had begun, according to Gallup.[65] William Hague and his shadow chancellors (first Francis Maude, later Michael Portillo) were like snooker players glued to their chairs as their opponent cleared the table of balls. They could do little but wait for Labour to make a mistake, but as the parliament wore on it became increasingly obvious that Labour would not make a serious misjudgement about the economy. As Philip Norton has noted in Chapter 3, the Conservatives made increasingly frantic efforts to make their economic policies more attractive, initially by pledging a "tax guarantee" (subsequently abandoned) and then by promising both to match Labour's spending plans and to cut taxes (including a popular promise to cut petrol tax). However, these proposals were counter-productive. They served to underline the widespread suspicion that the Conservatives did not really believe in the public services. Moreover, the pledges were not believed in themselves. In May 2001 Gallup asked voters, "The Conservatives say they can cut taxes by 8 billion pounds while keeping to the present Government's plans for increased spending on the NHS and education. Do you or do you not believe that a Conservative government, by saving money elsewhere, could combine tax cuts and increased spending in this way?"[66] Fully 68 per cent of all voters and nearly one in three (32 per cent) Conservatives doubted that this trick could be pulled off. Moreover, while many voters resented the petrol tax increases, the same survey revealed that a majority (54 per cent) of all voters thought that the Conservative proposal to reduce this tax would not be "the fairest way of reducing taxation".[67] Not only were the Conservatives thought to lack credibility, they were thought to lack heart as well.

The Conservatives and the Public Services: Safe in Our Hands?

Labour offered the Conservatives little scope to improve or retrieve their reputation for economic competence. However, Labour's failure to deliver on the public services, the issues that were uppermost in voters' minds, did offer opportunities to an appropriately positioned opposition. In fact, William Hague and the Conservatives did try to highlight Labour's failings. During the campaign itself they launched one poster showing a pregnant Tony Blair with the slogan "Four years Labour and he's still to deliver". Another poster showed a picture of a harassed nurse with the question, "You paid the taxes so where are the nurses?"; another a picture of a housewife walking through a dark housing estate asking, "You paid the taxes so where are the police?"

These attacks helped undermine Labour's already tarnished reputation for delivery. However, it is unlikely that they rebounded to the Conservatives' credit. The party's self-evident attachment to tax cuts did little to reassure voters that it really did wish to improve the public services. When Gallup asked in May 2001 which party was best able to handle the issue of the NHS, the Conservatives trailed Labour by 28 points. On education the Conservatives trailed by 26 points. Although many voters were disappointed with Labour, little about the Conservatives reassured them that the public services would be safe in their hands.

Unsurprisingly, a MORI poll in January 2001 found that only 16 per cent of voters thought that the public services would "get better" under the Conservatives while 32 per cent thought that they would "get worse".[68] The Conservative Party found itself out of touch with some of the deepest instincts of the British electorate.

A Not So Popular Populism: Europe and Asylum Seekers

Having abandoned much of the centre of British politics to Labour, the Conservatives tried to campaign on a series of populist issues where they appeared to enjoy an advantage. In particular, the Conservatives chose to emphasize their opposition to the European single currency, an issue that was thought to appeal not only to its core voters but to Labour voters on council estates too.

In opposing a single currency the Conservatives appeared to be speaking for Britain, since poll after poll indicated that some 60 per cent or so of the public would vote against a single currency in a referendum. However, emphasizing the single currency created several problems. One problem was that it simply made the Conservatives look rather odd. From January to May 2001 only 4 per cent of voters on average thought that Europe was the most important issue facing Britain, compared with 28 per cent on average who thought the same of the NHS. Instead of addressing the issues of greatest concern to voters — education and health — the Conservatives spent a great deal of time talking about what appeared, to most voters at least, a peripheral issue. Another problem was that as the campaign developed the Conservative position became increasingly bizarre. William Hague argued that Labour's guarantee of a referendum prior to entry was a device by which voters would be "duped" into entering the single currency: an argument that appeared to reveal a poor view of the average voter and further illustrated how out of touch the Conservative Party was. The final and greatest problem, however, was simply that the Conservatives had misread public opinion. Voters were not, on the whole, hostile to Europe. If asked whether they would support entry in a survey most answered "no", but when they were given more subtle choices — which matched those they were offered in the election — a more complex and variegated pattern of responses emerged. For example, when presented with three options on the single currency 14 per cent chose "definitely join" (roughly the Liberal Democrats' policy), while 47 per cent chose "wait and see how it develops" (roughly Labour's policy) and only 38 per cent chose "definitely stay out" (roughly the Conservatives' policy).[69] As with the tax-and-spend issue, many voters were deeply ambivalent about Europe. Even though 77 per cent of Conservative voters told Gallup that they would vote no in a referendum, 35 per cent said that "Britain should probably join the euro at some point, but not yet".[70]

The tendency of the party, its leaders, its activists and its supporters in the media to emote obsessively about the issue and dramatize the consequences of adopting the euro ("just ten days to save the pound") had many undesirable consequences. It simply made the Conservatives look out of touch. A Gallup survey in June 2001, for example, found that 65 per cent agreed that Conservative leaders "go on too much about Europe".[71] Talking about Europe served to underline divisions in the party and undermine its reputation for unity during the campaign. These divisions also reminded voters that the most popular Conservative leaders — Michael Heseltine and Kenneth Clarke — fundamentally disagreed with their party's position on the single currency and could not bring themselves to serve in Hague's shadow cabinet. Revealingly, 81 per cent of voters (including 69 per cent of Conservative voters) agreed with the proposition that "Conservatives do not have a strong team of leaders".[72]

Another supposedly "populist" issue that the Conservatives chose to emphasize was that of asylum seekers. The number of asylum seekers reaching Britain had risen sharply between 1997 and 2001 and had become an important issue in some areas of the country, such as Dover, where many of those claiming asylum entered Britain. The Conservatives enjoyed a sizeable 10-point lead on the issue of which party could best deal with the problem of asylum seekers and Conservative canvassers reported that the issue played well on the doorstep.[73] However, yet again the polls suggested that the asylum seekers issue was a secondary one for most voters. From January to May 2001, only 5 per cent of voters on average reported that asylum was the most important issue facing Britain. The Conservatives' "populism" did not appear to be so popular after all.

The Leadership Question

Many commentators were apt to ascribe the Conservatives' failures in the polls at the general election to William Hague's lack of a personal appeal.[74] Critics complained long and loudly that Hague's youth, his premature baldness and even his strong regional accent (he hailed from Yorkshire) all contributed to the Conservatives' woes. If only the Tories could have replaced him with a more acceptable leader, it is suggested, then they would have done much better. Certainly many of the public appear to have held this view. In March 2001 NOP asked voters, "Can you see the Conservatives winning a general election at any time in the future with William Hague as the party's leader, or can they only win by changing the leader?" Only 29 per cent thought that the Tories could win with Hague as leader, while 58 per cent thought that they could not.[75] Hague himself appears to have agreed. In his resignation speech he acknowledged that, "I have been [un]able to persuade sufficient numbers that I am their alternative prime minister", and he went on to argue that the Conservatives needed a leader who could "command a larger personal following in the country".[76]

At face value, both the public and William Hague appear to be right. Figure 7.4 shows that William Hague was considered the third best prime minister in Britain until Paddy Ashdown was replaced as leader of the Liberal Democrats,

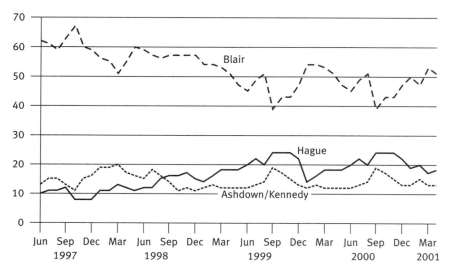

Figure 7.4 The Best Prime Minister, 1997–2001

Source: King and Wybrow, *British Political Opinion, 1937–2000: The Gallup Polls,* 203-4; *Gallup Political and Economic Index,* April 2001, Issue no. 489.

after which he was merely second best, lagging far behind Tony Blair. Surveys revealed that he was considered less "tough", less likely to "understand people like me" and to have less "personality" than Blair. However, Hague was considered less "arrogant" than Blair, while the Labour leader suffered from the allegation that he had "more style than substance".[77] The idea that Tony Blair was particularly popular or that the Conservatives could have faired much better had they simply replaced Hague with a personally more attractive leader is implausible. The Conservative Party's problems long pre-dated Hague. Suspicions about the Conservatives and the public services stretch back as far as the Thatcher governments, and doubts about the Conservatives' economic competence stretch back to Black Wednesday. Moreover, while there is much speculation about the impact of leaders' personalities in Britain, no one has ever demonstrated that they have much impact on vote decisions net of basic values, policy preferences and evaluations of the economy. Nor has anyone ever demonstrated that leaders' personalities have a significant impact on election outcomes net of all those other factors.[78] To be sure, voters thought that Tony Blair would make a better prime minister than William Hague, but these evaluations are almost entirely predictable on the basis of voters' predispositions, policy preferences and evaluations of party competence. William Hague was not the Conservative Party's problem. Quite the reverse: the Conservative Party was William Hague's.

The Labour government was vulnerable in June 2001. However, the Conservatives were unable to take advantage of the fact. Yet in 2001 at least some of those who were disappointed by the Labour Party chose another option: the Liberal Democrats.

THE LIBERAL DEMOCRATS: THE "NONE OF THE ABOVE" PARTY

To the surprise of many commentators it was the Liberal Democrats who had a minor triumph at the 2001 general election. Not only did they increase their share of the vote to 18.8 per cent, their highest vote since 1987: they managed to make a gain of six seats and were the only party to apparently gain support during the campaign. Liberal representation in the House of Commons now stands at its highest level since 1929. It is therefore worth speculating about the reasons for their success.

A simple reason why the Liberal Democrats retained so many seats appears to be a desire among some voters to protect the Liberal Democrat MPs first elected in 1997 (see below). This desire to retain the services of their Liberal Democrat MP may be partly a consequence of the great care that Liberal Democrats take to cultivate a personal vote in a constituency. Evidence from MORI, for example, suggests that, while 72 per cent of those living in Liberal Democrat seats were satisfied with their member of Parliament, only 40 per cent of those living in Labour seats and 38 per cent living in Conservative seats were satisfied.[79] This reason, however, does little to explain why the Liberal Democrats increased their national share of the vote. The most plausible reason for their advance during the campaign appears to be the increased media attention that campaigns bring (see above). In addition, it is clear that the Liberal Democrats' emphasis on improving the public services also contributed to their success. It may also be that their "honest" approach to tax and spending (pledging to raise the basic rate of income tax by 1 per cent and the top rate to 50 per cent) appealed to voters more accustomed to evasion from the other main parties. If these are the reasons for the Liberals' success, then they may have a bright future.

However, there are other reasons for thinking that support for the Liberal Democrats was based in large part on a general hostility to the main two parties. Closer inspection of the data suggests that there is little "issue basis" to Liberal Democrat support. Table 7.9 (p. 194), for example, shows the proportion of voters thinking the party they voted for was best able to handle certain issues. The proportion of Liberal Democrat voters thinking that their party was best able to handle issues is 37 per cent on average across all the six issues, compared with around 80 per cent for the other two parties. Moreover, the lack of faith that Liberal Democrats expressed in their party was not restricted to low-salience issues — such as Europe, where 28 per cent thought the Liberals best — but extended to the core issue of the NHS, where only 46 per cent thought their party was best.

Table 7.9 The Issue Basis of the Vote

"I am going to read out a list of issues facing the country. Could you tell me for each of them which political party you personally think would handle the issue best?"

	Percentage thinking that their party is best		
	Con	Labour	Lib Dem
The National Health Service	69	86	46
Education and schools	71	84	52
Law and order	86	73	28
Europe	84	71	28
Taxation	82	81	45
Inflation	71	85	20
Average	77	80	37

Source: Gallup website at
http://www.gallup.com/Poll/Surveys/2001/topline010523/index.asp.

Even on education, which constitutes one of the Liberal Democrats' most distinctive policy areas, only 52 per cent of Liberals thought their party was best able to handle the issue.

A lot of support for the Liberal Democrats, therefore, appears to take the form of "a plague on both your houses". Some indication that a lot of the support for the Liberal Democrats has this quality is provided by responses to the following question asked by Gallup: "Suppose at this election you had the choice on your ballot paper of a Conservative, a Labour candidate and a Liberal Democrat candidate or none of the above, which would you choose?" When faced with this question fully 24 per cent of all Lib Dem voters chose the "none of the above" option rather than their own party, far higher than the equivalent figures for Labour and Conservative voters (10 and 13 per cent respectively). While the Liberal Democrats' emphasis on adequate funding for the public services and Charles Kennedy's personal appeal clearly played a part, the Liberal Democrats were in many ways, and just as often in the past, the "none of the above party".

FROM A PLURALITY TO A LANDSLIDE

Despite the catastrophic failure of the Conservatives, election night 2001 had little sense of excitement compared with 1997. Four years earlier virtually every declaration had brought news of some terrible catastrophe for the Conservatives and some remarkable gain for Labour or the Liberal Democrats. Indeed the resulting drama had kept many voters glued to their seats until well into the morning. For many weeks after the 1997 election conversations with strangers invariably included the question "Were you still up for Portillo?", referring to the moment when the secretary of state for defence had been defeated at 3 in the morning. In 2001, however, the television monitors told a far less dramatic story.

As seat after seat declared, the screens flashed "Lab Hold" with a monotonous regularity. The day after the election few people could even say "Were you still up for Sunderland South?", the first seat to declare at 10.43 p.m. The sheer tedium of the whole evening's proceedings became the message. It appeared as if the country had made its mind up four years earlier and had chosen to hold to that decision, for the time being at any rate.

Although the constituency results contained none of the drama of four years before, they still told a fascinating story about the British electoral system. Had seats in the House of Commons been distributed in proportion to the vote Labour would have won 269 seats rather than 412; the Conservatives would have won 211 rather than 166 and the Liberal Democrats 122 rather than 52. Labour thus received a substantial "winners' bonus" of 134 seats. As is usually the case, the Liberal Democrats were penalized most, but the Conservatives received 45 fewer seats than they would have done under a purely proportional system. A simple comparison of the 1992 and 2001 general elections illustrates the "pro-Labour" bias in the system. In 1992 a lead of 8 points translated into an overall Conservative majority of 21 seats, while in 2001 a 9-point lead translated into a Labour majority of 167 seats. A 1 per cent larger lead — plus the British electoral system — made all the difference between a government that was permanently vulnerable to rebellion and one with virtually unlimited power.

The sources of this pro-Labour bias are easily understood.[80] Scotland and Wales continue to be over-represented at Westminster — that is, they have "too many seats" in proportion to their populations. Labour is traditionally strong in these nations and so needs fewer votes to win seats than the Conservatives. Similarly, Labour seats tend to have both smaller populations and lower turnouts. Yet again, therefore, Labour needs fewer votes to win those seats and a smaller national vote share to win an overall majority. However, the main — and, in recent years, growing — source of bias is that Labour tends to have a much more effective distribution of its vote, winning seats with smaller majorities and thus minimizing the number of wasted votes.

In 1997 the effective concentration of votes in marginal seats was assisted by a slight increase in anti-Conservative tactical voting.[81] In 2001, however, tactical voting appears to have been less widespread.[82] Nevertheless, tactical voting by Labour voters may have helped the Liberal Democrats retain seats in Bath, Colchester, Kingston and Surbiton, Ross, Skye and Inverness West, and Winchester.[83] Tactical voting may even have helped Labour retain seats such as Conwy, Enfield Southgate, Harwich, and Sittingbourne and Sheppey. However, with the exception of Guildford, Ludlow, Norfolk North and Romsey, tactical voting did not lead to further Conservative losses. Those who said that tactical voting was not important were only half correct: for the Liberal Democrats in particular it made the vital difference between progress and retreat.

Some commentators believed that in 1997 Labour had managed to win so many seats because it had targeted only those that they expected to win and ran skeleton campaigns elsewhere.[84] The party had poured resources, senior figures and party activists into selected constituencies in the effort to win. Evidence relating to targeting in 2001 is more impressionistic, since the parties have not made their target lists publicly available. However, it evident that Labour's vote held up well in its marginal seats. Indeed, in those 22 ultra marginals (where Labour had a majority of 5 points or less) its share of the vote rose on average by 1.4 points, compared with falls of 2 points in "fairly safe" and 4 points in "ultra-safe" seats. It is certainly striking that Labour retained a whole clutch of highly marginal seats such as Kettering, Wellingborough, Milton Keynes North East, Rugby and Kenilworth, Northampton South, Lancaster and Wyre, Harwich, and North West Norfolk, that would have been lost on a uniform swing of 2 per cent.[85] Labour's targeting of seats may therefore have ensured that what the party had won in 1997 it held onto four years later. However, there is little evidence that targeting seats had any effect on propensity to turn out and vote.

A LOW-TURNOUT LANDSLIDE

One of the most striking features of the general election was the dramatic reduction in turnout that took place. Just how dramatic this was can be seen in Table 7.10, which displays turnout figures for the United Kingdom since 1945. The largest previous drop occurred between February and October 1974 when turnout fell by 8.1 points. However, this reduction was largely the result of an ageing electoral register and two elections occurring exceptionally close together. The second most dramatic fall in turnout occurred between 1951 and 1955 when turnout fell by 7.2 points. However, the 1951 election had established a post-war record for turnout. The subsequent fall in turnout to 76.8 per cent can hardly be compared with what happened between 1997 and 2001 when it fell by fully 12 points from 71.4 to 59.4 per cent. In 2001 turnout fell by more than it had ever done before and from its lowest-ever base, to reach its lowest level since 1918.[86] Clearly this remarkable decline is important and requires explanation.

The first thing to note about the decline in turnout is that it was a pervasive phenomenon. To be sure, Table 7.3 (p. 170) does suggest that there were regional variations. The decline in turnout was most marked in North West England and Scotland where it fell by 14.6 and 13.2 points respectively, while the decline was least marked in South West England and East Anglia, where it fell by "just" 10.1 and 10.7 points respectively. The decline in turnout also appears to be particularly marked in safe seats and those constituencies with high proportions of younger voters and the unemployed. This suggests that Labour may have suffered from differential turnout among its core voters and in its heartland seats. However, this effect, if it existed, appears to have been offset to some extent by reduced turnout in constituencies with high levels of owner occupation and the fact that turnout held up in those seats with a higher proportion of non-white

Table 7.10 Turnout in British Elections, 1945–2001

Election	Turnout in U.K.	Change in turnout
1945	75.5	–
1950	83.6	+8.1
1951	84.0	+0.4
1955	76.8	-7.2
1959	78.7	+1.9
1964	77.1	-1.6
1966	75.8	-1.3
1970	72.0	-3.8
1974 (Feb)	80.9	+8.9
1974 (Oct)	72.8	-8.1
1979	77.9	+5.1
1983	72.7	-5.2
1987	75.3	+2.6
1992	77.7	+2.4
1997	71.4	-6.2
2001	59.4	-12.0

Source: House of Commons Library Research Paper 01/54, Table 22, 36.

residents. Indeed, controlling for prior variables, the decline in turnout was no greater in Labour-held seats than Conservative seats, though turnout in Liberal Democrat-held seats was two points higher.[87] The political context thus appears to have had some influence on turnout, but the differences by comparison with the general decline are tiny. Turnout in ultra-marginal seats, for example, where each vote was vital, was just 2.3 points higher than in ultra-safe seats, controlling for other constituency characteristics.[88] Although all these differences are interesting, worthy of comment and suggestive of lines of enquiry, they explain little of the downward step-shift in turnout that occurred.

Some explanation of why turnout fell in all regions and in all types of constituency is required. Possible explanations can be divided into two broad categories: those that suggest rather benign causes and those that suggest that there is something fundamentally wrong with the British political system.

One of the more benign sources of decline in turnout has been alluded to already: the way in which British society has become decidedly less tribal in recent years.[89] In the early twentieth century, British society was divided into a series of easily recognizable "tribes" based on social class or religious affiliation. Loyalty to class or faith represented potent mobilizing forces in British politics. While many individuals realized that their single vote by itself gave them little say in relation to politics, the sense of belonging to a wider group provided them with a sense of efficacy. Feelings of loyalty to tribe coupled with a genuine fear of "others" motivated many people to go out and vote. Certainly fear of others appears to be one reason, for example, why turnout in Northern Ireland bucked the national trend and rose slightly from 1997 to 2001 (see above).

In recent years tribal loyalties have waned and have less potential to motivate voters.[90] Moreover, New Labour has eschewed exclusive appeals to the working class, the north, ethnic minorities and youth, claiming that it is nothing other than the political arm of "the British people as a whole". This point is made in Table 7.6 (p. 176). As described earlier, between 1987 and 1997 the proportion of voters thinking that Labour looked after the interests of the middle class increased from 58 to 81 per cent. At the same time, the proportion thinking that Labour looked after the interests of the working class held serenely steady at around 90 per cent. However, by mid-2000, after three years of New Labour government, assessments had shifted. While 73 per cent thought that Labour looked after the middle class (a fall of just 8 points), only 70 per cent thought that Labour looked after the working class (a fall of 21 points). Similarly, while the proportion thinking that Labour looked after the interest of the trade unions fell just 9 points from 93 per cent to 84 per cent between 1987 and 1997, it plummeted by 24 points to just 60 per cent by three years later. The Labour government was thus widely thought to have carried out its pledge to "govern as New Labour". By embracing business and psychologically distancing itself from the trade unions, Labour could claim to be a "one nation" party.[91] Unsurprisingly, therefore, traditional Labour supporters were less likely to turn out and vote for a party that they thought does not act particularly in their interests. Equally unsurprisingly, many traditional Conservative voters, such as professionals and managers, felt far less threatened by Labour. Having been reassured that Labour was not out to tax them to the hilt, unleash trade-union power and mismanage the economy, many natural Conservatives were also less likely to go out and vote than they had been. As Nick Martin, the Conservative candidate in Swindon North, put it:

> I'm forty nine, so I can remember the trade unions trying to bring down the government, but people brought up in the 1980s don't remember that at all. There are no menaces now. Who is renationalizing what? What closed shops are there? All the threats are remote and secret.[92]

The idea that ideological convergence may have promoted the step-shift in turnout that occurred in 2001 is supported by evidence provided by the Electoral Commission in Table 7.11. Fully 38 per cent of voters agreed that "there was very little difference between what the main parties were offering", while only 58 per cent disagreed. Equally Gallup found 62 per cent agreeing with the proposition that "the main parties are all 'much of a muchness'".[93]

Another benign explanation for the sharp decline in turnout in 2001 has also already been hinted at. For four years the national polls beat out a relentless message: that Labour would win the general election, whenever it came, and win it by a wide margin. Indeed, Labour had a massive lead in the polls for nearly nine

Table 7.11 Attitudes towards Voting

"I am going to read out a number of statements some people have made about the general election campaign this year. Please tell me how much do you agree or disagree with each."

	Strongly agree	Tend to agree	Neither agree nor disagree	Disagree	Strongly disagree	Don't know	Net
I did not believe that voting would make much of a difference.	18	16	2	18	46	–	-30
None of the parties stands for the policies I would like to see.	12	19	6	36	25	2	-30
I didn't think it was important to vote.	4	5	1	11	78	–	-80
There was very little difference between what the main parties were offering.	12	26	3	31	27	1	-20
It was an interesting election campaign.	10	20	4	35	31	1	-36

Source: Electoral Commission website at
http://www.electoralcommission.gov.uk/moripoll.htm.

years before the election. For most commentators, therefore, the only real question about the election was the size of Labour's eventual majority. The message that Labour would win was undoubtedly absorbed by the electorate. Surveys conducted in May 2001 suggested that around 90 per cent of voters thought Labour would win.[94] Throughout the campaign many journalists could hardly conceal their own boredom with the whole process. Indeed, from a very early stage they began to discuss who would be promoted or demoted in the new Labour cabinet and what would happen to William Hague in the event of a second Labour landslide. One interpretation of the low turnout, therefore, is that just about everyone in the country knew that Labour was going to win — and many were content to let it happen without their intervention.

The explanations outlined above suggest that the sharp decline in turnout witnessed in 2001 is regrettable but has few serious implications for British democracy. If voters think that there are large enough differences between the parties or that the election is going to be close, then they will be prepared to go to the polls in just as large numbers as before. However, there is another set of explanations with altogether more pessimistic implications about the health of British democracy. If these interpretations are correct, then ideological divergence and a close election will not necessarily motivate voters to turn out and radical solutions may be required to fix the system.

Some commentators have suggested, for example, that the low turnout reflects a growing sense of alienation from the political process. This sense of alienation is often thought to be found particularly amongst the young. Indeed, according to one estimate, turnout among the 18 to 24-year olds may have been as low as 39 per cent on June 7.[95] Unfortunately, propositions about alienation are very hard to assess using survey techniques alone, since the questions posed are often ambiguous. Table 17.11 suggests that 34 per cent of respondents agreed that "I did not believe that voting would make much of a difference", but this may not reflect a sense that "if voting changed anything they'd abolish it", so much as a realization that individual votes are not likely to be decisive. Table 7.11 suggests that fewer than one in ten of those interviewed, for example, agreed with the proposition that "I didn't think that it was important to vote". It appears, therefore, that any alienation may be quite limited, though it may be more prevalent amongst the very young.

Other commentators have suggested that, since ideological differences between the parties have diminished and since performance in achieving consensual goals has become more important, the parties have started to spin information to their advantage. This new style of politics may have turned people off politics. Again, there is no direct way of assessing this proposition, though the surveys provide clues. Fully 77 per cent of all voters agreed that "all the politicians quote statistics and figures that are meaningless to most people", while 76 per cent agreed that "all you hear from politicians at the moment are slogans and sound bites — there is no real debate".[96] Evidence has already been provided that voters thought the Labour government should place more emphasis on "practical achievements and less on presentation". Moreover, surveys also indicated that voters wanted more emphasis on the issues and less on personalities and the horse-race aspect of the campaign. Certainly not all the blame can be placed at the door of New Labour. It may well be that the Conservatives' decision to emphasize secondary issues such as the euro turned off many voters. The media were obliged to cover these stories because a major party had raised them, but this focus on issues of little concern did not help to mobilize voters.

Many of those who have written about the decline in turnout have assumed that it damaged Labour more than any other party. In particular, they have argued that some of the decline was due to growing disillusion with New Labour — and in particular its failure to deliver on the public services — in its former heartlands. It has been suggested that a substantial left-wing constituency in Britain currently feel disenfranchised. However, not all the evidence on differential turnout suggests that Labour voters disproportionately stayed at home. In some cases turnout fell by more than expected in those constituencies whose characteristics should have predisposed them to vote Conservative. The idea that Labour suffered from differential turnout is based at least in part on the discrepancy between Labour's 42 per cent share of the vote and the final week's polls, which indicated that it would receive 46 per cent (see Table 7.5, p. 173). Yet some of this discrepancy may be simply the result of the polls overstating Labour support throughout the election. Moreover, even if the polls did not overstate Labour support, not all the discrepancy between the final polls and Labour's share of the vote was the product of Labour voters staying at home as a result of disillusionment. Some voters appear to have stayed at home simply because a Labour victory was inevitable. Many voters had the option of voting for a left-wing alternative in the shape of the Socialist Alliance and Socialist Labour Party, but few took it. Disillusionment with New Labour seems to have played a small part in the decline that took place.

One cause of the decline in turnout is speculative and relates again to the decline in the tribal element of politics: the decline of the parties as mass organizations. Between 1997 and 2001 membership of the two major parties fell.[97] Moreover, there is evidence that those who remained in the parties were far less active than they had been in the past, far less likely to work for the party on election day, to canvass support or to put up a poster. On general election day itself, therefore, there were probably fewer people knocking on doors than ever before and those who were active worked disproportionately in ultra-marginal seats. Labour's move to the centre may have de-energized many Labour activists, while the Conservatives' misfortunes in recent years could hardly have inspired many people to go out and work for them. Only the Liberal Democrats, with their relatively stable membership and strong activist base, appeared to be in a position to mobilize their potential support but, even then, only in ultra-marginal seats.

The causes of the remarkable decline in turnout are likely to be debated for some time, and it is not yet clear whether 2001 is a one-off or just the most dramatic example of a decline in participation. Nor is it clear that turnout *per se* is an indicator of a healthy democracy, as the example of Northern Ireland clearly shows. However, the most important lesson is that turnout declined across the board. If there is a problem with the political system, then all parties, together with many members of the political elite, are to blame, though Labour bears a special burden being the incumbent government. It follows that, if the system is to be fixed, it will require all parties to fix it.

CONCLUSIONS

The outcome of the 2001 general election was not determined by Britain's social structure. Voters are no longer, if they ever were, chained to parties by virtue of their social location. Yet nor was the outcome of the 2001 general election determined by the four-week campaign. The election was determined — both won and lost — in the long haul between May 1997 and June 2001. The election outcome thus represents a political verdict on both the government and the alternatives to it.[98]

The first factor underpinning Labour's victory was that it had managed to govern with a moderate degree of success. New Labour exploded the myth that governments must be either caring but incompetent or uncaring but competent by being both caring and competent (though, to be sure, some thought not caring enough). While many voters expressed disappointment about Labour's failure to improve the public services, few failed to recognize that Labour had managed the economy well, achieving low inflation, low unemployment and rising standards of living. It deserved more time to put things right, even if it did not deserve much positive reward. The second factor underpinning Labour's victory was, quite simply, the Conservative Party. By continually emphasizing their commitment to tax cuts, the Conservatives appeared just as hostile to many of the public services as they had four years earlier. Moreover, their tax policies singularly failed to erase voters' memories of the Major government's incompetence. In the 2001 general election many voters came to the conclusion that there was no alternative.

If this analysis is correct — or even largely correct — it follows that the next general election is still wide open. If New Labour fails in its promise to deliver on the public services or if there is an economic downturn, then either of the opposition parties could have the opportunity to capitalize on its failures. It is far from ridiculous to suggest that the Conservatives can make a comeback at the next election, though they would of course have to surmount formidable obstacles in the shape of Britain's electoral system. However, to do so they need to learn to love the public services; otherwise voters may choose to stick with the devil they know — whether it be Tony Blair or Gordon Brown. If they do not and Labour fails to deliver, voters may decide that Charles Kennedy and his Liberal Democrats are worth a try. The future is uncertain, but one thing is certain, "Governments are capable of losing elections — but only if there is an opposition party available that people are willing to vote for."

NOTES

1. Anthony King, "Why Labour Won — At Last", in Anthony King, ed., *New Labour Triumphs: Britain at the Polls* (Chatham, N.J: Chatham House, 1998), 177–207.
2. See Larry Elliott, "Labour to play on the feel-good factor", *Guardian*, January 22, 2001; David McKie, "I think it's all over, already", *Guardian*, January 18, 2001.
3. Bagehot, "Are the Tories dead and buried?" *The Economist*, May 3, 1997.
4. See David Butler and Donald Stokes, *Political Change in Britain: The Evolution of Electoral Preference* (London: Macmillan, 1974).
5. David Sanders, "Goodbye to all that", *Guardian*, July 3, 2000.
6. John Bartle, "Left-Right Matters, but Does Social Class? Causal Models for the 1992 General Election", *British Journal of Political Science* 28 (1998), 501–29.
7. See John Curtice, "Who Votes for the Centre Now?" in Don MacIver, ed., *The Liberal Democrats* (London: Prentice Hall, 1996); Ivor Crewe and Anthony King, *SDP: The Birth, Life and Death of the Social Democratic Party* (Oxford: Oxford University Press, 1995).
8. Ivor Crewe, "On the Death and Resurrection of Class Voting: Some Comments on *How Britain Votes*", *Political Studies* 34 (1986): 620–38.
9. This information will be made available by the British Election Study via the ESRC Data Archive at the University of Essex.
10. *New Labour Triumphs* included a large number of age groups. Data on the voting behaviour of

each age group is therefore derived from the authoritative British Election Studies. The large swing among the youngest cohort may be the result of differential turnout.

11. www.icmresearch.co.uk/reviews/2001. The poll gave the vote intention figures as Labour 46 per cent, Conservative 34 per cent and Liberal Democrat 15 per cent.

12. A more detailed breakdown of voters into a larger number of cohorts would probably have revealed more significant differences.

13. John Bartle, "Improving the Measurement of Party Identification", in Justin Fisher, Philip Cowley, David Denver and Andrew Russell, eds., *British Elections & Parties Review,* 9 (London: Frank Cass, 1999), 119–35.

14. King, "Why Labour Won — At Last", 12.

15. Colin Brown, "Labour fails women, Harman tells Blair", *Independent,* June 18, 2000.

16. Sanders, "Goodbye to all that".

17. See Ian McAllister, "Regional Voting", in Pippa Norris and Neil T. Gavin, eds., *Britain Votes 1997* (Oxford: Oxford University Press, 1997), 133–49.

18. See Simon Atkinson and Roger Mortimore, "The Liberal Democrats at the General Election: One Step Forward or Two Steps Back?" (paper presented at the Elections, Public Opinion and Political Parties Conference of the Political Studies Association, available at www.mori.com/digest/2000/c000908.shtml).

19. See Iain McLean, "The Semi-detached Election: Scotland", in King, ed., *New Labour Triumphs,* 145–75.

20. A House of Commons Research Paper comes to a similar conclusion. It notes that support for Labour fell by 2.3 in borough constituencies (i.e., predominantly urban) seats, compared with 1.7 points in county (i.e., rural) seats. This is not a perfect proxy for the urban/rural divide but does give an indication that the "countryside revolt" was overstated. See Bryn Morgan, "General Election Results, 7 June 2001" (House of Commons Research Paper 01/54).

21. The polls used to calculate this are:

Organization	Fieldwork	Con	Lab	Lib Dem
ICM	20–22 April	33	47	14
MORI	30 April–1 May	32	50	13
NOP	1–6 May	34	49	13
Gallup	2–8 May	32	49	13

22. This is calculated simply by multiplying the total votes cast in Great Britain (25, 558, 424) by 0.06.

23. Alan Travis, "Final opinion polls point to increased majority for Blair", *Guardian,* June 7, 2001.

24. See Ivor Crewe, "The Opinion Polls: Confidence Restored?" in Norris and Gavin, eds., *Britain Votes 1997,* 61–77; Patrick Dunleavy, "Slippery Polls", *Guardian,* January 30, 2000.

25. King, "Why Labour Won — At Last", 205.

26. Bagehot, "Are the Tories dead and buried?" *The Economist,* May 3, 1997.

27. The Labour Party, *New Labour: Because Britain Deserves Better* (London: Labour Party, 1997), 17.

28. The Labour Party, *Because Britain Deserves Better,* 12.

29. *Gallup Political and Economic Index,* No. 442, May 1997, 23, fieldwork, April 21–23.

30. The careful reader will note that the proportions thinking that Labour looked after the interests of the working class and trade unions did fall after three years of Labour government. The implications of this are dealt with in the section on turnout.

31. *Economic Trends,* April 2001, Table 6.8.

32. Faisal Islam, "Whatever happened to big economics?", *Observer,* June 3, 2001.

33. George Jones, "Things can't get any better for Blair", *Daily Telegraph,* February 15, 2001.

34. For 1997 figures, see *Gallup Political and Economic Index,* No. 442, May 1997, 19; for 2001 figures, see www.gallup.com, fieldwork, May 21–23.

35. *Gallup Political and Economic Index,* No. 442, May 1997, 18, fieldwork, April 29–30.

36. www.gallup.com, fieldwork, May 21–23, 2001.

37. *Gallup Political and Economic Index,* No. 442, May 1997, 20; for 2001 figures, see www.gallup.com, fieldwork, May 21–23.

38. *Gallup Political and Economic Index,* No. 442, May 1997, 21, fieldwork, April 30.

39. Tony Blair, "The big challenges lie ahead", speech to Scottish Executive Committee, Labour Party, February 18, 2001.

40. See David Sanders, "Economic Performance, Management Competence and the Outcome of the Next General Election", *Political Studies* 44 (1996), 203–31.

41. See Anthony Heath, Roger Jowell, John Curtice, Julia Field and Sharon Witherspoon, *Understanding Political Change: The British Voter 1964–1987* (Oxford: Pergamon Press, 1991), 138–43.

42. Ivor Crewe, "Now relax, it's a dead cert", *New Statesman,* February 12, 2001.

43. MORI, *British Public Opinion,* January–February 2000, vol. 23, No. 1, 7.

44. *Gallup Political and Economic Index,* No. 442, May 1997, 23, fieldwork, April 21–23.

45. Indeed, indications of discontent were apparent in the very first budget with 62 per cent disapproving of the 4p increase in the price of a litre of petrol. See *Gallup Political and Economic Index,* No. 444, July 1997, 6, fieldwork, July 2–3.

46. Question 40, British Election Study, rolling campaign survey.

47. *Gallup Political and Economic Index,* No. 447, February 2000, 7–8, fieldwork, February 2–6, 2000.

48. www.icmresearch.co.uk/reviews/2000/news-of-the-world-nhs-poll-jan-2000.htm.

49. www.gallup.com/Poll/Surveys/2001/topline/010525.index.asp, fieldwork, May 21–23.

50. *Hansard,*, July 18, 2000, col. 228.

51. www.icmresearch.co.uk/reviews/1998/guardian-poll-march, fieldwork, March 6–8, 1998.

52. The reduction is even steeper if those opting for the status quo are included with those who wish to reduce taxes and spending (from +47 to +35).

53. *Gallup Political and Economic Index,* No. 481, August 2000, 9, fieldwork, April 4–6.

54. John Curtice, "New blow to Tories as voters reject cuts in tax and public spending", *Independent,* May 15, 2001.

55. See John R. Zaller, *The Nature and Origins of Mass Opinion* (Cambridge: Cambridge University Press, 1992).

56. *Gallup Political and Economic Index,* No. 442, May 1997, 28.

57. www.mori.com/polls/2000/ms000722.shtml, fieldwork, July 20–22, 2000.

58. www.mori.com/polls/2001/ms010126.htm, fieldwork, January 25–26, 2001.

59. Anthony King, "Electors fed up with spin and sound bites", *Daily Telegraph,* June 11, 2001; John Bartle, Ivor Crewe and Anthony King, "Was it Blair who won it? Leadership effects in the 1997 British General Election", Essex Papers in Politics and Government, No. 128 (Colchester: University of Essex, 1998).

60. See David Denver, "The Government That Could Do No Right", in King, ed., *New Labour Triumphs,* 15–48.

61. John Bartle, 'The MPs who owe their seats to Tony Blair', *Times Higher Educational Supplement,* October 3, 1997.

62. Other evidence suggests that Tony Blair's personal appeal declined over time. In March 2001 ICM asked voters, "Do you trust Tony Blair more or less than you did in 1997?" Only 15 per cent indicated that they trusted him more, while some 42 per cent said they trusted him less. See www.icmresearch.co.uk/reviews/2001/notw-marginals-march-2001.htm, fieldwork, March 14–16, 2001.

63. www.gallup.com/Poll/Surveys/2001, fieldwork, May 21–23, 2001.

64. Graham Turner, "The traditional Tories who won't be coming back", *Daily Telegraph,* December 15, 2000.

65. Anthony King, *British Political Opinion 1937–2000: The Gallup Polls* (London: Politico's, 2001), 232–7.

66. www.gallup.com/Poll/Surveys/2001/topline010515/index.asp, fieldwork, May 14–15, 2001.

67. www.gallup.com/Poll/Surveys/2001/topline010515/index.asp, fieldwork, May 14–15, 2001.

68. See John Curtice, "Public doubts grow over Labour record", *Sunday Telegraph,* January 14, 2001.
69. Question 30, British Election Study, rolling campaign survey.
70. www.gallup.com/Poll/Surveys, fieldwork, May 28–29, 2001.
71. King, "Electors fed up with spin and sound bites".
72. King, "Electors fed up with spin and sound bites".
73. www.gallup.com/Poll/Surveys/2001, fieldwork, May 21–23, 2001.
74. See Sion Simon, "Hague's a loser just like Kinnock", *News of the World,* July 16, 2000; Andrew Rawnsley, "Prime Minister Hague? I think not", *Observer,* August 6, 2000; Jonathan Freedland, "Now it's getting personal—and it's just the business", *Guardian,* May 29, 2001.
75. David Smith, "Disease and sleaze fail to dent Labour", *Sunday Times,* March 18, 2001.
76. Hague's resignation speech from the *Guardian* website (http://politics .guardian.co.uk/election2001/story/0,9029,503732,00.html).
77. http://www.icmresearch.co.uk/reviews/vote-intention-reports/ party-leader-attributes.htm.
78. See John Bartle and Ivor Crewe, "The Impact of Party Leaders in Britain: Strong Assumptions, Weak Evidence", *Leaders' Personalities and the Outcomes of Democratic Elections* (Oxford: Oxford University Press, forthcoming).
79. MORI commentary column, "Election Commentary: MPs—Good or Bad", www.mori.com/ election2001/eco518.shtml.
80. David Rossiter, Ron Johnston, Charles Pattie, Danny Dorling, Iain McAllister and Helena Tunstall, "Changing biases in the operation of the UK's electoral system", *British Journal of Politics and International Relations* 1 (1999), 133–64.
81. Geoffrey Evans, John Curtice and Pippa Norris, "New Labour, New Tactical Voting? The Causes and Consequences of Tactical Voting in the 1997 General Election", in David Denver, Justin Fisher, Philip Cowley and Charles Pattie, eds., *British General Elections & Parties Review, Volume 8: The 1997 General Election* (London: Frank Cass, 1998), 65–79.
82. The British Election Study rolling campaign survey estimates that around 7 per cent of voters thought of themselves as tactical voters. This pre-election estimate almost certainly understates the true level of tactical voting.
83. In all these cases the Labour vote fell substantially while the Liberal Democrat vote rose substantially.
84. The effectiveness of targeting in 1997 is disputed. Curtice and Steed think that the effect was limited, while David Denver and his colleagues think that there was a far greater effect. See John Curtice and Michael Steed, "The Results Analysed", in David Butler and Dennis Kavanagh, eds., *The British General Election of 1997* (Basingstoke: Macmillan, 1998); and David Denver, Gordon Hands and Simon Henig, "Triumph of Targeting? Constituency Campaigning in the 1997 General Election", in Denver *et al.,* eds., *British Elections & Parties Review, Volume 8,* 171–90.
85. Labour lost five seats to the Conservatives: Newark, North West Norfolk, Romford, Upminster and Castle Point.
86. It has been pointed out that "It is very misleading to describe the turnout last Thursday as the lowest since 1918. It is worse than that. It is the lowest turnout ever in the UK because in 1918 40% of men got the vote for the first time, as did some women, and people were being moved around because of the war. So around 60% of the new total electorate were completely unused to voting." See "Worst ever turnout", *Guardian,* June 12, 2001.
87. The constituency-level analysis is based on data kindly provided by Professor Pippa Norris, Harvard University. The fact that turnout held up in Liberal Democrat seats again suggests that voters tried to save their MPs in those seats.
88. Ultra-marginal seats are those that would be lost on a 5 per cent swing. Ultra-safe seats are those that would be lost on a 30 per cent swing.
89. Anthony King, "Why poor turnout points to a healthy democracy", *Daily Telegraph,* May 23, 2001.
90. See David Sanders, "The New Electoral Battleground", in King, *New Labour Triumphs,* 209–48.

91. Paradoxically, as reports from the Institute for Fiscal Studies confirmed, Gordon Brown did engage in surreptitious redistribution from the rich to the poor. See Polly Toynbee and David Walker, *Did Things Get Better?* (London: Penguin, 2001).

92. Turner, "The traditional Tories who won't be coming back".

93. www.gallup.com/Poll/Surveys/2001, fieldwork, May 21–23, 2001.

94. Question 18, British Election Study rolling campaign survey.

95. www.mori.co/polls/2001/elec_comm_pr.shtml.

96. www.gallup.com/Poll/Surveys/2001, fieldwork, May 21–23, 2001.

97. Patrick Seyd and Paul Whiteley, "Middle class activists", *Guardian,* September 20, 1999; "A question of priorities", *Guardian,* September 27, 1999; and "Slow collapse", *Guardian,* October 5, 1999.

98. Bagehot, "Are the Tories dead and buried?"

CHAPTER 8

A New Political Hegemony?

Ivor Crewe

IF THE BRITISH general election of 2001 had to be summarized in a single phrase, it would be "no change". The outcome was almost a carbon copy of the previous, momentous, election of 1997. The Labour Party won a second landslide of nearly identical proportions, the Conservatives suffered a duplicate humiliation, and the Liberal Democrats consolidated their unexpected breakthrough. The net change in votes was the smallest for any election after a full parliament for almost fifty years and the net turnover of seats was the lowest for a hundred years.[1] The House of Commons that reassembled on June 12 resembled to an unprecedented degree the House of Commons that had been dissolved only five weeks earlier. In 1997, it turned out, the British people had elected Labour to govern for at least two terms and the 2001 election was merely a confirmation.

In only one major respect did the British electorate change their minds between 1997 and 2001. Fewer of them — 5 million fewer of them — bothered to vote. Turnout (59.4 per cent) fell to its lowest level in peacetime conditions since 1857. The most popular choice of the electorate was not Labour, but not voting at all. Barely more than a third of new voters dragged themselves to the polls. The poor turnout reflected a wider political apathy. Membership of the Conservative and Labour parties had declined, local party workers were in short supply, and there was noticeably little campaigning on the streets and doorsteps. The election was almost universally regarded as a yawn even for those generally interested in politics and a turn-off for those less so. The electorate gave Labour a second landslide victory, but without any enthusiasm.

In the previous chapter John Bartle gives a detailed account of why there was a landslide and why it was so half-hearted. This chapter takes a wider perspective and explores the long-term implications of the 2001 election for electoral politics in Britain. It seeks to answer two broad questions. The first is whether Labour's second emphatic win in succession signifies a new (and New) Labour hegemony, the beginning of a long period of consecutive Labour governments, equivalent to the Conservatives' dominance from 1951 to 1964 and from 1979 to 1992. If so, a number of subsequent questions need to be addressed. What is the social and political basis of Labour's new ascendancy? What are the new coalitions of social groups and issues that Labour has stitched together?

The second broad question is prompted by the historically low turnout. Does the 2001 election mark the emergence of an a-political, or perhaps anti-political era in Britain? If so, why, and why now? Is Britain coming to resemble low-participation democracies like the United States, where large proportions of the underclass exclude themselves from the democratic process? Does it matter, and, if so, what might re-energize British electoral politics and the democratic process?

NEW LABOUR HEGEMONY OR TWO GOOD STROKES OF FORTUNE?

There is a straightforward *prima facie* case for claiming that the 2001 election marks a new (and New) Labour hegemony. Never before, in the era of the mass franchise, has a non-Conservative government been re-elected with a decisive majority and thus enjoyed a full second term of power. The rare election triumphs of the left in the twentieth century were all short-lived. The 1906 Liberal landslide was followed by a hung parliament in the two elections that followed only four years later. Labour's massive majority of 146 in 1945 crumbled to an unsustainable five in 1950 and was overturned in 1951. Harold Wilson's two-stage advance to a majority of 102 in 1966 was wiped out four years later. His October 1974 government, elected with a wafer-thin majority, became a minority government dependent on Liberal support within three years and fell to the Conservatives under Margaret Thatcher in 1979. But where Herbert Asquith, Clem Attlee and Harold Wilson had all failed, Tony Blair succeeded. He not only led his party to two clear election wins; he led them to two landslide victories.

What Kind of Hegemony?

The party landscape created by the 1997 and 2001 elections is dominated by the Labour Party in two quite distinct ways. First, Labour controls the House of Commons with over three-fifths of the seats and a huge overall majority. Although its lead in the popular vote was not that overwhelming (13 points in 1997, but only 9 in 2001), the heavy pro-Labour bias in the electoral system, which is spelled out in later in the chapter, significantly increases the prospects of Labour being re-elected in 2005/06 for a third term. However nervous the prime minister is about the next election, the rest of the country will think in terms of at least eight to nine more years of New Labour government. To them the Labour Party has become the natural party of government.

It does not, however, face a natural party of opposition. The Conservatives are the official opposition at Westminster, being the second largest party in the House of Commons. But in much of the United Kingdom they are not the main contenders for power or even in contention at all. In the three provinces of the United Kingdom, they barely have a presence. In Northern Ireland's distinct four-party system, shaped by the Protestant–Catholic divide over the province's constitution, neither the Labour nor the Conservative party contests elections. But Labour, as the Westminster government, must contend with Nationalists and Unionists, divided into conditional and unconditional supporters of the Good Friday Agreement, for influence over the government of the province. In Scotland, where Labour prevails in both the Westminster and Scottish Parliaments, its main opposition is the Scottish Nationalists, and it has to negotiate with its junior coalition partner in the Scottish executive, the Liberal Democrats.[2] The Conservatives are barely visible on Labour's radar screen: they came fourth in both votes and seats in 2001. In Wales, similarly, Labour dominates at both country and Westminster elections, faces the Welsh Nationalists as the main opposition in the Cardiff Assembly, and must negotiate with the Liberal Democrats as its junior coalition partner in the Welsh executive. The Conservatives are again barely in contention, lacking a single Westminster seat. In England three different two-party systems operate at both Westminster and local levels: Labour versus Conservative in most of the suburbs and towns (outside the South West); Labour versus Liberal Democrat in the big cities of the North; and Conservative versus Liberal Democrat in the South West and most of the more prosperous suburbs and shires. At Westminster itself the Labour government may find that its main opposition in the 2001 parliament comes not from the opposition benches in front of them but from the Labour back benches behind. Thus in the United Kingdom the Labour Party dominates government, but no party dominates the opposition. Labour's hegemony as the party of government is reinforced by the fragmented pattern of opposition.

Prospects for Hegemony

Labour's double-landslide is undoubtedly a historical achievement, but it does not, in and of itself, mean that Labour is destined to win in 2005/06, let alone beyond. Perhaps sheer political luck smiled on Tony Blair but deserted each of his predecessors. Short-term electoral fortunes are easily reversible and could well work against Labour by the next election. What matters is whether the 1997 and 2001 victories came about through a planned, deep-seated and enduring improvement in the Labour Party's relationship with the electorate or through two lucky turns of the electoral roulette wheel.

How can one tell? A serious analysis of the prospects for a new Labour hegemony needs to be founded on a model of how such new hegemonies arise, based on an examination of past occurrences. Most of the modelling has been done in the United States and is heavily influenced by the "classical" instances of partisan realignment (the term used in American political science) in 1852–56, 1896 and 1932 and the fuzzier case of 1964–72; but it is assumed that this model can be adapted to British conditions.[3] Details vary, but generally realignments are depicted as going through three stages: a prior dealigning phase, then a critical realigning election, or perhaps series of elections, followed by a stable period of consolidation. Dealignment means a weakening of loyalty to the old hegemonic party, as manifested by, for example, a waning of its supporters' partisan identification or a continuously poor standing in the opinion polls. This is usually accompanied by the emergence of a new, intense cross-cutting issue that creates new divisions within the old hegemonic party and by the emergence of a new, minor party that makes inroads among its traditional supporters. Realignment means an enduring change in the normal level of electoral support for the new hegemonic party, accompanied by a favourable shift in the social and ideological basis of its support, arising from the replacement of old party divisions by the new cross-cutting issue cleavage. What distinguishes an enduring partisan realignment from mere electoral good fortune is the development of a distinctive social and ideological base for the new hegemonic party.

How well do the 1997 and 2001 elections match up to this model? It is easy to list the ways in which they deviate from it and thus fall short of establishing Labour as a new hegemonic party. First, there was no equivalent in 1997 or 2001 of the emotive, cross-cutting issues, such as slavery, federal intervention in the economy or desegregation, that have triggered realigning elections in the United States. No issue in 1997 or 2001 deeply divided both parties, provoked breakaway factions, dominated the election and redistributed voters between the parties. The closest was Europe, symbolized by the issue of whether to replace the pound currency by the euro. Europe did deeply divide the Conservative Party at all levels throughout the 1992–97 parliament and during the 1997 election campaign itself and contributed significantly to the Conservatives' downfall in 1997.[4] The issue also led to the creation of two new nation-wide parties on the right, the Referendum Party and the U.K. Independence Party, which inflicted some additional minor damage on the Conservative vote in 1997.[5] But Europe did not shape electoral politics after 1997. Under William Hague the Conservative Party united around the position of "no entry into the euro in the next parliament" and the small rump of unhappy pro-Europeans kept their dissent quiet. However, the issue remained remote, irrelevant and confusing to most ordinary people and did not influence how they cast their vote, as William Hague found to his cost during the 2001 campaign. It was an emotive cross-cutting issue for some politicians, but not for more than a small number of voters.

Second, as Chapters 1 and 7 show, between 1997 and 2001 Labour failed to forge the deeper and more positive relationship with the electorate that the conventional model of partisan realignment assumes. The 2001 election was an unpopularity contest that the Conservatives lost, not a popularity contest that Labour won. Voters did not so much rally to Labour — fully 2.8 million fewer of them voted Labour than in 1997 — as flee from the Conservatives. People were deeply disappointed with the Labour government's record on the things that mattered to them — in particular health care, crime and transport — but convinced that a Conservative administration would have done even worse. Labour's second landslide was a landslide by default.

Third, for the reasons just described, Labour partisanship among its own supporters almost certainly weakened rather than strengthened after 1997 (when it was wider but shallower than before). The qualification "almost certainly" is necessary because precise comparisons with earlier elections await the results of the 2001 British Election Study. But, given the well-attested link between strength of identification and turnout, and the sharp fall in turnout, it is safe to assume that the electorate's sense of attachment to all parties, including Labour, became even more attenuated in 2001 than in 1997. In terms of the classical model, the electorate had not realigned. It remained dealigned, and dealigned more than ever.

Finally, Labour's handsome win in 2001, like its win in 1997, can be explained in terms of favourable short-term political factors, which could easily go into reverse by 2005/06. For example, economic conditions were exceptionally benign. The currency was strong (except against the dollar) and the growth rate was above Britain's long-term average. Unemployment, price inflation and interest rates were all at historically low levels for the postwar period. Most people were better off in 2001 than in 1997, and felt it. But no government can insulate Britain from a downturn in the global economy before the next election and, if it occurs, the government will take some of the blame from the voters who suffer the consequences. In 2001 Labour also benefited (if not by as much as is generally assumed) from the fact that voters showed far more confidence in Tony Blair than William Hague in the role of prime minister. But by the next election the Conservatives will have a new leader who might prove much more appealing to voters, while Tony Blair, if still prime minister, is likely to have lost what remains of his gloss after eight years in Number 10. Voters also placed more faith in Labour than the Conservatives in most areas of policy, and by a wide margin in those areas that particularly concerned them, notably the public services. But by the next election the Labour government will have had at least four more years to deliver better health care, schools, transport and policing. If voters believe that the government has failed in this regard — and they probably will, for reasons explained later — they will be far less ready than in 2001 to swallow their disappointment, blame the last Conservative government and give Labour yet another chance. The huge if short-lived anti-Labour swing in the opinion polls in September 2000, when a widely supported protest blockade led to petrol shortages, testifies to the punishment that voters will mete out to a government that fails to prevent the disruption of their everyday working lives.

In at least four respects, therefore, the 1997 and 2001 elections look very different from the critical elections that usher in a new hegemonic party. No defining major issue cleavage emerged to reshape the party system. Labour failed to forge a new, lasting and positive relationship with the electorate. Indeed, voters loosened their ties of loyalty to all the parties even further. Labour won in 2001 simply because it compared favourably with the Conservatives on short-term considerations of governmental competence. However, it would be hasty to conclude that Labour is not poised for a period of hegemony, since that would be to assume that the classical model is the only model of partisan realignment. There may be alternatives.

The classical model of partisan realignment is a product of its place and time, the rapidly expanding United States of the mid nineteenth to twentieth century. It reflects the institutional particularities of U.S. presidential elections, such as an almost pure two-party system, voluntary electoral registration and the mobilization of large cohorts of newly enfranchised voters through successive waves of immigration. It does not export easily to other democracies and sets such exacting standards for partisan realignments that almost no postwar election in any European democracy has passed the test. It might account for Labour's replacement of the Liberal Party in the 1920s, when the franchise was massively extended, but it would not have foretold the Conservative ascendancies of 1951–64 or 1979–97, nor can it account for them satisfactorily in retrospect.

An alternative model for the emergence of a new party hegemony has recently been provided not by an academic political scientist but by a politician: Tony Blair. Most party leaders take an interest in short-term electoral tactics, but few devote much serious thought to long-term electoral strategy. Tony Blair, advised by a small personal entourage, has been the exception. No party leader has carefully planned as coherent and radical a strategy for electoral hegemony as Tony Blair did between becoming leader in 1994 and the general election of 1997. And no party leader has been as determined to stick to the plan as Blair was throughout the period to the second election of 2001.

The strategy was shaped by two considerations. First, the Labour Party had to find a way of ending eighteen continuous years of Conservative government. Second, it had to break the historical pattern of single-term Labour governments if it wanted to achieve anything of lasting value once elected to office. Previous Labour governments had lost power after only one term because their economic and social programme was over-ambitious, or raised unrealistic expectations, or was directed at too narrow a segment of the electorate, or lost the confidence of international markets, or had to be abandoned mid-way, or some combination of these. The Labour governments of the past, by the end of a single term, were left with a damaging reputation for good intentions but incompetent management, a reputation that lingered for many years. Blair's New Labour strategy was designed to win, from the outset, not one election but at least two.[6] The overriding aim of the first term of government would be to win a second term of government.

There were four connected strands to New Labour's strategy for hegemony:

- create a cross-class coalition of support (the social basis)
- occupy the centre ground (the ideological basis)
- establish the party's credentials for competence (the political basis)
- cultivate institutional sources of electoral support (the institutional basis).

Each was shaped by a hard-headed appreciation of electoral realities. Some resemble elements of a classical partisan realignment, others do not; together they constituted a quite different approach.

The first strand was the single-minded conversion of habitual non-Labour voters in preference to the mobilization of traditional Labour supporters. This required a frank recognition of the electoral implications of Britain's changing class structure, in particular the steady contraction of the industrial working class. Non-Labour voters were assumed to be concentrated in the growing ranks of middle-income, economically aspiring, home-owning, shopping mall-visiting, tax-paying — but public-service dependent — Middle England. They would make the crucial difference in dozens of marginal seats, particularly in the Midlands and South. Long-standing working-class Labour loyalists were too small in number to guarantee Labour victory even if fully mobilized; anyway, they mainly lived in safe Labour seats and, when it came to voting, had nowhere else to go. The Labour Party therefore needed to create a new social coalition of support. In this respect, its strategy did resemble the classical model. But the new coalition would comprise almost everybody — low-income, middle-income and large sections of the professional and managerial classes — by focusing on the interests and values that united rather than divided them. Labour would avoid becoming the party of one or more social groups: it would be a one-nation catch-all party. In this respect, its strategy departed from the classical model.

The second component of the strategy followed from the first: the repositioning of the party on the broad centre ground where British public opinion is largely concentrated. In this regard, too, New Labour deviated from the classical model. In a traditional partisan realignment, a party creates an electoral hegemony by associating itself with the new majority position on an established issue cleavage or the emerging majority position on a new issue cleavage. New Labour did neither. It studiously avoided associating itself with any one "Big Idea". It simply moved away from the left/liberal pole on the two separate ideological dimensions that define party and public opinion: "state versus market" on social and economic issues and "individual versus state" on citizenship issues.

Two particular features of New Labour's re-positioning were important. One was the special emphasis it placed on demonstrating to voters what it had changed from, what it no longer was. To make it crystal clear that Labour had re-invented itself, it made the double pledge not to raise income tax (repeated in 2001) and not to change the Conservative government's spending plans for its first two years. It reduced the trade unions' power in the party's organization and, in a move of huge symbolic importance, replaced the redundant Clause 4 of the party constitution, which nominally committed the party to public ownership of the economy. Old Labour policies that frightened the target non-Labour voter were not quietly dropped. They were ostentatiously thrown overboard.

The other feature of New Labour's move to the centre was its deliberate occupation of large tracts to both the left and the right of the centre point. Sometimes its policies skilfully combined both left and right, such as its proposal to tax the windfall profits of the privatized utilities to fund a welfare-to-work programme that cut welfare benefits. Sometimes it combined the left and right in vague policy formulations such as "tough on crime, tough on the causes of crime". The end result was that Labour appeared, Janus-faced, to be simultaneously a centre-left and a centre-right party.

The third strand in New Labour's strategy for hegemony was its determination to persuade voters of its competence to govern. It would lay the ghost of good-hearted ineptitude left by ill-fated Labour governments of the past. Classical realignment theory is cast in terms of "position" issues on which parties and voters divide in their view about the proper ends of government policy. New Labour strategists understood that British elections (as in most democracies) normally turn not on "position" issues but on "valence" issues,[7] on party *performance* (prospective as well as actual and reputational), not party *position*. The functional equivalent of a new cross-cutting position issue is a major shift in voters' association of the parties with a significant dimension of government performance. For decades voters have considered Labour to be the better party for the welfare state and public services — for jobs, pensions, schools and the National Health Service — and the Conservatives to be the better party for defence, law and order, foreign affairs and, above all, management of the economy. Labour was resolved to change these perceptions, by cautious commitments before 1997 and prudent government afterwards.

The final component of the Blairite strategy for a New Labour hegemony was a realistic appraisal of the institutional conditions for electoral success: a professional, disciplined and well-financed party organization, a friendly media and a hard-headed understanding of the operation of the electoral system. In this, it departed from the classical model which has nothing to say about the institutional, as distinct from the social and ideological bases, of electoral support. New Labour modernized the party machine, centralized power at the expense of local constituency parties and exercised maximum influence over candidate selection. Tony Blair and his close advisers cultivated the right-wing press, particularly the Murdoch stable, put almost obsessive emphasis on the management of the media and systematically analysed private polls and focus groups to take regular measures of public opinion. It took skilful partisan advantage of the public consultations over the constituency boundary revisions prior to 1997 and in both 1997 and 2001 ruthlessly targeted marginal seats to the neglect of safe and hopeless seats.

Judged by these four criteria, the prospects after the 2001 election for a New Labour hegemony look more promising than they do when judged against the predominantly American partisan realignment model. Let us explore each in turn.

The Social Basis: Labour as a Catch-all, Cross-class Party

In the 1980s Thatcherism's appeal to the "new working class" drove Labour back into its industrial and urban fastnesses of the North, Wales and Scotland. In 1997 New Labour broke out of its old ghetto with stunning successes in Middle England. The swing to Labour was even stronger in the affluent South and London than in the North, and even larger among the middle classes and owner-occupiers than elsewhere. On election night the drumbeat of Labour gains was a rollcall of the suburban and small town Home Counties: Brighton, Braintree, Hastings, Harrow, Hendon, Hemel Hempstead, Hove, Putney, St. Albans, Southgate, Watford. John Betjeman country had turned red.

In 2001 John Betjeman country stayed red. Labour consolidated and marginally extended its new middle-class support, demonstrating that it was not a flash-in-the-pan protest against John Major's Conservative government. The lowest swings from Labour to Conservative (other than in Scotland) were in the dynamic regions of the South East (0.5 per cent), London (0.5 per cent) and the South West (0.0 per cent). There was a further small swing of 0.5 per cent to Labour among the expanding groups of professional and managerial classes (the ABs) and 1.0 per cent among office workers and technicians (the C1s).[8] Although Labour still lagged behind the Conservatives in the preferences of the AB social classes (by 30 per cent to 38 per cent), it led the Conservatives by 38 per cent to 36 per cent among the C1s. The long-term weakening of social class as a basis for the vote continued. The larger numbers in these middle-class groups and the higher turnout among them meant that in 2001, for the first time, half of all Labour voters were middle-class. The majority of working-class voters continued to vote Labour, but the majority of Labour voters were no longer working-class. New Labour had become, as Tony Blair intended, a catch-all, cross-class party.

The one-nation character of Labour's electoral success was reflected in the range of constituencies Labour MPs represented. In 2001, as in 1997, Labour MPs were elected not only for the industrial heartlands, inner city and council estates, but for the outer suburbs, market towns, coastal resorts and commuter belts. Of the 21 seats with the highest proportion of professional and managerial workers, Labour holds even more (nine) than the Conservatives (eight). The party represents in Parliament almost the full range of communities and social groups in the country. In contrast, to the parliamentary Conservative party, once the proud claimant to being the party of one nation, the big cities, council estates, ethnic minority communities, the whole of Wales and almost the whole of Scotland are foreign planets. In 2001, as in 1997, the Conservatives were the party of the rural and small-town shires of England and of sizeable chunks of the more affluent commuter belt. They were no longer the national party of the United Kingdom or even of England.

Of course, at a normal election, with fewer MPs, the Labour Party's span of representation would not be as wide. But given the more even social and geographical basis of support for New Labour than Old Labour, even a sizeable adverse swing at the next election would leave it with a more balanced representation of Britain's groups and communities.

The Ideological Basis: New Labour as a Centrist Party

By 1997 New Labour had succeeded in rebranding itself in the eyes of the electorate. The British Election Study showed that in 1997 voters placed the Labour Party closer to their own positions on critical left–right issues (and the Conservatives further away) than they had in 1992.[9] Labour exchanged places with the Conservative Party as the more "moderate" rather than more "extreme" party. Policy areas in which voters had preferred the Conservatives for a generation, irrespective of the Conservatives' overall popularity — such as taxation, law and order and Europe — were captured for the first time by New Labour in 1997.[10] They stayed captured, even more firmly, in 2001. Labour was preferred by an even wider margin over the Conservatives as the best party on inflation and taxation and by nearly the same margin on Europe and law and order.[11] And it continued to be labelled as moderate rather than extreme while the Conservatives suffered the reverse.[12] New Labour consolidated its reputation as the moderate party of sound management and sensible policies. In the coming parliament its centrist location is likely to be bolstered by the Liberal Democrats, whose clear campaigning for higher taxes to fund more spending on the public services place them firmly to the left of Labour on the social and economic spectrum. The noticeable pattern of swings from Labour to the Liberal Democrat in constituencies with concentrations of the public sector salariat indicated that this switch of positions had registered with the relevant sector of the electorate.[13] The government's programme of "modernization" of the public services will give the Liberal Democrats ample opportunity to challenge New Labour from the left and thus underscore its centrist location.

The Political Basis: Establishing Credentials for Competence

The principal reason for New Labour's win in 1997 was that it persuaded the majority of voters that it would be better than the Conservatives at doing the job of governing. It would be more moderate, more united, more strongly led and more committed to high-standard public services. Most critically of all, it persuaded voters — for the first time in a British election — that it was more capable of running the British economy. This was partly by default after Britain's humiliating withdrawal from the European Exchange Rate Mechanism and effective devaluation in September 1992 and partly through Gordon Brown's repeated pledges to limit public expenditure, to desist from raising income tax and to adopt pro-business policies. Gallup regularly asks its respondents which party can best handle Britain's economic difficulties. In April 1992, despite the recession at the time, respondents preferred the Conservatives by a 7-point margin. In April 1997, they preferred Labour by a 9-point margin. New Labour, unlike Old Labour, seemed safe and sensible.

The overriding objective of the 1997 government was to consolidate New Labour's new-won claim to competence at governing. Determined to exorcize its reputation, buried deep in the collective memory, for presiding over economic and industrial crisis, it engaged in the politics of reassurance. The setting of interest rates was handed over to the Bank of England, with a remit to limit annual inflation to about 2.5 per cent. Public expenditure was tightly controlled. The standard rate of income tax was reduced and the top rate was left alone. When the spectre of recession loomed in 1998 the government managed a "soft landing" and avoided a new round of "stop–go". The result was that throughout the 1997–2001 parliament voters continued to regard Labour as the more competent at managing the economy, and usually by a wide margin.[14] In the April 1997 Gallup poll Labour led the Conservatives by 48 to 39 per cent as the better party for managing the economy. Four years later (March 2001) it had extended its lead to 53 to 31 per cent. It was the first Labour government in history to finish with a stronger reputation for economic management than it began with. In the eyes of voters, it had replaced the Conservatives as the natural steward of the British economy, an achievement of enormous electoral significance.

The Institutional Basis of Labour's Hegemony

Labour's prospective hegemony has social, ideological and political foundations. It has become a cross-class party with a centrist ideology and a new reputation for governmental competence. It also has an institutional foundation: the media and the electoral system.

As we saw in Chapter 5, a large majority of the press supported the Conservatives during the Conservative era of 1979 to 1992, often with gusto. Of the national dailies, only the *Daily Mirror* and the *Guardian*, comprising under a quarter of total circulation, backed the Labour Party. In 1997 they were joined by the *Financial Times*, the *Independent*, the *Daily Star* and, most important of all, the *Sun*, comprising 60 per cent of total circulation. In 2001 *The Times* and the *Daily Express* also endorsed the Labour Party, leaving the Conservatives with the support of only the *Daily Telegraph* and the *Daily Mail*. This was a remarkable change for a party that throughout the twentieth century had found most of the press ranged against it. It was the fruit of New Labour's careful wooing of the Murdoch press but also of its new respectability in the eyes of editors and proprietors and its new popularity with their readers. How much Labour's new backing from the press influenced the vote is hard to estimate: whether readers' newspaper preferences influence how they vote or voters' party preferences influence what they read is notoriously difficult to disentangle. What is clear, however, is that readers of the two newspapers endorsing Labour for the first time swung more heavily to Labour than other readers.[15]

However, newspapers are fickle in their political allegiance. The association of landslide election victories and newspaper backing suggests that New Labour will feel bound to continue to cultivate the press, especially the mass tabloids, and may allow its critical political choices, for example the timing of any referendum on the euro, to be influenced. However, there are limits both to how far government policy can be adjusted to the prejudices of newspaper owners and editors; and, if the Labour government became deeply unpopular, for whatever reason, with voters, some newspapers would abandon New Labour in order to retain their readers.

A more reliable source of electoral ascendancy is the electoral system. Since 1987 the British electoral system has become increasingly biased in favour of Labour at the expense of the Conservatives. Some of the bias would have occurred irrespective of New Labour stratagems. For example, Labour benefits from representing constituencies that have smaller electorates and lower turnouts than the Conservatives. This is partly due to the steady migration from Labour inner-city constituencies to Conservative small-town and rural constituencies and partly because the Representation of the People Act stipulates that Scotland and Wales, which happen to be overwhelmingly Labour, should have smaller constituencies than England. But some of the bias has been encouraged by New Labour's deliberate courting of the Liberal Democrats as an anti-Conservative ally. Anti-Conservative tactical voting, which first emerged in 1992 and spread in both 1997 and 2001, has distributed Labour and Liberal Democrat support more efficiently across constituencies.[16]

In 2001 Labour's appeal to the South and the middle classes, the further spread of anti-Conservative tactical voting and the small electoral bonus that new incumbents tend to gain when seeking re-election for the first time, all combined to shore up or even increase the Labour vote in its most marginal seats. The Conservatives gained only four of Labour's 30 most vulnerable seats and moved closer in three others; in the remaining 23 there was a further swing to Labour. Similarly, among the eighteen Liberal Democratic seats under greatest threat from the Conservatives, only two were lost and only two moved closer to the Conservatives. The other fourteen swung further to the Liberal Democrats.

This pattern of swings left the electoral system even more biased against the Conservatives than before. One measure of bias is the difference in the number of seats the Conservative and Labour parties would win if a uniform national swing produced a tie in terms of their overall vote at the next election. If the outcome were be an equal number of seats, then there would be no bias in the system; but if either party stands to win more seats than the other on equal shares of the vote, then there is clearly a bias in that party's favour. After the 1987 election the answer was: 303 Conservative, 299 Labour, a tiny bias in favour of the Conservatives. After the 1992 election, the answer was: Conservative 282, Labour 320, a significant bias, worth 38 seats, to Labour. After the 1997 election, the answer was: Conservative 258, Labour 338, a huge bias of 80 seats in Labour's favour. After 2001, the skew in Labour's favour has become greater still. A uniform national swing of 4.5 per cent, resulting in the Conservatives and Labour each winning 36.2 per cent of the vote, would leave the Conservatives with 219 seats and Labour with 370 seats, a massive bias of 151 seats for Labour. The system has become so disproportional to Labour's benefit that at the next election, on the assumption of uniform national swing:

- If the Labour and Conservative parties take an equal share of the vote, Labour would nonetheless have a comfortable overall majority of 79.
- Even if the Conservatives led by 3 per cent of the popular vote, Labour could remain in office for a full term with a majority of 23.
- Even if the Conservatives led by 5 per cent of the popular vote, Labour would remain the largest party in Parliament and with the Liberal Democrats could form a coalition government.
- To become the single largest party in Parliament — but still short of an overall majority — the Conservatives would need to be ahead by nearly 9 per cent.
- To win an overall majority of one — not enough to last a full parliament — the Conservatives would need a 12 per cent lead in the vote.
- To win a sufficient overall majority to govern for a whole term, the Conservatives would need to be at least 13 per cent ahead in the popular vote.

In other words, to win the next election the Conservatives need to secure an 11.0 per cent swing — even more than Labour achieved in its historic landslide of 1997.

The electoral system never works in precisely the same way from one election to the next and the national swing is never, in fact, uniform across constituencies. Some of the factors that have so distorted the electoral system in Labour's favour will change or go into reverse by 2005/06. The next election may be contested on revised boundaries which would reduce (but by no means eliminate) the unequal size of constituencies. The number of constituencies in Scotland will be reduced to bring them into proportion with England, now that Scotland has its Parliament, but the resulting disadvantage to Labour is likely to be minor. But other factors, such as anti-Conservative tactical voting, Labour's above-average performance in its marginal seats and its continuing benefit from unequally sized constituencies, are more likely to persist than not. The new Conservative leader, Iain Duncan Smith, has a huge mountain to climb at the next election.

STRATEGIES FOR CONSERVATIVE RECOVERY

How can the new leader of the Conservatives steer his party to electoral victory and destroy New Labour's hegemony? How can he retrieve the six million Conservative voters lost since 1992 and achieve the national swing of approximately 11 per cent needed to form the next government? It is a formidable task which will very probably take more than one election to accomplish. Yet it is not an impossible task, as Labour's ending of the Conservative ascendancy in 1997 shows. Over the ten preceding years Labour gained 3.5 million votes and a swing of over 11 per cent.

Answers to these questions are inevitably speculative but serve two useful purposes. They point to the range of possible directions in which British party politics might develop. They also describe the limited options available to the Conservative Party and thus underline the strength of New Labour's hegemony.

The Conservative Party can adopt a cautious or a radical strategy for electoral recovery. The cautious strategy is based on the assumption that elections are lost by governments rather than won by oppositions. The Conservatives should therefore be poised to exploit the blunders, failures, divisions, scandals and exhaustion that will eventually afflict the New Labour government as they do all governments. They can do this most effectively by being united, by avoiding major or controversial policy commitments of their own and by waiting patiently for voters' memories of the Conservatives' record in office to fade. This is indeed the manner in which party ascendancies of the past have come to an end, such as the Conservative ascendancies of 1895–1906 and of 1951–1964.[17] The weakness of the strategy is that it can take a very long time for governments to die naturally.

The radical strategy would take its inspiration from the New Labour project. The new Conservative leadership could choose to re-invent the party as New Conservatives, think the unthinkable and implement major changes of direction and policy. Like New Labour it could seek to relocate its ideological home, reach out to habitual non-Conservatives, reclaim its traditional reputation for sound government and make a cool appraisal of potential institutional sources of electoral success.

The Conservative Party of 2001, however, has less scope for rebranding itself than the Labour Party had in the mid-1990s, for three reasons. First, in the mid 1990s the ideological centre ground was inhabited by one small tenant, the Liberal Democrats, whereas in 2001 the whole area is occupied by New Labour. Second, the Conservative Party, despite its dire electoral position, is not crippled by as many unpopular policy positions on important issues for the voters. There is no equivalent of Clause 4, the sacrament of Old Labour, and thus no opportunity for a symbolic gesture of fundamental change. Third, Conservative Party members are probably not yet as desperate for victory as Labour Party members were after four successive election defeats and are therefore less ready to stomach major reversals of direction.

In the 2001 election the Conservatives competed with New Labour on both the left–right dimension of social and economic policies and the liberal–authoritarian dimension of what might broadly be described as issues of citizenship. As regards the former, the Conservatives sought to differentiate themselves from Labour in terms of performance rather than policy position. Labour had failed to improve schools, modernize public transport and improve the health service; the Conservatives would do better. As regards the latter, the Conservatives sought to differentiate themselves from Labour in terms of both performance *and* policy position. They would do a better job of cutting crime and catching bogus asylum-seekers. But they also took opposing positions on the reform of the House of Lords, the banning of fox-hunting, the status of homosexuality[18] and, of course, the euro (which they treated as a constitutional issue of national sovereignty rather than as a commercial or financial matter). The strategy completely failed because Labour won the battle on performance and because the issues on which the Conservatives took positions were matters of low priority for most voters.

The radical options available to the Conservatives are summarized below. All but the last, which is the least radical, do not appear promising and illuminate the difficulty of competing against a party that dominates the centre ground.

Option 1: Economic Thatcherism

New Conservatism could seek to distinguish itself from New Labour by embracing different economic and social positions. It could move to the right and adopt low-tax, low-spend policies involving the privatization of welfare and most public services such as health care and higher education. This option would win support from a substantial minority of Conservative MPs and members. The disadvantage of this strategy is straightforward: surveys consistently report that the large majority of voters oppose the privatization of public services and welfare.[19] It would lose many more votes than it gained.

Option 2: Populist Authoritarianism

New Conservatism could seek to distinguish itself from New Labour by adopting a larger set of different positions on cultural and citizenship issues. It could move to the right by, for example, opposing the equal opportunities agenda and multi-culturalism, championing "family values" as an alternative to homosexual rights, and increasing the powers of the police, courts and prisons at the expense of the accused and convicted. It could engage in a "cultural war" on the side of mainstream society and national tradition against ethnic, sexual and other minorities. It could continue to oppose any further integration of the United Kingdom into the European Union, including adoption of the euro, on grounds of national sovereignty. It could link these themes together in terms of stopping Britain (or, more likely, England) "turning into a foreign land". This strategy does have the advantage of appealing to the emotions, often quite intense, of large segments of the electorate, including working-class Labour voters and abstainers. The critical disadvantage is that, however strong their opinions, most people are not influenced by cultural and citizenship issues when it comes to voting, as the failure of William Hague's campaign in 2001 to "save the pound" demonstrated. To increase the salience of these issues for voters, the Conservative Party would have to give them a much higher priority than before, with the danger that the party would divide between its authoritarian and liberal wings, losing votes as a result.

Option 3: Social Libertarianism

Alternatively New Conservatism could differentiate itself from New Labour by moving to its left on citizenship and cultural issues. Michael Portillo floated this option in his abortive leadership campaign. The party could promote itself as the party of personal freedom and minority rights. It could abandon its current ambivalence about gay rights, equal opportunities and asylum seekers. It could go further and propose the decriminalization of drugs, an extension of homosexual rights (e.g. the legal recognition of same-sex marriages) and a much less restrictive immigration policy (not least on economic grounds). Combined with Option 1, this approach would turn New Conservatism into a classically liberal party. It might make inroads into Liberal Democrat support. The problem with this strategy is that it has all the disadvantages of Option 2 with the added drawback that most social-libertarian policies appeal only to minorities.

Option 4: Constitutional Reform

New Conservatism could also choose to outflank New Labour on its left by thinking the unthinkable on the constitution. It already advocates a wholly elected House of Lords, having hitherto stoutly defended the hereditary principle. It could reverse its long-standing opposition to electoral reform for both local and Westminster elections. This would have the double advantage of gaining an increment of votes from Liberal Democrats while simultaneously making an ally out of the Liberal Democrat Party, which would be useful in a hung parliament. There would be parallel advantages to reversing its equally deep-rooted opposition to the extension of the powers of the devolved parliaments, thus helping to make allies of the Nationalists in Scotland and Wales. These proposals are probably too radical for the party to accept in the short term but might be more palatable if it again loses heavily at the next election.

Option 5: U-turn on the Euro

Opposition to further integration of the United Kingdom into the European Union, and to adoption of the euro in particular, attracts the strong support of the majority of Conservative Party MPs, members and voters and the less committed support of the majority of voters as a whole. It might seem perverse, therefore, to jettison opposition to the euro in favour of, for example, a non-committal position similar to New Labour's in which party members would be free to campaign on either side if and when a referendum is held. However, campaigning against the euro proved not to be a vote winner in either 1997 or 2001. For most voters it was both a low-priority issue and a symbol of Conservative Party obsession, division and lingering Thatcherism, similar in some ways to Labour's commitment to unilateral nuclear disarmament in the 1980s. The electoral benefit of ditching principled opposition to the euro is that it would be the single most potent signal that the Conservative Party was no longer dominated by the right. The electoral drawback is that the attempt to change the policy would probably exacerbate internal divisions, at least on this side of the next election, and thus inflict further electoral damage.

Option 6: The Party of Public Services

Finally, New Conservatism could acknowledge that election outcomes in Britain typically hinge not on voters' policy preferences but on their judgement of which party is the more competent at governing. It could also recognize that the criterion for competent government has shifted from management of the economy to management of the public sector, from delivery of economic growth and prosperity to delivery of public services. On the morning after his election victory Tony Blair declared to party workers that the task of his second Government was "to deliver reform and investment in the future". The most promising strategy for the Conservatives is to challenge Labour on its own territory.

The electoral politics of delivering high-quality public services offer more favourable opportunities to the opposition than the electoral politics of delivering economic prosperity. There are a number of reasons. First, it is more difficult for any government to achieve an improvement in public services than in the economy during a single parliament. Changes in tax and interest rates have an almost immediate effect, whereas increased investment or structural reforms in the public services can take years to show results. It takes three years to train teachers and nurses, six years to train doctors and up to twenty years to modernize an underground railway system. Second, even where there are real improvements, these are usually less obvious to the voter than improvements to the economy. Voters are directly aware of tax cuts, lower interest rates, higher wages and a stronger pound but often unaware of the much less visible improvements in, for example, training or equipment in the public services. Third, the majority of voters do not come into contact with public services on a frequent basis, the exception being public transport, where rapid and evident improvement is particularly difficult. They must rely for their judgement on the reports of others or the media; and in the media failure has more news value than success. Finally, governments can blame economic downturn on factors beyond their control such as the world economy, at least for a time, whereas voters assume that government is exclusively responsible for the state of public services. For all these reasons any opposition should have plenty of material with which to castigate the government. The more difficult task will be to persuade voters that the Conservative Party is more seriously committed to the public services than New Labour and would do a better job.

However, if the critical issue at the next election is the management of the public services, as seems probable, it may well have one consequence that is not immediately obvious. The issue is likely to be contested between the parties in a manner that depresses rather than encourages participation. It is likely to turn people off voting rather than turn them out. The next section explains how and why.

ABSTENTION AND ITS SIGNIFICANCE IN 2001

So far this chapter has examined the long-term implications of Labour's second landslide. It now turns to the implications of the other significant feature of the election, the record level of abstention.

Why might it matter that two in five of those eligible to vote in 2001 decided not to bother? One or more of four reasons tend to be given, all in terms of the health of British democracy.

The first is that the low turnout undermined a critical task of elections, the conferring of popular legitimacy on the government. Less than a quarter of the electorate (24.1 per cent) voted for the Labour government. For every person who voted Labour, three people voted for one of the other parties or, most likely, did not vote at all. No government with an overall majority has ever received such a slender mandate.[20] It could reasonably be asked whether the newly elected government, despite its huge parliamentary majority, had received a mandate for its programme at all. The prime minister's low-key response to his election victory, notably lacking in the exultation of 1997, suggested that he had registered how half-hearted, even truculent, the voters' endorsement of him had been.

The second is that elections have an egalitarian function, which the low turnout subverted. Elections confer equal citizenship on all adults, as a counterweight to the inequalities of the market and natural endowment. In 2001 turnout fell to an exceptionally low level in the most deprived areas of Britain's cities. In 67 constituencies, all in such areas, the majority of the registered electorate failed to vote; in a few, under 40 per cent did so. The majority of the poor, the unemployed, the unqualified, single mothers on benefit and blacks disengaged from the election. The socially excluded felt politically excluded and so excluded themselves from the electoral process.

Third, low turnout matters because it suggests that elections are failing in their critical task of making British government representative and responsive. If 40 per cent of the electorate choose not to exercise their right to vote — the simplest of acts—it must be because they do not think it worthwhile. They must either believe that the parties on offer do not represent their interests and views or that, even if they do, they are ineffective when in government. Arguably, the poor turnout in 2001 showed that British democracy was not working properly, that the relationship between politicians and public had broken down.

The fourth cause for concern about low turnout is the danger that it could pose to British democracy. The 40 per cent who abstained amount to a huge pool of presumably disaffected citizens potentially open to anti-democratic methods of exerting political pressure and to extreme parties and movements. The popular support for the coercive blockades by protestors against the petrol tax, and the violent anti-police riots in Oldham, Bradford, Burnley and other ethnically mixed towns in the North are cases in point.

Whether the 2001 election does bear out these concerns depends on the motives of the 40 per cent who were eligible to vote but decided to abstain, in particular those who normally vote but chose not to in 2001. Abstainers can be divided into four categories:

1. *Apathetic abstainers* lack any knowledge, interest or involvement in politics: "I don't know anything about politics." Politics and their everyday personal lives are two completely separate worlds: they never read, listen, watch or talk about politics. There are almost no circumstances in which they would vote. They account for turnout never approaching 100 per cent, but they cannot account for the sharp increase in abstention in both 1997 and 2001.

2. *Alienated abstainers,* by contrast, do engage with the world of politics. They are often better informed about politics, and more interested and involved, than the average voter. They abstain out of antipathy, not apathy: antipathy to the failure, as they see it, of the parties and politicians to address their particular interests or values. They may be struggling farmers complaining that "none of the parties understand the problems of small holders" or idealistic environmentalists convinced that "none of the parties talk about the important global issues". They might vote if a radically different choice of parties or politicians was available.

3. *Indifferent abstainers* choose not to vote because they are indifferent to the election outcome. They perceive the main parties as so similar in their policies, effectiveness or relevance that little is at stake: "It makes no difference who wins." Unlike the *apathetics* they take some notice of political affairs and unlike the *alienated* they are not necessarily angry about the absence of a meaningful choice. They shrug their shoulders rather than raise their fists. They would vote if for whatever reason they came to prefer one of the main parties more (or less) than the others.

4. *Instrumental abstainers* do not vote because they calculate that it would make no difference to the result, nationally or locally: "Labour is bound to win." They are not necessarily apathetic about politics, or alienated from the system, or indifferent to the result (although they are unlikely to be strongly engaged in the outcome). They stay at home not because the result will make no difference to them but because they believe they will make no difference to the result. They would probably vote if they believed that the national or local outcome was uncertain.

Which type of abstention increased in 1997 and 2001? Firm conclusions must await analysis of the 2001 British Election Study, but interim deductions can be made from the aggregate electoral statistics and the opinion polls.

Any assessment should bear in mind that turnout in every type of British election began to fall after 1992. Local election turnout in England fell from the 40–45 per cent range of the 1980s to an average of 37 per cent in 1992 to 1996 and down further to the 30 per cent level in 1998–2000.[21] In by-elections, the customary drop in turnout compared with the preceding general election lengthened from 13 percentage points between 1966 to 1992 to 24 percentage points during the 1992–97 parliament and 27 percentage points during the 1997–2001 parliament.[22] In the 1997 general election, turnout fell to 71.4 per cent — the lowest level since 1935 — from 77.7 per cent in 1992. Despite the six-week campaign, saturation media coverage, the entry of a new national party (the Referendum Party) and the exciting or dreaded prospect of ending eighteen years of Conservative government, 2.3 million fewer people turned out to vote. In 2001 another 5 million decided not to bother. The particular circumstances of the 2001 election explain a sizeable part of the slump in turnout, but by no means all, because the growth of abstention was the culmination of a long-term trend.

Instrumental abstention was undoubtedly an important contributor to the slump in turnout. The large majority of voters regarded the result as a foregone conclusion and had done so since long before the campaign began.[23] The media repeatedly hammered home the message from the opinions polls that Labour was not only going to win, but win big. "TORIES FACE EXTINCTION", "TORIES FACE POLL MELTDOWN", "BLAIR HEADS FOR SECOND LANDSLIDE" were typical front page headlines during the campaign.[24] Indeed the opinion polls had been reporting a large lead for the Labour government ever since 1997 (except for September-October 2000). The drop in turnout in 1997 can be explained in similar terms because the polls had been reporting a large lead for the then Labour opposition continuously since early 1993. No period since opinion polls began has shown one party, whether in or out of office, with such a sustained and commanding lead. Historically, turnout at general elections has reflected the expected closeness of the result. It was low in 1983 (73 per cent) because everyone expected Labour to be trounced. It was high in 1951 (82 per cent), despite the wholesale absence of Liberal candidates, because people expected a close result. It was high in February 1974 (78 per cent) and 1992 (78 per cent) when the polls fed media speculation about hung parliaments.

To the extent that instrumental abstention accounts for the low turnout in 2001 and 1997, the implications are optimistic. It would mean that most of the new abstainers were not particularly dissatisfied with the parties and their leaders or vulnerable to anti-democratic appeals. It would make the Labour government's mandate stronger than the turnout figures imply: many of the abstainers would

have voted (and in roughly the same proportions for the parties as actual voters) if they had thought the result was in doubt.[25] Low turnout did not weaken
Tony Blair's mandate, but the reverse: the expected size of his mandate weakened turnout. Turnout would recover in 2005/06 if by that time local elections,
by-elections and opinion polls were signalling a much closer contest.

Turnout would recover, but by how much? Instrumental abstention is far
from being the full explanation for the poor turnout in 2001. It cannot easily
account for the parallel increases in abstention at local elections and by-elections
where the outcome was usually less certain and there were no cues from opinion
polls. It does not explain why turnout fell so much more sharply in 2001 (and
from a lower base) than it did in past elections where the result was predictable.
Nor does it square with the fact that in 2001 turnout declined by almost as much
in the ultra-marginal seats as in the super-safe seats.[26] As Peter Kellner, the election analyst, put it: "a shroud of apathy descended upon the nation".[27] There
must have been additional factors.

The most likely explanation, although there is no statistical proof, is that the
number of indifferent abstainers grew substantially. The proportion of people
who could see a good deal of difference between the parties has steadily fallen
since the high point of the Thatcher years — 82 per cent in 1983 and 84 per cent
in 1987 — to 55 per cent in 1992 and 33 per cent in 1997. In January 2001 the
proportion appeared to have slipped again, to 27 per cent.[28]

There are probably two main reasons, and both are the direct product of New
Labour's strategy for hegemony. The first is that Tony Blair's abandonment of Old
Labour thinking markedly reduced the number of policy positions on which the
Labour and Conservative parties differed. In the 1980s it was easy for voters to distinguish between the two parties. Margaret Thatcher's Conservative Party stood
for monetarist macro-economic management, privatization, cuts in income tax,
the reduction of trade-union powers, the sale of council houses and the retention of NATO nuclear bases on British soil. The Labour Party of Michael Foot
and Neil Kinnock stood for the opposite: an "Alternative Economic Strategy"
of Keynesianism and protection, no state sell-offs, tax increases for high-income
earners, the maintenance of trade-union rights, an extension of council housing
and unilateral nuclear disarmament. The two parties wanted to gain power for
very different ends.

Once Blair became the Labour leader, no such list of opposing policies could
be drawn up. New Labour quickly adopted the Thatcherite policy prospectus and
chose to compete with the Conservatives on the question of performance and
competence. In 2001 the two parties in the main claimed to be in favour of the
same, widely acceptable, things, but each argued that it was better than the other
at delivering them. The only significant position issue in the campaign was the
euro, but for most voters this was a low priority. (In the one part of the United

Kingdom dominated by a position issue, Northern Ireland, where voters can easily tell the parties apart, turnout was much higher than elsewhere and actually increased slightly, from 67 to 68 per cent.) Voters were asked to judge the parties on their performance, past and prospective, not their position. It is much harder to distinguish the parties on these grounds. Each trades selective statistics, brags of its own achievements and exaggerates its rival's blunders. Each side spins. The debate is confusing and tedious. How is the ordinary voter to know which party is right and how to tell them apart?

In the past British voters could also distinguish the parties in terms of the social groups they stood for. The Conservatives were the party of the self-employed, managers, the professions, country dwellers, home-owners and tax payers. Its leaders and MPs were overwhelmingly upper or middle class. Labour was the party of workers, the trade unions, big-city dwellers, council house tenants and welfare-dependants. A substantial minority of Labour MPs, including cabinet ministers, were former workers and trade unionists. However, New Labour's deliberate sidelining of the trade unions and cultivation of the middle classes and the business community, including the very wealthy, has muddied these clear social distinctions in voters' eyes. In 1987 (see Table 7.6, p. 176), fully 93 per cent of Labour voters associated Labour with the trade unions and only 58 per cent associated it with the middle classes.[29] In 2000 Labour's social image had reversed: only 60 per cent associated Labour with the trade unions whereas a larger proportion — 73 per cent — associated it with the middle classes. The university-educated, professional background and life style of almost all Labour's leading politicians, personified by Tony Blair, has reinforced voters' sense that nowadays both the main parties are middle class. In many voters' eyes they are not only indistinguishable politically. They are indistinguishable socially.

If indifferent abstention is linked in the manner suggested to New Labour's long-term hegemonic strategy, it is unlikely to subside in 2005/06. Thus, even if the next election proves to be a close contest, turnout will probably not revert to the mid-70 per cent level of the 1980s and earlier. Low turnout would appear to be the inevitable price of New Labour's long-term hegemonic strategy.

The contribution of alienated abstention to the poor turnout of 2001 is impossible to estimate with any confidence in the absence of suitable survey data.[30] Impression and anecdote suggest that alienated abstention increased. The broadsheet press gave notably more space than before to alienated abstainers. Live meetings between party leaders and ordinary voters in the streets and television studios seemed unusually sour and angry in tone. A rough indicator of the trend in alienation from the established party system is the vote of the fringe parties. Most of them improved their vote.[31] For example, the Greens, who tend to do poorly in Westminster as distinct from European elections, doubled their share of the vote where they stood and for the first time saved their deposit in ten seats. Socialist parties did better than the Marxist parties of the past. The Scottish Socialist Party won 3 per cent of the vote, saving its deposit in all the Glasgow seats, and winning 10 per cent in its strongest areas. More significantly, the British National Party, the far-right white racist party, benefited from the recent violent racial tensions in Oldham. Its leader took 16 per cent of the vote in Oldham West and Royton, almost beating the Conservative into second place, and the party also won 11 per cent of the vote in two neighbouring constituencies. It was by far the best performance of the far right at a general election since the war and demonstrated how a sizeable alienated minority could be rapidly mobilized by an extremist party. It was notable that the turnout in Oldham West and Royton fell by considerably less than the average for similar seats in the region.[32]

The most spectacular example of voting against the established parties, however, was the victory of the retired hospital consultant, Richard Taylor, with no known attachments to a party, standing as an Independent in the West Midlands seat of Wyre Forest (see Chapter 7, p. 181).[33] This was an extraordinary achievement for a British general election. Party rebels aside, only one other Independent has been elected at a general election since the war, Martin Bell at Tatton in 1997. But Martin Bell was a well-known television personality for whom the local Labour and Liberal Democrat candidates withdrew so that he had a clear run against the corrupt sitting Conservative MP, Neil Hamilton. In Wyre Forest the Liberal Democrat withdrew, but otherwise none of the favourable circumstances of Tatton applied.

Richard Taylor's victory represents a brand new phenomenon in British politics: the election, in competition against the mainstream parties, of a non-politician standing on an anti-party platform. He campaigned to save the local general hospital from downgrading, inevitably a popular cause. Describing himself as a "fighter against spin" he blamed party politics and "a very powerful government that overrides the will of the people", pouring scorn on a government that "seeks to enforce inferior health services upon people by describing them as improvements".[34] In the past, party loyalties would have overridden voters' sympathy for a local-cause Independent. It was a reflection of the depth of disaffection from party politics in 2001, elsewhere expressed by abstention, that three out of five voters in Wyre Forest plumped for one. They trusted an inexperienced non-politician more than a mainstream MP to put the interests of Wyre Forest before party. Significantly, turnout in the constituency fell by much less than the national or regional average.[35]

A NEW POLITICAL HEGEMONY?

In politics the foreseeable future is short and the long-term future cannot be foretold at all. It is impossible to know whether the Labour Party recreated by Tony Blair will become the natural party of government for the new century in the way that the Conservatives were for the old. The most that can be said is that Labour looks poised for a period of ascendancy comparable to that of the Conservatives in the 1950s and that by historical standards this amounts to a remarkable change. The change was partly brought about by the particular political circumstances of the mid 1990s but also by a deliberate strategy for hegemony planned and seen through by Tony Blair and his close supporters. If the hegemony comes about, it will not take the form of a classical realignment of the party system in which new social and issue cleavages repolarize voters' partisan loyalties. It will take the form of a non-ideological party, occupying the broad central ground of British political debate and appealing across the social spectrum to a national constituency of increasingly non-partisan voters on the basis of performance in government, not policy for government. The opportunities to create a successful New Conservatism will be very limited. Under the new hegemony, if it transpires, the politics of competence will replace the politics of conviction. There will be a price to be paid in terms of the clarity of choice offered to the electorate, unfulfilled expectations, trust in politicians and government and, therefore, electoral participation. British politics may be, probably will be, duller and more dispiriting. It will certainly be different.

NOTES

1. Labour lost a mere six seats on a 2.5 percentage point slip in its vote. The Conservatives gained just one seat on a tiny 1.0 point increment to its vote. The Liberal Democrats edged up six seats on a 1.5 point addition to their vote. The Pedersen index of volatility, i.e. the sum of the net percentage change since the previous election in the Conservative, Labour, Liberal Democrat and other parties' vote was 5.0, the lowest since 1955, when it was 4.0. The net turnover in seats of fourteen for Great Britain (21 if Northern Ireland is included) was the smallest since 1900 (ten) although in December 1910, the second election that year, net turnover was only eight.

2. In fact, the Liberal Democrats won more seats than the Scottish Nationalists but fewer votes in both the 1997 and 2001 general elections.

3. See V.O. Key, "A Theory of Critical Elections", *Journal of Politics* 17 (1955): 3–18; V.O. Key, "Secular Realignment and the Party System", *Journal of Politics* 21 (1959): 198–210; Walter Dean Burnham, *Critical Elections and the Mainstream of American Politics* (New York: Transaction Books, 1970); James L. Sundquist, *Dynamics of the Party System: Alignment and Realignment of Political Parties in the United States* (Washington, D.C.: The Brookings Institution, 1973).

4. See John Curtice, "Anatomy of a Non-landslide", *Politics Review* 7 (September 1997), 2–8; and Peter Kellner, "Why the Tories Were Trounced", in Pippa Norris and Neil Gavin, eds., *Britain Votes 1997* (Oxford: Oxford University Press, 1997).

5. See John Curtice and Michael Steed, "Appendix 2: The Results Analysed", in David Butler and Dennis Kavanagh, *The British General Election of 1997* (Basingstoke: Macmillan, 1997).

6. The best account of how the strategy was formulated and implemented is Philip Gould, *The Unfinished Revolution: How the Modernisers Saved the Labour Party* (London: Little, Brown, 1998).

7. The distinction was first made in Donald Stokes, "Spatial Models of Party Competition", in Angus Campbell *et al.*, *Elections and the Political Order* (New York: Wiley, 1966).

8. Market & Opinion Research International, *British Pubic Opinion*, XXIV (June 2001): 3. The MORI figures are based on "all MORI's surveys during the election, involving interviews with 18,657 British adults aged 18+. The data is weighted at regional level to the final result and turnout of the election (taking those who said they were 'certain to vote' as having voted in line with their voting intentions, and the remainder as having not voted)."

9. David Sanders, "The Impact of Left–Right Ideology", in Geoffrey Evans and Pippa Norris, eds., *Critical Elections: British Parties and Voters in Long-Term Perspective* (London: Sage Publications, 1999), 181–206.

10. *Gallup Political and Economic Index,* No. 440, May 1997.

11. See Ivor Crewe, "Everything Is in Blair's Favour", *New Statesman,* March 26, 2001, 21–22.

12. Market & Opinion Research International, *British Public Opinion,* XXIII (November/December 2000): 8.

13. Examples include Cambridge (8.6 per cent from Labour to Liberal Democrat), Durham (7.8 per cent), Edinburgh South (7.2 per cent), Hampstead & Highgate (9.3 per cent), Hornsey & Wood Green (13.2 per cent) and Manchester Withington (7.6 per cent).

14. In 1997, 1998 and 1999 it was preferred by a 20 percentage point margin. At the lowest point of the government's popularity, in the third and fourth quarters of 2000, it was still preferred by an 8-point margin.

15. By 5 per cent among *Daily Express* readers and 1 per cent among readers of *The Times;* the country as a whole swung by 2 per cent to the Conservatives. See Market & Opinion Research International, *British Public Opinion,* XXIV (June 2001): 3.

16. See Curtice and Steed, "Appendix 2", in Butler and Kavanagh, *The British General Election of 1997,* 314–18.

17. See Anthony Seldon, ed., *How Tory Governments Fall* (London: Fontana Press, 1996), especially 453–62.

18. The Conservative government had (effectively) placed a statutory prohibition on the inclusion of homosexuality in sex education in schools. Schools were concerned that Section 28 of the Local Government Act, which prohibited local authorities from promoting a homosexual life style, precluded them from using books which referred to homosexuality in neutral or positive terms. The Labour government tried to repeal Section 28. The issue made quite a splash, especially in Scotland.

19. For example, in a MORI poll of June 2001 respondents split 86 to 5 per cent in favour of local education authorities rather than private companies managing schools and 78 to 14 per cent in favour of the NHS rather than private companies managing specially built surgical units. See Market & Opinion Research International, *British Public Opinion,* XXIV (June 2001): 13.

20. The last government to take office on the vote of such a small proportion of the electorate (20.9 per cent) was the short-lived minority Labour government of 1924.

21. See Colin Rallings and Michael Thrasher, *British Electoral Facts, 1832–1999* (Aldershot: Ashgate, 2000), 236.

22. Ivor Crewe, "Elections and Public Opinion" in Anthony Seldon, ed., *The Blair Effect: The Blair Government 1991–2001* (London: Little, Brown, 2001), 82.

23. MORI reported that in May 2001 a Labour win was expected by 78 per cent and a Conservative win by only 5 per cent (the remainder expected a hung parliament or did not know). In January 2001, the proportions were 60 per cent and 13 per cent respectively. See Market & Opinion Research International, *British Public Opinion,* XXIV (June 2001): 28.

24. For further details, see Ivor Crewe, "The Opinion Polls: Still Biased to Labour", in Pippa Norris, ed., *Britain Votes 2001,* special issue of *Parliamentary Affairs* 54 (October 2001).

25. Preliminary analysis suggests that intending voters who eventually abstained were disproportionately Labour supporters. See Paul Whiteley *et al.,* "Turnout" in Norris, ed., *Britain Votes 2001.* This implies that had turnout in 2001 been at normal levels Labour would have won by an even larger majority.

26. Turnout fell by 11.2 percentage points in ultra-marginal Con–Lab seats (majority under 5.0 per cent in 1997) and by 11.1 points in super-safe Con–Lab seats (majority over 20.0 per cent). The parallel figures for Con–Lib Dem seats are –9.3 per cent and –11.4 per cent and for Lab-Con seats –10.3 per cent and –13.6 per cent respectively. I am grateful to Pippa Norris for providing these figures. It could be argued that many voters will not have known whether their local constituency was safe or marginal and will therefore have responded to the national situation, in other words treated the whole country as a "safe seat".

27. *Evening Standard* (London), June 8, 2001, 43.

28. The figures for 1983 to 1997 are the proportion answering "a great difference" to the question "Considering everything the Conservative and Labour parties stand for, would you say that there is a great difference between them, some difference or not much difference?" The figure for 2001 is the proportion answering that there are "differences" to the Gallup poll question: "Do you think that there are any really important differences between the parties, or are they all much of a muchness?" See *Gallup Political and Economic Index,* Report 485, January 2001, 13. The wording and timing of the question may have slightly deflated the proportion perceiving differences between the parties.
29. "Associate" is short hand for agreeing that the party "looks after the interests of the trade unions [middle classes etc.] very closely or fairly closely".
30. In a MORI survey of non-voting for the Electoral Commission, 11 per cent of abstainers (representing a mere 2 per cent of all respondents) appeared to be alienated, giving as their reasons a dislike of all the parties and candidates or the assertion that none were worth voting for. However, this may well be an under-estimate. Non-voters were seriously under-represented in the sample (constituting 18 per cent of respondents, when abstention at the election was over 40 per cent), as is universal for political surveys. We may assume that the survey under-polled the alienated, not only as a proportion of the electorate, but as a proportion of the non-voters.
31. The exception is the U.K. Independence Party, dedicated to Britain's withdrawal from the European Union, which fell short of the 2.6 per cent of the vote won by the Referendum Party in 1997.
32. By 8.5 percentage points compared with 14.9 points for the Greater Manchester area.
33. He turned a Labour majority in 1992 of 6,946 into a majority of 17,630 for himself, taking 58 per cent of the vote.
34. See *Evening Standard* (London), June 8, 2001, 5.
35. By 7.3 percentage points, compared with 11.2 points for the whole of the county and 12.2 points for England.

Appendix: Results of British General Elections, 1945–2001

		Percentage of popular vote						Seats in House of Commons					
	Turnout	Con.	Lab.	Lib.a	Nat.b	Other	Swingc	Con.	Lab.	Lib.	Nat.	Other	Government majority
1945	72.7	39.8	48.3	9.1	0.2	2.5	-12.2	213	393	12	0	22	146
1950	84.0	43.5	46.1	9.1	0.1	1.2	+3.0	299	315	9	0	2	5
1951	82.5	48.0	48.8	2.5	0.1	0.6	+0.9	321	295	6	0	3	17
1955	76.7	49.7	46.4	2.7	0.2	0.9	+2.1	345	277	6	0	2	60
1959	78.8	49.4	43.8	5.9	0.4	0.6	+1.2	365	258	6	0	1	100
1964	77.1	43.1	44.1	11.2	0.5	0.8	-3.2	304	317	9	0	0	4
1966	75.8	41.9	47.9	8.5	0.7	0.9	-2.7	253	363	12	0	2	96
1970	72.0	46.4	43.0	7.5	1.3	1.8	+4.7	330	288	6	1	5	30
Feb 1974	78.7	37.8	37.1	19.3	2.6	3.2	-1.4	297	301	14	9	14	-34d
Oct 1974	72.8	35.8	39.2	18.3	3.5	3.2	-2.1	277	319	13	14	12	3
1979	76.0	43.9	37.0	13.8	2.0	3.3	+5.2	339	269	11	4	12	43
1983	72.7	42.4	27.6	25.4	1.5	3.1	+4.0	397	209	23	4	17	144
1987	75.3	42.3	30.8	22.6	1.7	2.6	-1.7	376	229	22	6	17	102
1992	77.7	41.9	34.4	17.8	2.3	3.5	-2.0	336	271	20	7	17	21
1997	71.4	30.7	43.2	16.8	2.6	6.7	-10.0	165	419	46	10	19	179
2001	59.4	31.7	40.7	18.3	2.5	6.8	+1.8	166	413	52	9	19	167

a. Liberal Party 1945–79; Liberal/Social Democrat Alliance 1983–87; Liberal Democrat Party 1992–2001.

b. Combined vote of Scottish National Party (SNP) and Welsh National Party (Plaid Cymru).

c. "Swing" compares the results of each election with the results of the previous election. It is calculated as the average of the winning major party's percentage point increase in its share of the vote and the losing major party's decrease in its percentage point share of the vote. In the table, a positive sign denotes a swing to the Conservatives, a negative sign a swing to Labour.

d. Following the February 1974 election, the Labour Party was 34 seats short of having an overall majority. It formed a minority government until it obtained a majority in the October 1974 election.

Index

Contributors

John Bartle is lecturer in government at the University of Essex and co-editor of *Political Communications Transformed: From Morrison to Mandelson.*

Ivor Crewe is vice-chancellor of the University of Essex and professor of government. He is the author of numerous books and articles on British electoral politics and co-author with Anthony King of *SDP: The Birth, Life and Death of the Social Democratic Party.*

David Denver is professor of politics at Lancaster University and author of *Elections and Voting Behaviour in Britain and Modern Constituency Electioneering.* He appears frequently on BBC Scotland.

Anthony King is professor of government at the University of Essex and writes widely on British, American and comparative politics. He is coauthor with Ivor Crewe of *SDP: The Birth, Life and Death of the Social Democratic Party* and sole author, most recently, of *Does the United Kingdom Still Have a Constitution?*

Philip Norton is professor of government at the University of Hull, director of the university' Centre for Legislative Studies and author of books on Parliament, the Conservative Party and the British constitution. He sits in the House of Lords as Lord Norton of Louth and is chairman of the Lords' constitution committee.

Patrick Seyd is professor of government at the University of Sheffield and co-author of survey-based studies of rank-and-file Conservative and Labour party members, *True Blues and Labour' Grassroots.*

Colin Seymour-Ure is professor of government at the University of Kent at Canterbury and author of numerous books and articles on politics and the mass media in Britain.